Virtual Environments for
Teaching & Learning

Series on Innovative Intelligence

Editor: L. C. Jain *(University of South Australia)*

Forthcoming Titles:

Neural Networks for Intelligent Signal Processing
    (A. Zaknich)

Complex-Valued Neural Networks: Theories and Applications
    (ed. A. Hirose)

Biology and Logic-Based Applied Machine Intelligence: Theory and Applications
    (A. Konar & L. C. Jain)

Levels of Evolutionary Adaptation for Fuzzy Agents
    (G. Resconi & L. C. Jain)

Series on Innovative Intelligence – Vol. 1

Virtual Environments for
Teaching & Learning

Editors

L. C. Jain
University of South Australia

R. J. Howlett
Brighton University, UK

N. S. Ichalkaranje
University of South Australia

G. Tonfoni
University di Bologna, Italy

World Scientific
New Jersey • London • Singapore • Hong Kong

Published by

World Scientific Publishing Co. Pte. Ltd.

P O Box 128, Farrer Road, Singapore 912805

USA office: Suite 1B, 1060 Main Street, River Edge, NJ 07661

UK office: 57 Shelton Street, Covent Garden, London WC2H 9HE

British Library Cataloguing-in-Publication Data
A catalogue record for this book is available from the British Library.

VIRTUAL ENVIRONMENTS FOR TEACHING AND LEARNING

ISBN 981-238-167-8

This book is printed on acid-free paper.

Printed in Singapore by Uto-Print

Foreword

Distance learning has been a vision for decades. For example, in the 1960s Brazil set up a national satellite based network to make education available to its citizens via their television sets.

Satellite-linked Distance Education studios were built in many teaching institutions. After the overblown flurry of the 1980s they lost favor as the ideal medium due to their high transmission costs, difficulties with simultaneous student access and changing student requirements. Lack of sufficient understanding of the medium at large did not help. Teaching was being forced into this medium, rather than being naturally catered for by it. It does work and still is in use, but it has been largely overshadowed by the potential of the global web. This has provided an everyday, potentially every person, information support network. It arrived in force in the 1990s and expanded at previously unseen rates of take-up with billions of computers now connected in every imaginable location.

It enables two-way communication via sound, vision and text media. It seems to be the ultimate answer. Its limitation is the slow transmission time but that has not held up development of educational programs that can be taken synchronously and asynchronously with participants being located at home, in the city or in a Bedouin tent in a desert.

The printing press of Gutenberg times made knowledge available to the many. Allied with it was an enlightened attitude to freedom of access to the knowledge of the times. That event has been heralded as an epoch in the dissemination of knowledge.

We are living in the next such epoch – the use of the web in the delivery of knowledge and as an extension tool for supporting the use of knowledge for education and learning. It allows access to many more people than any publishing medium has before. It is not overstating it to suggest that it can, hopefully will, make knowledge available to everyone on the Earth.

The potential of the Internet to assist in education and learning is vast. It is only just being tapped. Discovering how to make best use of it is not an easy field for it requires the integration of numerous disciplines spanning the sciences and the humanities.

The learning environment is a most complex system situation. The good lecturer and learning environment easily stand out from the pack. What makes them so is not easy to capture for this is a situation in which the reductionist science approach is not well suited to investigation and problem solving. It is not an energy/mass network type of problem that is comfortably described with the laws of physics. This is not a mere data transmission problem but one involving many of the science and humanities disciplines. Soft thinking approaches are needed to create virtual teaching environments that will one day seriously compete with the best human practitioners.

This field is not a solution looking for a problem, but a suddenly emergent, major opportunity looking for overdue solutions. This is not a fad built to find new uses for a fading technology; it is a 'killer' application. It does not take the mind of the proverbial rocket scientist to imagine the potential of the Internet for knowledge gathering, storage and use. Mankind is again lagging behind the technological capability provided by electronic computers and the Internet. Researchers need to run very fast here.

Fortunately there is considerable research and development work in progress. This book pulls together the findings and visions of key research groups from several countries. This is fitting for the spread of knowledge and learning is now an international issue like never before. This book provides a set of up-to-date readings specifically generated as state-of-the-art reports.

Whether the establishment likes it or not, this mode of learning will assuredly replace much of the learning role currently carried by educational institutions. It so well matches the learner's requirements for access. Whether we like it or not, given more development in the quality of the virtual learning environment, it will replace much of current offerings.

The editors and contributors are to be congratulated on pooling their thoughts and creating this position statement.

Peter H Sydenham, Adjunct Professor
University of South Australia
Joint Editor-in-Chief, MeasureMentor, Wiley (Europe)

Preface

When considering any new and rapidly evolving area of research, a deeper insight and a better understanding can be gained by exploring the roots of the research that originated from its founders and pioneers. Scientists in general, and engineering designers more specifically, can fully comprehend where they stand now and why they use their current methodologies only through careful analysis of what came before.

Significant discoveries about teaching and learning were made during the golden age of artificial intelligence during the late fifties as a very precise and focused effort was made to explore natural intelligence. The human capacity of learning was considered to be a crucial domain to be accurately explored, comprehensively grasped and fully understood. Analyzing in detail the many and remarkable contributions which were made at the time of discovery, would require a whole book in itself, rather than just a preface. However, the early research into learning certainly showed the complexity of the field, as so many kinds and diverse forms of "learnings" were identified. Some of these have been investigated while others still remain to be explored. As soon as a particular learning problem was considered to be solved and a consistently designed model of learning was completed, a new learning problem would manifest itself. Just like an iceberg, the visible peak could be small, but there is a lot more to emerge under the surface.

Another important discovery was that learning is so strictly bound to other equally complex aspects of natural intelligence such as reasoning, perception, knowledge representation, knowledge expression through natural language, concept abstraction, analogy recognition and more. Learning is fundamentally connected with teaching. If consistent models of learning are available, they should be of direct relevance to the design of teaching support systems. The discovery of possible links and interconnections is unlikely to ever end. This is the beauty of a pioneering field, for example, the study of the mind and human intelligence is primarily: if a lot has been discovered much still remains to be unveiled and explored.

It took a long time for linguists to realize that, while natural language generation and natural language understanding are very much connected, and both belong to the more general domain of natural language processing, they are nevertheless not alike. Generation and understanding are not isomorphic processes at all. A speaker may create a perfectly well formed sentence, which may be unheard, or its untended meaning may not be understood by the listener.

There is a commonly found problem in communication between speakers and listeners which also extends to the comprehension of written documents. This is based upon discrepancies existing both at the perceptive and cultural levels. Models of reality and knowledge passed around throughout the different cultures, even if through the same language, may not necessarily be consensually shared. Frequently they are not even based upon common representations of the same concepts.

E-communication is therefore substantially different to physical communication, as roles, channels, time-frames and space have been so radically modified by the new technologies. Just as e-speakers are not just speakers, able to check if the intended meaning is transferred, e-readers differ from readers too. Similarly, e-teachers and e-learners deeply differ from other teachers and learners. They are part of an entirely different context of interaction, which is a virtual one.

Many behavioral observations, that apply widely to our highly interconnected world today in relation to e-communication, can be extended and applied to the field of e-teaching and e-learning. A really appropriate definition would actually require the use of the plural for both teaching and learning, as those are such complex processes, which also apply to the many and most different areas and disciplines and sub-disciplines we have today.

So it is really much better to talk about 'teachings' and 'learnings' of various kinds, which may be applied to the most diverse fields and disciplines. Similarly it is better to extend these observations to e-teachings and correspondingly to 'e-learnings' as well, according to the areas of expertise and knowledge to be analyzed at each different time.

We should not underestimate the importance of the wealth and variety of research contributions made in the field of cognitive science and psychology, especially over the last fifty years. A wide diversity of theory concerning learning and teaching has deeply influenced methodologies and policy concerning the teaching system, both in relation to priorities and to roles to be assigned, given a new selection of tasks to be achieved in a continuously shifting scenario.

Meta-learning theories have been predominant in this field. These stress the most substantial role of the learner as a self monitoring individual able to decide and control not only the kind of knowledge to be acquired, but also the overall process of knowledge acquisition, so as to be able to make decisions both for the quantitative and qualitative aspects involved.

As for the complexity of learning options and modes of learning and areas of knowledge to be addressed, knowledge in today's world of exploded information resources is growing as rapidly as never before. What we may think of in terms of optimized teaching may not trigger an optimized learning process, as there are so many variables at play and a completely fluid situation too, which is hard to cope with and fully account for.

Some particularly careful attention should be devoted to the term "optimization" and a very clear-cut distinction should be drawn once again between learning and teaching versus e-learning and e-teaching.

Learning is a highly complex and delicate process, based upon many capabilities still to be confronted in different areas of learning and related to the types of competence and expertise to be promoted. Optimizing learning immediately poses the challenge to choose among the various aspects of learning to be optimized.

E-learning is a complex process as it refers to a whole variety of e-learning abilities and applies to so many and diverse areas today. Any optimization process needs to be then referred to a very specific aspect of e-learning, which is therefore likely to become the target of attention.

Just to give a sense of the complexity of natural learning explored and the number of categories set up accordingly, consider these categories of learning found and defined but still not considered to be exclusive, for example: learning by analyzing differences, learning by managing multiple models, learning by explaining experiences, learning by correcting mistakes, learning by recording cases, learning by building identification trees, learning by training neural nets, learning by training perceptions, learning by training approximation nets, learning by simulating evolution (Winston 1993).

What is most interesting to observe in the science of engineering design is what happened at some point, that created the conditions for one of the major sudden shifts and biggest switch ever experienced in the history of science and of scientific reasoning: which is precisely the advent and pervasive diffusion of both the internet and the world-wide web.

The pre-web era of research in engineering design was in fact dedicated to the exploration of the many varieties of learning. Some of these are still to be discovered and fully analyzed as they certainly require a real in-depth exploration, which is destined to take much longer. In the current post-web era of research in engineering design, the focus of interest has moved in a different direction, and this has even changed the very nature of problems addressed, as it happens in the course of scientific revolutions (Kuhn 1962).

In previously described scientific revolutions, a paradigm shift was caused by the increasingly obvious inadequacy of the already existing paradigms in use to cover a whole set of expected problems. In contrast, what happened with the sudden introduction of internet and with indiscriminate web access world-wide, was that previous problems still to be resolved, were neglected and forgotten, as new and previously unheard problems manifested themselves and took priority as urgent issues to be resolved.

This explains why research topics and interests in the area of learning and teaching have recently changed so dramatically as new emergencies have emerged. The latest priorities now concern how to cope with exploded information sources and flows, multiple learning resources up to overlapping and often competitive teaching opportunities. They are also about overlapping up to colliding offers and, more generally, about how to cope with the biggest amount of information ever experienced in the whole history of mankind (Tonfoni 2002). Choices about future actions have become limited, as the overwhelming flow of information to be organized, filtered, packaged and absorbed was not an option and just a fact. So the "emergence" of a new problem of this entity also became an "emergency" for the engineering design community and almost real time solutions to problems of increasing complexity have been asked and solicited.

Very differently where scientists in the past were in charge of deciding the kind of problems to be prioritized and solved (even if any scientific community may have debates on choices and also disagreements, still scientists could take decisions on where their field should be heading) is the engineering design community today, who are more and more called on tasks of major urgency of finding solutions to an increasing number of problems. Most of the time these problems have not even been defined or identified as the important ones to solve. Rather, ill posed problems often surface as a consequence of a major, and mostly uncontrolled, technology implant.

In this very new scenario, even the concept of learning, previously seen as one of the many possible and desirable options, has turned into a necessity and a need for survival, so that toolkits are required to provide resistance to the overwhelming flow of information (Tonfoni 1998).

Seeking learning, selecting a specific domain of interest, nurturing the very pleasure inspiring individuals throughout their intense desire to see their dreams materialize as a result of a search among a few learning opportunities, heightening their motivation and creating the most solid platform for successful outcome has been abruptly substituted by an absolutely mandatory requirement, a real demand on each individual today just to survive in the information workload era.

Learning has become a must today and is no longer a real option, whereas a huge variety of options, which may at times look alike, seem to be provided continuously to individuals; this is definitely the case when we think of e-learning opportunities more specifically.

Of course we should now specify that learning as personal, progressive, day by day acquisition continuously occurs anyway, as we learn something every day as a consequence of our experiences in the world. This natural kind of learning is very enriching and somewhat very unstructured too, as we may not necessarily know what we are going to learn each day throughout a whole set of unplanned learning experiences. Besides different individuals exposed to different experiences are likely to learn naturally but in very different ways, according to the diversity and uniqueness of experiences they may have and in a different sequence of actions and order of time too. It is actually out of their own perception modes and it is by carrying on their daily life, elaborating on their own experiences and out of their own trials and mistakes, that individuals have constantly been able to learn, which means that they are able to perceive and experience and acquire new knowledge to be organized and packaged in ways, which may be retrieved and accessed to be used later on.

This kind of experiential learning, very synthetically described, is most times not really a systematically observable process, as it is only very rarely a linear one. As a consequence of a direct and personal exposure to a certain environment, each individual may actually evolve a comprehensive and quite unique background of knowledge.

Thanks to this kind of expertise, accumulated over time and out of multiple learning opportunities, benefited out of learning by making mistakes, individuals were considered as real repositories of unique competence in various fields and at different levels of depth and breadth. Those individuals, considered to be really knowledgeable in a certain field, were also assigned the role of experts, entitled and also required to pass their knowledge, assisting and teaching newcomers in a really meaningful master-and-apprentice relationships. The level of expertise reached could not be determined *a priori*, but rather discovered at the end of the coaching process.

This has also been the concept, which some expert systems and advisory system designers at the very early stages of artificial intelligence intended to model and to then implement. According to such interpretation and vision, would the teaching leadership be attributed to those human experts, who had accumulated a body of knowledge as a result of their complex learning and reasoning abilities, based upon their ongoing experiences, continuously subject to revision and update.

Common sense by individual experts was considered to be an essential part of so-called expertise to be then passed along through generations. Nonsense and information, which was found not worth retaining, was also taken away by those same individuals, who were acknowledged to be experts in their field and therefore in charge of making decisions as for what should be passed along and taught, and what should be eliminated instead. Guidelines as to avoid previously made mistakes, carefully indicating what should not be done and why, were taken as most significant means to advance the overall learning experience by not repeating mistakes.

Still, at this level was the technology component considered to be an integrated element, within a broader learning and teaching environment, filled with a whole set of diversified information resources, where the real role of the individual human expert had in fact never been diminished, or challenged up to even jeopardized. The exponential growth of information available and speeded up tremendously throughout the web and the internet, has indeed changed the scenario completely and most substantially over the last twenty years.

Some e-learning models have in fact emerged showing how the web may be presented as a learning environment in itself. Many academic programs have been activated as e-learning activities and advertised as a real substitute to more conventional teaching, therefore opening up a whole new market and a parallel teaching infrastructure.

There is no debate that both the web and the internet are the most amazing learning resources in terms of access to a massive amount of information, and because of their persuasiveness. But in order to really understand the meaning of this new and completely different set up, we need to carefully discriminate between learning and e-learning processes, as they do indicate in fact two separate acquisition paths, which certainly entail radically different attitudes leading toward entirely distinct output results.

We do not need to create new words if they are not strictly needed, but we certainly may want to introduce new words or redefine old words, when the original meaning seems to have been so deeply affected as to make the word become a very fuzzy term.

It has proved useful to differentiate between emotions and e-motions. Emotions are deeply rooted perceptive experiences, which are not intentionally designed and planned, as they come as a consequence of exposure to spontaneous unpredicted situations. In contrast, e-motions derive as a consequence of triggering events accurately planned and meant to cause shallow sequences of short term mental states, changing rapidly over time. It is equally useful to discriminate between learning and teaching and e-learning and e-teaching and to classify research, which previously occurred in learning and teaching prior to the web advent, separately from research going on as for e-learning and e-teaching throughout the web and the internet. We are now talking about very different subjects, which need to be interpreted and labeled according to very different sets of categories.

Traditional teaching is definitely based upon common sharing and synchronous interactions, and it is certainly very much bound to personal identities, preferences and styles. Connections and relationships established among students, and between each student and each teacher do have a very significant impact on the success of teaching and learning outcome. The personal and the affective component is very evident, whereas e-teaching is not intended to be affective, rather to be effective. In so many ways may e-learning facilities enhance solitary learning, by providing support available just where and when requested and needed. Personal acquisition to take place in context is somewhat replaced by personalized packages of knowledge to be accessed easily.

We need to be reminded that 'personal interaction' and 'personalized interaction' may sound phonetically and morphologically close words, but they certainly represent very different concepts. A personalized package in e-learning may actually be even more effective than a personal interaction between learner and teacher at some point, but it is quite evident that it is really indicated for those learning phases, which do require a more solitary kind of behavior as time for acquisition and mode of acquisition may significantly differ among individuals.

There are some phases in the process of knowledge acquisition, where the collaborative effort and the presence of the leading figure of a teacher is most important, whereas there are other phases, where solitary efforts and privacy in self-monitoring and progressive acquisition are in demand. It is therefore most important to respect the learning cycle as to be able to determine when some e-learning support may not only be welcome, but be absolutely most relevant.

In e-learning environments, asynchronous interaction facilities are meant to make possible e-conversations, which would not otherwise even be conceivable, connecting individuals long distance and opening up totally new scenarios.

Memories about the very process of acquisition, which are a very important component in any learning process are virtually established as a consequence of virtual experiences had in e-learning, differently than those memories, which are built and consolidated as a result of real experience within a really conventional learning environment.

At the very beginning and at the early stages of the e-learning adventure the web was seen as a way to actually include those individuals, who would be normally excluded from receiving any other kind of learning support otherwise. It became obvious later on that those e-learners, who had been included, and had become part of an interconnected acquisition experience, should in fact not be secluded into e-learning. In other words e-learners should not be brought to think of themselves, as if they were in fact undergoing a full and complete learning experience, as in fact they were not.

Availability of knowledge and being really knowledgeable are two very different and diverse issues. An e-learner may be taught how to access some information easily, but may still remain cut off from the very process of knowledge acquisition in its full complexity.

Personalized knowledge provided through e-learning is also obviously subject to standardization. In other words, a personalized package to be delivered to an e-learner is conceived to suit a category of individuals, and once again personalized interaction does not mean personal interaction. Designing a personalized course is first about designing both a realistic model and an ideal model of e-learner. In some ways personalized packages are also standardized packages, which may more or less approximate the ideal process of acquisition planned as the one to be prioritized.

If conventional learning may be somehow conceived in terms of distributed learning as it is based upon a set of different learning resources of different kinds, e-learning may be reframed in terms of ubiquitous learning, where you may think of the same facilities available and accessible in many different locations.

In depth and in breadth, analysis in the field of e-learning has shown that major differences occur regarding acceptance of those new set ups in different cultures. E-learning facilities within the U.S. may be accepted as they are thought to carry the same content, which could be provided at one of the major institutions. E-learning opportunities may somehow create the illusion that if someone cannot go to one of the most prestigious educational institutions, there is nevertheless availability of contents, though obviously still the whole real learning experience is missing.

More realistically, should e-learning be presented as for its real opportunities, not to generate illusions that could easily turn into disappointments later on. No discussion, even one experienced on a major institution's e-learning track, is a substitute for the full experience of a real campus. It would be very unfair to present e-learning as more or less equivalent to 'being there' for years, attending classes regularly, sharing the overall experience with other learners and with teachers in presence.

E-learning facilities, when extended overseas and reaching out to other cultures, show the two different sides of a same coin; on the one hand they may represent a real opportunity of access to information, which otherwise would not be available, but they may be also perceived as a real short cut and, more than that, even as aggressive tools. E-learning facilities may be threatening when interpreted and viewed as a means to infiltrate knowledge packaged according to ways and principles, which are not shared by the very same community where the technologies are already reaching out. In this last case, e-learning resources are perceived as a means for standardizing learning in countries, which have not at all made the decision to promote that kind of learning among their own people, as they may want to do it in their own ways instead.

If it is true that we are what we learn, an aggressive e-learning technology may be perceived as that kind of infrastructure, which is rather meant to make individual ways of thinking change in ways they are not likely to be controlled and according to a progression and time frame, which are considered to be alien.

E-learning may also be perceived as a real threat to the very hierarchical structure of the teaching institution. The fear of being replaced has been somehow interiorized in the western world as one of the side effects of the advent, growth and persuasiveness of the technologies. Concepts of 'ever changing conditions' and 'continuous learning' have been presented as challenges or opportunities for each individual at any level of teaching in our high tech world of today. Like it or not, faculties are brought back to school to make sense of the new tools and master them, and have to acknowledge the fact that in some areas their own students may be more knowledgeable than themselves. In the western world, teachers are presently required to reinvent themselves and their roles continuously; any time a new technology threatens their own niche and their actions, they need to find a new spot to justify their presence. In this restless search for identity, most of the conventional and strong identities are jeopardised.

Teachers in a traditional sense were in fact viewed as real models of action and masters of research: the younger generation would learn by identifying with those individuals and by emulating them. This very delicate process of knowledge transfer was also bound to a real transfer: the model of actions performed by the knowledgeable teacher would be appreciated and admired and therefore incorporated during the acquisition process.

In today's world of high tech devices, teachers are very busy struggling to retain their identity, role and job too: their influence or impact on the student population has therefore changed radically. Teachers rarely look as real experts in the field and sometimes even struggle to keep up with the latest criteria that needs to be handled, to decide how to act and what should be considered a priority out of the overwhelming flow of information they are continuously exposed to in their own knowledge areas. A most puzzling question for them is about what should be considered stable knowledge to be packaged and presented as research outputs with times of processing much accelerated, that there is just no way to understand what should be kept, focused or rather ignored, especially for disciplines where contrasting and too fast inputs are continuously provided.

It is therefore really difficult to see how much of the so-called conventional knowledge should in fact be passed along. If teachers are expected to present really most updated information and knowledge in a field, it will be very unlikely that they will have adequate time and opportunities to consider imparting some of the old knowledge which may help learners understand where we all stand now.

Probably that time will never come, as learners may themselves feel compelled to just ask for the very new, without being willing to explore the connections with what was there before. E-learning is not just about new learning technologies, but it is also about making a lot of previous knowledge look obsolete, under the constant search for the new and innovative.

Research generations in science and technology would normally be apart by a separation of twenty years, whereas we now see only a difference of just a few years between generations. Contributions by a previous generation are rarely considered. Innovation is about reinventing, with a tremendous loss of those experiences, which were there before, which may even still be available on the web, but are no longer read.

Innovation interpreted as bound to tools has primarily caused, even if unintentionally, a real compulsion toward innovation of contents, at the expense of continuity. If continuity is disrupted, meaningfulness is also in jeopardy. And even if it may indeed sound as a real paradox, in a world of interconnected opportunities for learning of any kind and at any time, the pleasure and the real wish for learning has dramatically decreased. Continuously increasing numbers of individuals are learning today, as reported by statistical analysis. But this does not necessarily mean that learners are being led toward a learning experience by their own real wish and will, as they may rather have just adapted to the idea that they need to be continuously involved with some kind of learning, for advancing their career or just for the media push and systematic advertising. By adapting to the concept of continuous learning, they trust that their own identity will be preserved, be it both their professional identity and their personal sense about themselves.

Some cultures, which are not part of the western tradition, may not wish to adapt to this new and extraordinarily pervasive model of knowledge packaging and dissemination. Consequences of such resistance may manifest themselves as some real deep rooted resentment toward the radical change imposed throughout technologies, which shows up to be considerable. Certainly, this change seems as powerful as to discard any previously existing model and system of traditional learning.

E-learning as distributed learning facilities also require maintenance over time. The need for rapid integration in the era of internet has led e-learning designers to anticipate that both heterogeneous and homogeneous systems should be maintained and made to evolve.

One of the major threats posed by the overall e-learning idea is that structured knowledge disseminated around is based upon contents manufactured according to some very precise ideological structure and very specific cultural model of reality, which is totally alien to some cultures and even heavily disliked. In some cultures, the very same act of selecting and passing knowledge has an extremely precious value: the very real process of knowledge transfer is the result of mutual trust, appreciation and care. Possessing knowledge is for some cultures the end result of an inner growing path of wisdom, where the learner becomes eligible for that growth as for many skills, abilities and attitudes accumulated over time. Patience over time and progressive accumulation of knowledge and wisdom do not easily match with widely advertised concepts of accelerated and targeted learning.

Envisioning learning as that very unique endeavor, where each piece of solid knowledge built up as a result of experience, is carved and selected as to be strong enough to be passed along to a new generation and to be considered by the new generation as a gift to be preserved, and also of course expanded and further carved, is quite incompatible with 'serial learning'.

Serial learning is in fact that kind of learning, where it does not really matter which context individual learners are in as long they are connected. Some ways of conceiving e-learning may easily look like serial learning, where standardized packages of knowledge are passed around in a time and space vacuum. The web is in fact a no-space and no-time environment, due to the way it has been conceived, where contexts may be easily made up and taken away, and even names and personalities are likely to fade away as easily as they have surfaced. Everything on the web is as temporary and transient as the entire model of producing knowledge of our world today. Something, which is considered to be most valuable these days, may be gone and forgotten by tomorrow for reasons that cannot be determined or controlled.

Power and teaching have always been very highly interconnected concepts: there is power in deciding what should be taught and when and where, and to whom and to what extent, these is no doubt about power acquisition in learning. Individuals do become more powerful as they acquire knowledge, which will enable them to better understand the world they live in, and make changes.

These statements have certainly proved valid according to the conventional teaching mentality, as individuals seek learning opportunities to empower themselves, as a consequence of a major breakthrough caused by new and relevant knowledge and experience acquired during the learning process and as a result of their own decision and choice.

But how does this actually apply to our world of today? A lot of what is presented to be acquired is actually taken away from the teachers' community and packaged by other experts (with some exceptions, of course). Teachers are likely to be asked to provide opinions based on their own expertise in teaching, but their directions may or may not necessarily be followed. On the other hand, individuals acknowledged as experts in a field, as for the compartmentalized structure of knowledge today, and the exponential growth and tremendous speed of research areas, are, most of the times, just experts in a very specific sub-field. So-called meta-experts, individuals who are really able to decide due to a broader competence and a real vision, are not so easy to find. But major promises are made today in our highly interconnected world and exciting opportunities are provided, which represent challenges that are actually extremely difficult to be met.

If in traditional teaching individual learners naturally seek tools that are meant to add value to their professional lives and to their own lives in general, today the individual learners are exposed to a whole variety of options that they do not necessary know the real value of.

Today any form of value is affected by continuous change, then how may anyone have a correct estimate of what value is to be attributed to a certain task, topic and ability and how may added value even be predicted and measured? What is added value to already existing value, which we are not sure will last? What is sure is that the traditional way of measuring value and added value has been taken away too, whereas new ways for deciding about new values are available in a very fluid manner.

Individual learners today are not even certain about their own time investment: how about if value attached to a specific kind of learning, highly suggested and recommended, disappears all of a sudden in the stock market of teaching opportunities, provided on a world-wide basis?

What are the abilities currently being promised and which are the tasks to be prioritized? If we proceed toward some case studies, we may well see how fast those promises and priorities are being updated and upgraded all the time, up to even being turned upside down and fully reversed.

In the present world of knowledge reshuffling, making the right choice about what kind of learning should be chosen, the contents and methods and teaching tools, is just by luck or coincidence.

Obviously, making the right choice implies and requires having precisely the consistent tools available for action and immediate response; which means possessing both tools and the technological abilities and skills, but hopefully also some conceptual tools to have a broader vision. But what about the real wealth and solid background, that is based on harmonious merging of knowledge and wisdom and only comes from direct experience growing over time? This harmonious process is the only way to guarantee the cultural uniqueness and symmetry when acquiring and sharing concepts and values.

E-learning, even if standardized, is very likely to produce asymmetrical learning. Symmetry in learning is based on the possibility of observing each individual's knowledge acquisition process in a real environment like in a traditional classroom.

In a conventional learning environment is a teacher also a supervisor meant to ensure that the whole group of learners present may share a common background and be part of a homogeneous acquisition path. Symmetrical conditions are a task to be achieved and individual learners may undertake collaborative efforts as a consequence of it. In other words, at a certain time in a given teaching path teachers may assume that each individual has a certain skill and ability as a consequence of a commonly shared learning experience.

E-learning is not meant to create symmetry as its tools reach out to a dispersed community, whose individuals are asked to move along according to their own personal time frame as in acquisition. E-learning is likely to produce asymmetrical learning conditions, as individuals may at a "same time" have reached completely different stages even if along a common learning trajectory. The very same concept of collaboration needs to be therefore radically reinterpreted.

Symmetrical collaboration in a group may only happen when each member of the group has reached a certain level of acquisition at a "common time", so that expertise required is considered to be part of a common background, and different roles and tasks may be assigned to various participants present.

E-learning technologies provide users with opportunities to e-collaborate, which means to pass information and advice from their own experience, which is packaged and transported out of each individual's context. Context shifts and time and space variables are very likely to affect interaction, so that we need to think of "group-ware" as an e-collaborative tool, which cannot resemble a classroom interaction where real time practice and feedback are on, all the time.

This edited volume, is actually an anthology of selected contributions meant to be a response to challenging questions on the future of technology in education, posed already by Jain (2000):-

"It is important to consider the wisdom-based thinking of eminent researchers as a starting point in the design of innovative teaching and learning paradigms. It is most important to consider the need for life long learning and the need of the society during the development phase of curricula and learning strategies."

In some ways we may consider this selection of chapters to be representative of the many approaches taken and the diversity of applications is to be seen as really positive too. Different perspectives and different solutions adopted are the result of choices made contextually. These chapters may constitute a real platform for further discussion and for verification in the future years, as they provide different and diverse views of e-learning approaches in various countries and educational contexts. We may add that it would be interesting to come back, reread and verify the guidelines and suggestions made here some twenty years from now. This will pose the real challenge to this volume, which consists of ten contributed chapters:

- Chapter 1 gives the reader an interesting illustration of ongoing research, that is very representative of a leading U.S. e-learning perspective. A new teaching framework is presented and the concept of the teacher-centered lecture is challenged so as to encourage a more active attitude by the learners.

- Chapter 2 provides an accurate description of specific examples of traditional distance education in Israel. The main aspects and

problems relating to the transition and integration of the technology into distance learning are described. Techniques for
compensating for the lack of direct communication with the
faculty and the absence of a real campus, are clearly illustrated.

- Chapter 3 contains a comprehensive analysis of a well-
  documented set of e-learning experiences that were made in
  Hong Kong. Guidelines are provided by drawing on the experiences. The relative positive and negative aspects are contrasted.
  In addition, the resulting side effects are well illustrated and
  carefully balanced.

- Chapter 4 accurately describes the development of internet-
  based courses within a European framework and access to
  them. Specific attention is given to the provision of student
  support in different ways to ensure the personalized guidance
  that can be easily lost in the internet.

- Chapter 5 illustrates current ways of considering e-learning in
  the context of other distance learning paradigms. The innovative and important concept of the distance ecological model is
  presented and some of its direct implications and possible
  applications are discussed in depth.

- In Chapter 6 the reader is presented with a model, which is
  based on an agent concept, for guiding students through course
  material accessed via the internet. As there are many interpre-
  tations of the term "agent" and the concepts of "agent",
  "agency" and "autonomy" in the current literature, some of the
  most current definitions are considered and explored.

- Chapter 7 contains a general view of the state of the art in relation to problem generation in web-based tutoring systems. A
  complete framework is presented to allow the reader to form an

interpretation of the past and present research in the field so as to be able to envision and move on to the future.

- Chapter 8 provides an interesting description of internet-based interactive suggestion group learning for targeted students. Specific methods illustrated show the deep interest and involvement of governmental policy in support of the explosive spread of e-learning in Japan.

- Chapter 9 contains a discussion of the major concerns existing in Europe relating to the issue of personalization. The major role played by the user interacting and working collaboratively poses the need for accurate and individually acceptable solutions.

- Chapter 10 provides a very illuminating description of how video may consistently be used for distance education. Very precise skills are needed to ensure quality. The chapter explains that audio-visual education is in fact based on an entirely different set of perceptive capacities, which need to be accurately explored and certainly cannot be taken for granted.

Each of the ten chapters presented in this anthology is meant to pose further questions and challenges, which may be only fully verified later on as it is common practice in the field of technology.

This is the 'temporary conclusion' of the present preface, whereas the real anthology of chapters to follow and its extension and evolution, are meant to stay in time, for future verification to come.

A book is a co-operative venture with many contributors. The editors would like to thank the many people who made this volume possible. Of course the authors made a major contribution and we offer them sincere thanks for the chapters they wrote. We are grateful to the reviewers for their time and comments and extend our thanks to them. We thank Berend Jan van der Zwaag for his wonderful contribution, and Ms Lakshmi Narayanan of World Scientific Publishing Co. for her professional help in publishing the book. We hope to work with these colleagues again on future exciting ventures.

References

Jain, L.C. (ed.) (2000), *Innovative Teaching and Learning*, Physica-Verlag, Germany.

Kuhn, T. (1962), *The Structure of Scientific Revolutions*, University of Chicago Press, Chicago, Ill.

Tonfoni, G. (1998), *Information Design: the Knowledge Architect's Toolkit*, Scarecrowpress, Lanham, MD.

Tonfoni, G. (2002), *Changing Perceptions on Documentation Management*, Intellect, U.K.

Winston, P.H. (1993), *Artificial Intelligence*, 3rd edition, Addison-Wesley, Reading, Mass.

Contents

Chapter 4
Developing and Accessing Adaptive Internet-Based
Courses... **111**
R.M. Carro, E. Pulido and P. Rodríguez

Chapter 5
Towards Intelligent Media-Oriented E-Learning
Environments **153**
M. Kayama and T. Okamoto

Chapter 6

An Intelligent Tutoring System for Student Guidance in Web-Based Courses.. 195

B. Özdemir and F.N. Alpaslan

Chapter 7

Automatic Generation of Problems in Web-Based Tutors.... 237

M.V. Belmonte, E. Guzmán, L. Mandow, E. Millán and J.L. Pérez de la Cruz

Chapter 8
The Design of Internet-Based Interactive Learning Models Using Agents and Their Applications **283**
T. Ichimura, M. Nakamura, K.J. Mackin, K. Yoshida, S. Otsuki and T. Yamashita

Chapter 9
**Supporting Personalization in Distance Education Virtual
Communities** **327**
E. Gaudioso and J.G. Boticario

Chapter 10
**An Intelligent System for Capturing Presentation on
Desktop Manipulations — Supporting for
Video Contents Production** **363**
Y. Nakamura, M. Ozeki and Y. Ohta

Chapter 1

Use of Virtual Worlds
to Teach the Sciences

**B.M. Slator, J.T. Clark, L.M. Daniels, C. Hill, P. McClean,
B. Saini-Eidukat, D.P. Schwert and A.R. White**

Innovations in educational technology have taken many forms over the last decade. Courses are now taught online and at a distance, and computers have made increasing inroads into instruction at all phases and at all levels. At the same time, the spirit of educational reform has been felt across the curriculum in all corners of the globe. The watchwords of constructivism, active learning, and learning-by-doing, coupled with the idea of engaging students through one or more sensory modalities, have found increasing support in both the literature and in modern practice.

This chapter describes a set of research and development activities aimed at realizing the potential of computers both in and out of the classroom through an active, constructivist paradigm called role-based learning. In role-based learning, students are afforded the opportunity to join an active learning environment and immerse themselves in the role of a scientist. They are presented with authentic science goals, provided virtual scientific instrumentation, and given access to a range of reference materials. The challenge for the student is to operate within these simulated worlds in order to achieve the goals set for them, and in so doing learn to think and act like a scientific problem solver.

The Worldwide Web Instructional Committee (WWWIC) at North Dakota State University (NDSU) constructs active simulated worlds, populates them with intelligent software agents for atmosphere, infrastructure, and tutoring, and makes them available online. These virtual environments, for Geology, Biology, Archeology, and a range of other disciplines, are constructed according to a uniform set of principles which guide design and promote sharing of techniques and approaches. The research described here is aimed at both developing new innovations in instructional media, and exploring the limits of the strategy.

Assessment activities conducted with a large number of students over the course of several years, using an approach called scenario-based assessment have shown these techniques to be effective and statistically significant in a range of controlled studies. This chapter describes the progress of WWWIC and the results achieved so far.

1   Introduction

The North Dakota State University (NDSU) Worldwide Web Instructional Committee (WWWIC) is engaged in developing a range of Virtual Environments for Education spanning a variety of disciplines, from Earth Science to Anthropology, and from Business to Biology. However, all of these projects share a strategy, a set of assumptions, an approach to assessment, and an emerging tool set, which allows each to leverage from the insights and advances of the others.

These projects are designed to capitalize on the affordances provided by virtual environments. For example, to
- control virtual time and collapse virtual distance,
- create shared spaces that are physical or practical impossibilities,
- support shared experiences for participants in different physical locations,
- implement shared agents and artifacts according to specific pedagogical goals,
- support multi-user collaborations and competitive play.

Each project has the following properties in common. They are role-based and goal-oriented; they are immersive simulations intended to promote learning-by-doing; they are spatially-oriented, exploratory, and highly interactive; they are multi-user and game-like; and they employ software agents as tutors.

2 Project Overviews

Geology Explorer is a virtual world where learners assume the role of a geologist on an expedition to explore the geology of a mythical planet. Learners participate in field-oriented expedition planning, sample collection, and "hands on" scientific problem solving. The Geology Explorer world is simulated on an Object Oriented Multi-user Domain (a MOO). To play the game, students are transported to the planet's surface and acquire a standard set of field instruments. They are issued an "electronic log book" to record their findings and, most importantly, are assigned a sequence of exploratory goals. The students make their field observations, conduct small experiments, take note of the environment, and generally act like geologists as they work towards their goal. A scoring system has been developed, so students can compete with each other and with themselves.

The Virtual Cell (VCell) is an interactive, 3-dimensional visualization of a bio-environment. VCell has been prototyped using the Virtual Reality Modeling Language (VRML), and is to be available via the Internet. To the student, the Virtual Cell looks like an enormous navigable space populated with 3D organelles. In this environment, experimental goals in the form of question-based assignments promote deductive reasoning and problem-solving in an authentic visualized context.

The ProgrammingLand Museum implements an Exploratorium-style museum metaphor to create a hyper-course in computer programming principles aimed at structuring the computer science curriculum as a tour through a virtual museum. Student visitors are invited to participate in a self-paced exploration of the exhibit space where they are introduced to the concepts of computer programming, are given demonstrations of these concepts in action, and are encouraged to manipulate the interactive exhibits as a way of experiencing the principles being taught (Duffy and Jonassen, 1992).

The Virtual Archaeologist is designed to give students an authentic experience that includes elements of a) exploration of a spatially oriented virtual world, b) practical, field-based decision making, and c) critical thinking for scientific problem solving. The objectives of the project include assessment of student performance, evaluation of instructor feedback, and incorporation of that information into the continuing design of the system. The larger objective is the distribution of this experience to archaeology students around the world.

The Blackwood Project is a simulation of a mythical 19th Century Western river town. Participants who join the simulation will accept or be assigned a role in the simulation that is primarily economic in nature. In Blackwood, gameplay is influenced by historical events and players are assigned roles designed to promote collaboration and interaction. Players assume roles in the simulation, such as a blacksmith, but are not expected to learn blacksmithing. Employee software agents actually do the day-to-day chores. The players are "only" expected to manage the retailing and business elements of the game.

Another key element in the research is devising non-standard and qualitative methods of evaluation and assessment to determine the benefit to students derived from their "learn by doing" experiences. Like the educational environment projects themselves, assessment is designed to apply across disciplines.

3   Project Details

WWWIC is an ad hoc group of university faculty dedicated to developing internet-based education and research software. Members of this group foster cross-disciplinary, collaborative relationships with WWWIC faculty, students, and staff as well as those from other universities and institutions. The content of WWWIC immersive environment projects includes subject matter across a variety of disciplines such as anthropology, archaeology, cell biology, commerce, computer science, geology, and history.

3.1   Geology Explorer

The Geology Explorer project implements an educational game for teaching the Geosciences. This takes the form of a synthetic, virtual environment, Planet Oit, where students are given the means and the equipment to explore a planet as a Geologist would.

We describe a pedagogical architecture and an implemented application designed according to these principles. Students assume a role in a simulated environment and learn about real science by exploring in a goal-directed way and competing with other players. The game, which teaches principles of geology, is an implementation of a networked, multi-player, simulation-based, educational environment that illustrates the principles of learning by learning roles.

The Geology Explorer has been built to explore the following beliefs: (1)Educational technology should capitalize on the natural human propensity for role-playing, (2)students will be willing to assume roles if the environment makes it easy to do, and if the environment reinforces role-playing through careful crafting of the explicit tutorial components of the game, and (3) that educational software should be engaging, entertaining, attractive, interactive, and flexible: in short, game-like.

Planet Oit is simulated on a MOO ("MUD, Object-Oriented", where MUD stands for "Multi-User Domain"). MUDs are typically text-based electronic meeting places where players build societies and fantasy environments, and interact within them [Curtis 1992]. Technically, a MUD is a multi-user database and messaging system. The basic components are "rooms" with "exits", "objects" and "players". MUDs support the object management and inter-player messaging that is required for multi-player games, and at the same time provide a programming language for writing the simulation and customizing the MUD.

The usual platform for operating a MUD or MOO is a machine running a Unix-based operating system, although there have always been alternatives, such as a MacIntosh server or a PC running Windows NT. Participants (usually referred to as players) connect by using Telnet or some other, more specialized, client program, which establishes a text-based session on the MOO.

Because the Geology Explorer project is intended to be a platform independent distance education system, the first client software for the project was a Telnet client developed in Java. This enabled connections from either MacIntosh, Microsoft Windows, or Linux X-Windows machines, using either Netscape or Internet Explorer browsers, although for technical reasons the Windows- and Linux-based browsing has been faster and better.

Research in active learning environments includes implementing "live" simulations for exploration and discovery that engage learners while treating them to a plausible synthetic experience. We have implemented the Geology Explorer as a synthetic environment using the freely available Xerox PARC LambdaMOO, which is a development environment for creating text-based virtual worlds, to simulate a portion of Planet Oit (very similar to Earth, and in the same orbit, but directly opposite the Sun). Students "land" on the planet to undertake an exploration exercise armed with tools and instruments implemented as LambdaMOO objects. They are given an authentic geosciences goal, e.g. to locate and report the position of potentially valuable mineral deposits. Accomplishing these goals will entail mastering several geoscience concepts and procedures, and will demonstrate student mastery of the material.

In many respects, Physical Geology is an ideal course for a role-based environment. Unlike many of the other sciences, Physical Geology is highly visual, with landscapes ranging from mountain tops to ocean floors, from arid badlands to intensely-leached tropical soils, from gently-flowing streams to violent volcanic eruptions.

However, it is obviously impractical to take large numbers of students into the field to experience first hand how a geologist makes decisions. However, students can do so in synthetic environments. Within this context, the student makes decisions similar to those of a geologist, using the tools and techniques of geoscience.

The first module mostly involves mineral exploration, where students are expected to plan an expedition, locate and assess potential mineral and ore deposits, and survive to report on it.

The first step was to develop a storyboard for the project which directed the development of the synthetic Planet Oit. A map was then developed to show the different environments on the planet (for example, Brown Dunes) and what will be encountered when the student travels southeast, the red beach, or south, the Lake region. A group of summer school students originally implemented multiple locations from which the geological expedition can begin. Geological tools were developed (such as streak plates, hammers, and Geiger counters), and the appearance and response of 40 minerals and 40 rocks to a series of interactions are described.

Once the layout and artifacts of Planet Oit had been implemented, the "rules of the game" were imposed. In particular, we have built an environment where students are transported to the planet surface and acquire a standard set of field instruments (a rock pick, a small bottle of hydrochloric acid, a magnet, and hand lens, a small glass plate and a streak plate). Students are issued an "electronic log book" to record their findings and, most importantly, are assigned an exploratory goal. These goals are intended to motivate the students to view their surroundings with a critical eye, as a geologist would. Goals are assigned from a principled set in order to leverage the role-based elements of the game.

The students can make their field observations, conduct small experiments, take note of the environment, and generally act like geologists as they work towards their goal of, for example, locating a Kimberlite deposit. A scoring system has been developed, so students can compete with each other and with themselves.

An on-line rock and mineral resource is being developed to allow students access to common reference materials. A simple tutorial browsing mechanism is also planned. Finally, a tracking mechanism has been implemented to follow students through the course of their explorations, in order to identify the way students are using the technology, and to implement software tutors.

On Planet Oit, tutoring is done through non-intrusive but proactive software agents. Agents monitor student actions and "visit" a student when the need arises. Tutors give advice, but they do not mandate or insist on student actions, nor do they block or prevent student actions.

The equipment tutor has been implemented to detect when a student has failed to acquire equipment necessary to achieving their goals The equipment tutor is mainly called by the *purchase* verb (which is how instruments and tools are acquired. The tutor checks whether the student has the instruments needed to satisfy their goals. If not, the tutor remediates on that topic (i.e., the need to buy instruments that serve to satisfy goals). For example, an acid bottle is necessary to identify limestone. If the student has a limestone goal, but has no acid, the student cannot possibly achieve the goal.

The exploration tutor has been implemented to detect when a student has overlooked a goal in their travels. The exploration tutor is called by the exit(s) from each of the locations (rooms) on Planet Oit. The tutor checks whether the student is leaving a room that might satisfy a goal; i.e., if their goal is to locate Kimberlite, and there is Kimberlite in the room they are leaving, the tutor visits the player to inform them.

The science tutor is implemented to detect when a student makes a mistake in identifying rocks and minerals. This tutor will activate to tell a student a wrong guess has been made and why (i.e., what evidence they are lacking), or to tell a student making a correct guess that insufficient evidence has been gathered (i.e., a lucky guess).

3.2   The Virtual Cell

The long term goal of the Virtual Cell development project is to create an environment in which students can learn about the structure and function of the cell. Active learning is our objective. We have decided to introduce our students to the material through the use of experiments. For example, a student might be asked to travel through the cell and identify each of the key organelles. They may come up to a chloroplast and state "This is a chloroplast." Although they may be correct, we want to encourage decision making based on experimentation. So the program will ask them how they know it is a chloroplast.

This line of questioning will motivate the student to collect evidence from experiments that will provide them with the information necessary to distinguish the chloroplast from other cellular organelles. The student will present that evidence to the program, and if it is distinguishing evidence, points will be awarded for completing that task. Similar interactions between the student and the program are planned for all aspects relating cellular structure and function.

VRML (Virtual Reality Modeling Language) was chosen as the language for the development of the Virtual Cell environment because it provides the kind of active, navigable environment we need. Another positive aspect of VRML is that it can be delivered through the familiar browser interface.

Finally, we are planning to create the Virtual Cell as a multiple user environment. To this end, we have chosen LambdaMOO as the server to control the multiple rooms and domains. The cell itself will be a room, and the interior of each organelle will also be room in the LambdaMOO environment. Using a MOO poses unique research opportunities because software must be developed that manages the multiple, simultaneous interactions between objects defined in LambdaMOO, Java, and VRML and synchronized in the Virtual Cell" multiple, simultaneous interactions with the Virtual Cell VRML world. Therefore, we are researching ways in which the MUD/MOO approach can be extended to virtual worlds.

The Virtual Cell (VCell) is an interactive, 3-dimensional visualization of a bio-environment. VCell has been prototyped using the Virtual Reality Modeling Language (VRML), and is available via the Internet. To the student, the Virtual Cell looks like an enormous navigable space populated with 3D organelles. In this environment, experimental goals in the form of question-based assignments promote diagnostic reasoning and problem-solving in an authentic visualized context.

The initial point of entry for the Virtual Cell is a VRML-based laboratory. Here the learner encounters a scientific mentor and receives a specific assignment. In this laboratory, the student performs simple experiments and learns the basic physical and chemical features of the cell and its components. More notably, our laboratory procedures are crafted such that they necessitate a voyage into the Virtual Cell where experimental Science meets virtual reality. As the project progresses, students revisit the laboratory to receive more assignments. Periodically, the student will bring cellular samples back to the virtual lab for experimentation. The Virtual Cell prototype can be visited at http://vcell.ndsu.edu/ .

3.3   The ProgrammingLand MOOseum of Computer Science

The Programming Land MOO at Valley City State University which is being developed as an adjunct to programming classes. The MOO contains material that parallels an introduction to programming in C++. The MOO server is called WinMOO (Unkel, 1997) which is a port of the original LambdaMOO server from UNIX to Windows NT. The original database was the enCore database, which is the LambdaMOO database enhanced with numerous objects of educational merit, such as moderated classrooms, lectures, etc. The server is version 1.8.0p6 and database is enCore Beta 2.

Student visitors to the Virtual Lecture museum are invited to participate in a self-paced exploration of the exhibit space where they are introduced to the concepts of computer programming, are given demonstrations of these concepts in action, and are encouraged to manipulate the interactive exhibits as a way of experiencing the principles being taught.

The museum is being used with one class in the fall 1997 semester and will be used with two in the spring. There are two MOO entryways to the Virtual Lecture. The first leads to a series of rooms that describe the basic commands of the MOO. The other leads to the C++ Foyer exhibit. This takes the student to one of several topics. Each of these lessons may lead to one or several further lessons. A lesson is an amount of instruction that could reasonably be completed in one sitting, whereas a topic is usually several lessons and hence too large for a single session. It should be noted that both lesson and topic are arbitrary terms without specific boundaries in the MOO. If a student wants to learn one lesson in several settings, they have the freedom to progress at their own pace in whatever way they choose. Thus, students do not perceive lesson boundaries or topic boundaries. All they see are single exhibits, which are single rooms and the brief amount of information that is present in that context.

A single exhibit will convey a very limited amount of text. This text may be any of several types. One common exhibit is a signpost. A signpost exhibit does not convey much technical information, instead it is usually the entrance to several other lessons and topics. The C++ Foyer is a signpost directing students in any of several directions. Figure 1 shows the Function Lesson which is a signpost exhibit and an example of what a touring student would actually see in this Virtual Lecture.

```
Function Lesson
  This is the start of a number of lessons about
functions.
  Consider the following menu that may be selected by
letter or topic:
  a) The importance and usefulness of functions (why)
  b) Using functions or calling functions (call)
  c) Overview of function definition (define)
  d) Function parameters (parms)
  e) Function return values (type)
  f) Function and variable scope (scope)
  You may choose any of these and enjoy.
  Obvious exits: [exit] to C++ foyer, [define] to
Function Definition, [call] to Calling Functions,
[parms] to Function Parameters, [scope] to Scope Les-
son, [why] to Why use functions?, [type] to Types
that functions produce
```

Figure 1. An example of a Signpost Room.

The first line "Function Lesson" is the MOO room name. The next ten lines are the room description. The last four lines are a listing of the exits from this room. This description as a signpost does not convey any significant technical information, but does direct students to a series of lessons. This particular signpost is arrayed like a menu. A student may type either "b" or "call" and go to the same room. The name of the room is given when the room is created. The description of the room is written after the room is created and is the main means of conveying information. The last four lines are generated by the MOO server to indicate the available exits. Each of these exits may have one or more synonyms that cause the student to progress to the destination room.

The most common type of exhibit is informational, a room where some content is given. This can take any of the forms that a lecturer would use. For example on the menu of Figure 1 the first option is mostly motivational – why is this feature useful to the student. In an actual lecture this is needed to pique the curiosity or otherwise show the need of the concept about to be discussed. Lecturers do not need to motivate the good students, but a lecture has to be inclusive, so motivational comments are required for a good lecture. Yet in the virtual lecture students may pick and choose what they view and in particular a student may skip the first part of the function lesson if they desire. Other rooms may have the informational content of other parts of a lecture: simple descriptions, a variety of longer descriptions and examples. No oral lecture can have the number of examples of a virtual lecture since the student does not need to view them all, only enough to grasp the concept.

The example of the Virtual Lecture so far presented could be easily implemented with a series of web pages: a hypertext reference document. The next part considers some of the aspects of the MOO that are not readily implementable with web browsers and these enhance the mostly passive hypertext reference document into the active Virtual Lecture.

The MOO attaches to each student a list of exhibits they have visited. This list of exhibits is available to the instructor and is a record of progress and a diagnostic tool for that student. This list cannot consider comprehension, but does demonstrate exposure. For distance learners it is a concrete measure of activity for a student that may have no other communication with the instructor. A student who has a problem, may just have missed the part of the Virtual Lecture that dealt with the item in question, so that an obvious course of remediation can then be suggested.

This history of exhibits also enables an improvement to the structure of the museum. In order to keep the hypertext reference document convenient many more paths must be created than a novice should be allowed to use. Designing a Virtual Lecture requires a balance between the single linear path, which penalizes advanced or returning students, and the potential for too many choices which invites the novice to exhibits where they are more likely to be confused than educated. The solution to this dilemma is the active exit.

The active exit checks the prerequisites for the room. A student taking a path to an advanced topic has their history checked against some possible background exhibits. If the student has visited rooms that form the foundation for the room to be entered, they are allowed in without knowing that their prerequisites have been tested. If they have not visited the rooms needed then the exit suggests that this room may be more confusing than helpful and asks them if they really want to proceed. An advanced student may have acquired the needed knowledge outside the Virtual Lecture and thus can go forward, while a merely curious novice has been warned and at least knows there is potential confusion ahead.

A very important consideration for any educational tool is the interest level that the tool maintains in the student. Consider public libraries: most of those that lend video tapes are actually lending more tapes than books, which is especially remarkable when considering the selection of book dwarfs that of video tapes in most libraries. The implication is clear, video tapes are more engaging than books. Similarly, the Exploratorium model for a museum is more interesting than the older museums with glassed in exhibits and no interaction. If interest level was not a consideration we would write good textbooks, hand them to the students and administer examinations at the end of the time. The impracticality of such an approach is obvious. A web implementation of the reference document will hold a student for a while, but will eventually become essentially the reading of an electronic text. What is needed is something even more interactive than the reference document or even the Virtual Lecture possible in a MOO.

In the web implementation this may be accomplished by Java applets, but in the MOO this will be accomplished by software agents. Such an agent may appear as a code machine that occupies the room and has various commands that operate it. It may also be a robot, that the student might or might not distinguish from another student, who comes alongside and questions or tutors the student as they walk through the museum.

3.4   The Virtual Archeologist

We have started to develop an immersive multi-user 3D virtual environment that faithfully reproduces an archeological site: Like-a-Fishhook/Fort Berthold (LF/FB). The site is rendered as two discrete models, the first representing the site in 1954 (just prior to its destruction by the Garrison Dam flooding), and the second being a mirror of the first, but representing how it was in 1854.

This mirroring will support "time travel" that will enable students to visit both times, and to visualize the relationships between a "dig" and a village a century earlier. The 1954 world is built from "distribution maps" of archaeological features and floor plans (or bird's-eye views) of those features. These archaeological features include linear trenches with wooden post remnants, circular depressions where earth lodges stood (20 excavated) with a series of stains from structural posts, and a variety of soil discolorations from pits, fireplaces, and other features. In the 1854 world, the archaeological traces are seen as timber palisades, "remarkable" earth and timber lodges, cache pits, scaffoldings, etc.

3.4.1   Background: The Like-a-Fishhook Story

Prior to the coming of European Americans, the Mandan, Hidatsa, and Arikara tribes of the Middle Missouri River resided in sedentary earth-lodge communities. Despite a basic similarity of economic and social life, these peoples differed remarkably in language and customs; the Mandan and Hidatsa speak a Siouan dialect, while the Arikara, related to the Pawnee, are members of the Caddoan linguistic group.

One of the most important historic sites of the Northern Plains was Like-a-Fishhook Village, which was occupied simultaneously by all three, known today officially as the Three Affiliated Tribes. Like-A-Fishhook Village, also called Fort Berthold, was located north of the confluence of the Missouri and Knife rivers in central North Dakota. As the last earth-lodge settlement of the Northern Plains, the site documents an extraordinary episode of cultural transformation (Smith, 1972). The village was initially founded in the aftermath of a devastating smallpox epidemic in 1837. The Mandan population was most heavily affected by the epidemic, being reduced to fewer than 200 individuals. Though not as severely struck by this terrible disease, the Arikara and Hidatsa populations shrank as well. Ethnohistorical evidence suggests that the first permanent residents of Like-a-Fishhook Village were Hidatsa who arrived in 1845 (Smith, 1972; pp. 4-5). They were joined shortly thereafter by a smaller group of Mandan. At about the same time as the Hidatsa built their first earth lodges, a white trading company (the American Fur Company), established a post at the site, with log structures and a stockade, which eventually became known as

Fort Berthold (dubbed Fort Berthold I by G. Hubert Smith). By 1862, a new trading post (Fort Berthold II), by a different trading company, had replaced the first, which had burnt to the ground. Also around 1862, the Arikara arrived, establishing themselves in a new section of the village, building on the site of the first fort.

Over the decades, more European Americans moved into the region and the area surrounding Like-A-Fishhook/Fort Berthold Village changed significantly. In the 1860s, Fort Berthold (by then a mixed community of Native Americans, European Americans, and mixed bloods), "was a base for Federal military units campaigning in the Dakota Territory against fugitive remnants" of Native American tribes in the region (Smith, 1972; p. 17). In the late 1880s the village was abandoned, as native residents were forced to leave the site and take up occupation on new areas of the then Fort Berthold Indian Reservation.

Data recovery projects (archaeological salvage excavations) were carried out at the site in 1950-52 and 1954 by the State Historical Society of North Dakota, under contracts with the National Park Service (NPS) and by the River Basin Surveys of the Smithsonian. Rising waters from the Garrison Dam and Reservoir project ultimately inundated the site, which now rests about a mile offshore under the waters of Lake Sakakawea (Garrison Reservoir).

To achieve these goals, we have begun to construct a highly interactive virtual environment (on two levels: 1954 and 1854) that provides "live" simulations for exploration and discovery that will engage learners while treating them to a plausible synthetic experience. Within this context, the student makes decisions similar to those of an archaeologist, using simulated tools and the techniques of archaeology in conjunction with actual data from a real excavation. We have implemented similar systems to teach in a "learn by doing" manner the scientific method and the strategies of deductive problem solving, along with fundamentals of geology [4] and biology [5].

The 1954 level is being constructed using an engineering drawing tool (AutoCAD 2000), to precisely replicate the site according the archeological record. This gives us a "to the inch" model of the location of structural features; wooden posts, underground caches, etc. The 1854 level is being constructed by loading these AutoCAD models into an architectural modeling program (we are currently using Form-Z), and then "extruding" the architectural features to give a faithful-as-possible rendering of the village as it is likely to have looked. We have accomplished one such extrusion of Hidatsa Lodge #1, and we are in the process of creating more (see http://atl .ndsu.edu/props/fishhook/slide.htm for a 2D view of this preliminary work). We propose eventually to capture the entire 40-acre site in this manner, using the archeological and topographical data as recorded in 1954. This includes the village site, the fort, an associated cemetery, and the flood plain where crops were grown. This "mirroring" of time levels is needed to support the "time travel" that we propose.

3.5   The Blackwood Game

The Blackwood Project provides a computer-based educational application for teaching fundamental, economic skills and knowledge, with an emphasis on the marketing and administrative dimensions of the discipline. This takes the form of an authentic, virtual environment where students are given the means and the opportunity to undertake active role-based discovery and learning.

Blackwood is periodically enhanced and improved upon by a new crop of students in Computer Science courses. In order to take advantage of the values of role-based learning, students in these classes act out roles while simultaneously improving the Blackwood game itself.

The Blackwood game implements a mythical town, set in the Old West (circa 1880), where players with Java-enabled browsers connect across the Internet and "inherit" a virtual store. The game is designed to impart the time-independent principles of microeconomics and the practice of retailing, but within an historical context, and by promoting the social and symbiotic relationships that sustain a business culture in the long term. As each turn progresses, players learn their role in the environment and see the results of their actions as well as the impact of other players' actions within the constraints of the simulated world. Students learn about culture (the ideas, values, and beliefs shared by members of a society) and society (e.g., social structure and organization) while at the same time developing historical cross-cultural awareness and understanding. And they will do so in a role-based manner, immersed in an authentic context, assigned authentic goals, and given the opportunity to learn to operate in an historical context.

The Blackwood Project is hosted on the Internet and provides a platform for opportunities for research into distance education, intelligent agents, economic simulation, and assessment of pedagogical approaches.

Following is a description of the game, as it existed prior to January 2001. The implementation of the game had been created through a collaborative effort of the WWWIC and student volunteers at NDSU.

3.5.1   Time Frame

The simulation begins in the Spring of 1880 and continues until the Great Flood destroys the town in the Spring of 1886. Since each virtual week lasts about 8 clock hours, there are three virtual weeks in each human day, and therefore the entire simulation takes approximately three months.

3.5.2   The Impact of History

Players of Blackwood "experience the effects" of history. This is accomplished by the following mechanisms:

1. Newspapers: The simulation tracks events in the 1880-1886 time frame. As events happen in the nation and around the world, they are reported in "Special Editions".
2. Economic Trends: The simulation reflects the impact of western expansion, the advance of railroads, and the discovery of silver deposits, in terms of fluctuations in population. This has immediate and discernible effects on player's businesses as demand (and prices) rise and fall.
3. Atmosphere Agents: The simulation supports a range of software agents that lend "color" to the environment (buffalo hunters, fur trappers, street entertainers, and the like)

3.5.3   The Economic Simulation

An economic model was developed to generate consumer behavior for the game (Hooker and Slator, 1996). The model takes as input the decisions the players have made, and returns a level of demand for each of the stores. In the game, players compete for market share against other human players trying to learn the same role in the simulated environment.

3.5.4   Software Agents

The Blackwood environment is populated by software agents of the following types:

1. Customer Agents: These have been implemented and form the foundation of the economic simulation (Farmers, Ranchers, Railroad Workers, Soldiers, Lumbermen, Transient Settlers, Riverboat Workers, Teamsters, Miners and White Collar Townspeople, and several others). These represent psychographic groups or clusters of consumers (Hooker and Slator, 1996) and their shopping behaviors simulation demand.

2. Merchant Agents: These are not currently implemented but are intended to simulate the activity of agents who run businesses in competition with human players. There are eight merchant roles to be filled by players or merchant agents (Blacksmiths, Cartwrights, Wheelwrights, Dry Goods Store Operators, Tailors, Wood Lot Operators, Stable Operators, and Leather Makers)

3. Employee Agents: These agents see to the daily operation of retailing outlets and conduct the actual transactions with the customer agents.

4. Banker Agents: These agents write loans depending on the player's financial profile.

5. Teamster Agents: These agents deliver goods from the Riverboat landing and the Railroad depot, when they are ordered by players.

3.5.5 Player Roles

Players are assigned a role in the Merchant class. The system arranges that plausible ratios are preserved so the game is not populated with 100 blacksmiths but no tailors. Players are required to procure food and fuel in order to run their households and keep their employee(s) warm and fed. In addition, of course, players must run their businesses as profitably as possible to succeed.

3.5.6 Neighborhoods

Neighborhoods include the Town Square neighborhood, the Old Business District, the Middle/Working Class neighborhood, the New Business District, the Wagon Train Staging Area, the Riverside neighborhood, the North Shanty Town, South Shanty Town, the Government/Financial District, the Wealthy neighborhood, the Lumber Town, the Western Outpost and the Fort Wood Trading Post. Neighborhood populations change over time to simulate the various ebbs and flows of the demographic landscape.

4   Assessment Studies

Education, like many other disciplines, needs computer-aided assistance. Most educational endeavors focus on an instructor, in a classroom, on a campus, at a particular time. Administrators prefer large lectures because that minimizes cost in an era of increasingly tight budgets. The ones who lose out in this scheme are the traditional students, who get very little instructor contact, and those non-traditional learners who cannot take the time to travel the distance to those campuses where knowledge is dispensed.

Education is very labor-intensive. Numerous organizations have applied technology in one form or another to make the instructor more efficient and the process more cost-effective. Diversity University (www.du.org) is a well known example. This paper suggests another approach.

Consider the most common means of teaching in this country: the lecture. In one session the teacher may give out information in a cost-effective way. Unfortunately, this method has some serious deficiencies. Lectures are very much teacher-centered, the teacher is elevated as the only one who really has something to share and is proclaimed the master of the students' destiny. Communication is typically uni-directional, the instructor speaks and the students listen. If well done, in a small group setting, it can be quite good with student involvement, interaction among all members of the group, a sense of ownership. Yet, the practical realities are that a small group is an expensive luxury. Instead, the lecture model views students as passive information sponges. Students are to be quiet, hanging on every word the teacher utters and carefully copying every single mark recorded on the blackboard. There is to be no comprehension at this time, for if a student considers an item for too long the instructor is on to a new topic and they have missed forever some valuable information. On the contrary, their task is to faithfully record every bit of information and, while outside of the classroom, attempt to make sense of it all. In rare cases a student might ask a question during a lecture, but self-consciousness prevents most of these. The problem, even with small group settings, is the experience is more passive than active, and the value of "active" versus "passive" learning has become increasingly clear (Reid, 1994).

There are many students whose learning style makes it quite difficult for them in a lecture setting. They have been branded as slow learners, in high school and shuffled into vocational programs that are much more hands on. It such a situation many of these flourish, not because they were incapable of the higher reasoning needed, but because coincidentally the vocational programs happened to match their learning style. It is no wonder that many people decry the use of the lecture mechanism, yet what is there to replace it?

The content of a lecture can be communicated by a number of means, to make it even more cost effective. Instead of concentrating the students in a single classroom, use some broadcast media, such as television to disseminate the image and sound to a much wider audience. This still has the disadvantages of a single time and the expense of broadcasting, but can effectively communicate nearly as well as a live performance. A videotape can capture the performance, but may be harder to distribute than a video signal. It does have the notable advantage that the student now has control of the time of presentation. Some of the power has been wrested from the instructor and given to the student. However, the presentation itself is very much linear. The student must start at the beginning and process it sequentially. The fast forward, rewind and pause buttons give them some options not available in a real lecture, but the format is still essentially linear. The corresponding disadvantage is the experience is almost totally passive.

The ubiquitous Internet can make a contribution in active learning. The lecture can be reduced to text and graphics and then put in a succession of world wide web pages. Although, they can still be arrayed in a linear order, hypertext may be structured in many other shapes as well. A link to an example may be viewed or skipped. Now the learner has control of many aspects of the presentation. They choose which pages to visit and in what order; the experience is now primarily in the hands of the learner. In this respect, a collection of web pages may be superior to either a traditional text book or a traditional lecture. To be sure, there is a loss of interest as we proceed from the teacher speaking live in a classroom, to the captured image on tape, to merely text and graphics on a web page. The web page is not as engaging as the lecture, but the web page is learner-centered: the learner has control of the process. However, browsing through hypertext is still largely passive in nature.

One possible implementation is, as has been suggested, a collection of web pages. Each page contains a small amount of text and supporting graphics. Each page is then linked to appropriate other pages. The links then structure how a student can browse; this approach is similar, in certain respects to the way traditional museums are organized. In the museum metaphor, each page is an exhibit.

There are some obvious advantages to this type of implementation that need not be belabored here. HTTP servers are quite common, with most higher education institutions already having a server. Authoring web pages is relatively easy. Many applications, such as word processors, have some facility in this area. The hard part is not the web authoring, but that the content is technically and educationally appropriate. The web is available continually to anyone, anywhere; distance education is becoming reality.

Despite the obvious advantages of the world wide web, it is still a relatively passive mechanism. The active learning alternative is the synthetic environment where learners can experience their education in a "learn by doing" way. The Virtual Lecture approach implements an Exploratorium-style museum metaphor to create a hyper-course aimed at structuring the curriculum as a tour through a virtual museum. Student visitors to the Virtual Lecture museum are invited to participate in a self-paced exploration of the exhibit space where they are introduced to the concepts of the particular domain, are given demonstrations of these concepts in action, and are encouraged to manipulate the interactive exhibits as a way of experiencing the principles being taught.

Virtual Lectures are implemented using freely available MOO environments (for example, the Xerox PARC LambdaMOO (Curtis, 1992) or the High Wired Encore MOO (Haynes and Holmevik,1997)). A MOO is an Object Oriented MUD where a MUD is a Multi User Domain. The most common use of these has been for role-playing games and the like. The metaphor of a MOO is of a text based virtual reality, with rooms and players. In this kind of educational setting a MOO room corresponds to a web page. When a student enters the room, an amount of text is presented in a way analogous to the browsing of a web page. The exits to the room are marked and the student may weave through the museum in the same way as the web. This minimal use of the MOO is equivalent to the hypertext reference document.

However, exploring a MOO is quite different from browsing a series of web pages. MOOs can be much more interactive. A MOO allows the interaction between one student and other students, interaction between the student and the environment, and between a student and software agents. Furthermore, record keeping is possible and even easy in a MOO in contrast with a web implementation. Using a MOO, the capabilities of a web reference document can be enhanced into a virtual lecture.

A MOO contains all the capabilities of an Internet chat room. Thus, students are aware of each other's presence in the room. They may inquire as to whom is presently in the museum and where these people may be. If either other students or instructors are present in the room then they may enter into a conversation. This conversation may be public, received by everyone currently in the room or private, only heard by two participants. A person not in the room may be paged, that is signaled that a conversation is desired and where the originating person is. A student (or a teacher) may disguise their identity. This has the effect of freeing them to ask questions they may not be brave enough to make if their identity is known. Two students at different physical locations may thus communicate and engage in collaborative work, which would be impossible on a web site. The student has all the control they had in the web implementation and substantially more as well. A MOO may also contain software agents. These are programs that occupy the MOO in approximately the same way as a student. They may interact with the student in the form of a tutor or peer.

Record keeping in a web site is very difficult. A server may record what page was served but the identity of whom received the page is usually only an IP address. In contrast a MOO requires a real login and password. Because of this login process, a variety of record keeping is kept automatically and more is available with special programming. It is therefore possible to track students' progress through the simulation.

5 Assessment Results

All WWWIC projects are based on the idea of authentic assessment (Bell, Bareiss, and Beckwith, 1994), within authentic contexts, where the assessment goal is to determine the benefit to students derived from their "learn by doing" experience using our virtual environments. Our scenario-based assessment protocol is a qualitative one that seeks to measure how student thinking has improved.

When learners join the synthetic environment they are assigned goals, selected by content matter experts to be appropriate to the learner's experience. Goals are assigned point values, and learners accumulate objectively measured scores as they achieve their goals. The goals are taken from a principled set, where easier goals are followed by more advanced ones. Similarly, certain goals in a set are required while others are optional. In this way, designers can insure that highly important concepts are thoroughly covered while allowing the maximum flexibility to the learner. Subject matter experts identify teaching objectives in more-or-less traditional ways, while learner outcomes are assessed in terms of the performance of specific and authentic tasks. This is the particular strength of learn-by-doing immersive environments, that a learner's success in achieving their goals provides an automatic measure of their progress.

In addition to these outcome-based measures, all students are asked to answer open-ended scenario-based questions before and after the experiment. These scenario questions are word problems that present the student with a situation that a scientist might be confronted with (the complete set of Planet Oit scenarios can be viewed at http://www.cs.ndsu.nodak.edu/~slator/html/PLANET/assess-scen.html). Students respond to the question with a narrative answer, which is evaluated according to an established protocol.

5.1   Geology Explorer Experiment Results

Students were divided into three experimental groups: two groups completed a self-evaluation in which they rated their abilities and experience working with computers and computer software. These were asked to experience Planet Oit or an alternate internet-based activity equal in estimated time-on-task; a third group did no additional activity. Then, after the players had experienced an extended exploration of Planet Oit (or alternative exercise), they were given a similar post-test survey with different but analogous problem solving scenarios, and asked again to record their questions and impressions. These documents were then compared with the pretest versions, looking for evidence of improved performance. If players score better on the problem solving scenarios, this creates the clear implication that they have learned from the experience. Analysis of the data shows that students who participated in the Planet Oit experience performed significantly better on scenario questions compared to those that participated in the alternative exercise or those who did no additional activity.

Lately you and your best friend have been experimenting with "new age" forms of relaxation and health improvement. One day your friend tells you that there is going to be a Crystal Power Retreat at a nearby national park and you can't resist.

It's a beautiful summer night, and you spread out your sleeping bag after a fun day of looking at exhibits and demonstrations. Your souvenir of the day is a beautiful quartz crystal you purchased from a vendor. You are tired from the day's activities, but are unable to sleep as something hard is digging into your back.

You grope around and dislodge a hard, clear, thumbnail-sized crystal.

Your friend says, "Cool! I'll give you five bucks for that."

What do you do?

List the things you would consider in your decision.

List the questions you would ask yourself, and reasons behind those questions.

Figure 2. A sample scenario from the Geology Explorer.

Scores were evaluated using a one-way analysis of variance and the Duncan's means separation test (Table 1). No significant difference ($P = 0.393$) was detected among Pre-experience group means. In contrast, Post-experience group means demonstrated a significant difference ($P = 0.002$). Among these means the Post-experience mean of the Geology Explorer group was significantly higher mean test score than the other two groups.

Please note this is the first ever result of its kind, and its importance cannot be over-stressed. We have discovered an effect. While a few others have shown significance in controlled studies over the years (e.g. Huppert et al., 1998; Mestre et al., 1992; Van Haneghan et al., 1992), this is the first where significant improvement in student learning provably resulted as a direct consequence of student use of an immersive (and self-paced) virtual environment, without direct intervention from a teacher or indeed any additional classroom experience at all. These results unequivocally support our methods and justify the approach.

Table 1. Performance results of 1998 Geology Explorer experiment.

Group	Group size	Pre-experience mean score	Post-experience mean score
Control	161	9.3a	25.6a
Alternate	95	8.5a	24.4a
Geology Explorer	78	6.8a	35.9b
		$F = 0.094$	$F = 6.320$
		$P = 0.393$	$P = 0.002$

5.2 Virtual Cell Experiment Results

To test whether users of the Virtual Cell have an increased ability to solve cell biology problems in a manner reminiscent of a professional in the field of cell biology, we collaborated with instructors teaching the large enrollment General Biology (NDSU Biol 150) class during the fall semester, 1999. General Biology is an introductory course for science majors which concentrates on cellular and molecular biology, genetics, and evolution. Students were recruited to the experiment by offering them the opportunity to earn extra credit points. As in the Geology experiment, two groups were matched to ensure equal distributions of technological ability. The volunteers were assigned to the Virtual Cell and Alternate experimental groups so that computer literacy was equal for both groups. Those students who did not volunteer formed the Control group which did not participate in any activities beyond normal lectures and labs.

Members of the Virtual Cell experimental group completed two Virtual Cell modules. The first module, *Organelle Identification*, was completed at the beginning of the semester. The second module, *Cellular Respiration*, was completed six weeks later. Students were given ten days to complete each module. Student progress through the modules was followed by a game-like point scoring system.

The alternate group was included to serve as a computer-based, time-on-task control. Students in this group were sent to a series of WWW sites that contained content material similar to that offered in the Virtual Cell modules. Participation was monitored by completion of an on-line quiz. Each quiz was evaluated to determine the student made an "honest effort" to study the WWW sites. Specific questions were included that could only be answered if the student visited the site.

All students, whether in control or test groups, were asked to complete two scenario-based questions at the beginning of the semester, before their Virtual Cell or alternative assignments. One question asked them to act as a cell biologist and design experimental approaches to solving a problem in which they must distinguish between cellular organelles (Figure 3). The second question tested the students' ability to determine experimentally why reactions related to mitochondrial electron transport were not functioning properly. Similar scenario questions were given to all students at the end of the semester. 332 of the students answered both the pre and post questions.

Two M.S. students in Biology independently graded each of the 1328 answers (= 332 students * 4 questions each, two pre and two post). Prior to grading, these students were trained according to a standard evaluation protocol. Our grader training appeared to be effective. Because the correlation between the 1328 scores assigned by each of the two graders was significantly different from zero

(r=0.75), we used the average grader score as the experimental observation.

You are on a foreign fellowship to work with Dr. Larsson in Sweden. Dr. Larsson is a cell biologist who specializes in human diseases. A new group of patients arrived recently exhibiting myopathy, a severe muscle weakness. The most prominent symptom is the severe muscular weakness that occurs after only a short period of exercise. Using his vast experience with cellular diseases, Dr. Larsson immediately suggests the Golgi apparatus is not functioning properly. This strikes you as not quite right. You suspect another organelle is not functioning correctly. You quickly volunteer to test Dr. Larsson's hypothesis.

While thinking as a biologist, list the things you will consider when designing your experiments.

Briefly describe the experimental results that will allow you to determine which organelle is not functioning properly.

Figure 3. An example scenario from the Virtual Cell.

One-way analysis of variances were performed to compare the mean scores for the pre- and post-experience scenario scores on the data combined between the two class sections (Table 2). From the group means, it can be concluded that students who completed the Virtual Cell modules performed significantly higher on the post scenario tests than either the control or alternative groups. This result was observed for questions relating to both the *Organelle Identification* and *Cellular Respiration* modules. In contrast, the pre-experience test scores among the three groups were not significantly different for the *Cellular Respiration* module.

This large experiment clearly demonstrates that the Virtual Cell experience has a significantly positive effect on the ability of students to solve problems in the manner of a cell biologist. The fact that the Virtual Cell group mean value is significantly higher than the Alternate group strongly suggests the improved ability is not simply the result of computer-based time-on-task, but rather is directly related to the Virtual Cell experience. This is encouraging because the experimental effect is identical to that observed with the Geology Explorer.

Table 2. Mean and F-probability for the 1999 Virtual Cell experiment.

	Organelle Identification Module		Cellular Respiration Module	
	Pre-test Scenario	Post-test Scenario	Pre-test Scenario	Post-test Scenario
Control Mean*	11.5a	17.4a	7.6	10.6a
Alternate Mean	13.5ab	19.7a	8.8	13.7a
Virtual Cell Mean	15.5b	22.7b	8.0	17.3b
F-probability	0.005	0.001	0.431	0.001

*Population sizes are: control = 145; alternate = 94; and Virtual Cell = 93.

6   Related Work

Over the past two decades there have been a number of meta-analyses of the literature pertaining to the effectiveness of technology on learning. According to Phipps and Merisotis (1999), Russell recently concluded that most of the research indicates no significant difference in effectiveness of learning when comparing the use of technology at a distance with conventional classroom instruction. According to Gormly (1996), in spite of great expectations, the overall impact of technology on education has been very small.

Some meta-analyses have reported favorable results from the use of technology in learning (Roblyer, 1989; Moore and Thompson, 1990; Kulik and Kulik, 1991; Snowman, 1995). However, a number of authors have cautioned that much of the research is flawed and that results should be questioned (Phipps and Merisotis, 1999; Moore and Thompson, 1990; Lookatch, 1995; Lookatch, 1996; Regian and Shute, 1994). Kulik (1994) points out that meta-analyses usually ignore factors such as experimental design that may affect the evaluation results of the meta-analyses.

Criticism of past research includes the lack of control for extraneous variables by random assignment of subjects to experimental and control groups (Phipps and Merisotis, 1999), and the use of measurement instruments with questionable validity and reliability (Phipps and Merisotis, 1999). Other problems include lack of research with regard to critical thinking skills (Phipps and Merisotis, 1999; Kearsley, 1998; Trotter, 1998; Coley et al., 1997; Dunlap and Grabinger, 1996), the lack of consideration of differences such as preferred learning styles and gender, small sample size (Phipps and Merisotis, 1999; Trotter, 1998). Very few studies have been found which randomly assigned subjects to groups.

Some studies have been reported as exemplary in recent literature (Phipps and Merisotis, 1999; Viadero, 1997; U.S. House of Representatives, 1997; Coley et al., 1997; Huppert et al., 1998; Regian and Shute, 1994). One, *The Adventures of Jasper Woodbury*, is a set of twelve video-based adventures designed by researchers at Vanderbilt University's Learning and Technology Center to improve complex mathematical thinking ability of students. A number of studies with different experimental designs have been conducted to test the effectiveness of Jasper (Viadero, 1997; Van Haneghan et al., 1992; Vye et al., 1997; The Cognition and Technology Group at Vanderbilt, 1997; Goldman et al., 1994; Young et al., 1996). Jasper classrooms perform as well as traditional classrooms at solving standard, one-step word problems, but they are significantly better than traditional classroom control groups at solving multistep word problems that require complex reasoning. Random assignment to groups was used in some of the studies.

These studies are among the few to show that it is possible to positively effect student thinking skills through the use of technology. The technologies, though, are all much different from our virtual world studies, with generally smaller sample sizes.

Educational computer games have a history dating back to the 1950s when business colleges began requiring their students to compete in a simulated business environment. These attempts have persisted through to the present, with a vast array of implementations ranging from math drill-and-practice, such as MathBlaster, to keyboarding skills, such as Mavis Bacon Teaches Typing, to problem-solving adventures like Oregon Trail. Many of these have worked their way into the schools, and form a productive niche. These systems are almost universally single-user and, with notable exceptions like Oregon Trail, are usually quite inflexible and focused on narrow teaching goals.

Recently, several projects have emerged implementing immersive virtual reality such as a tool called ScienceSpace at George Mason University (Nadis, 1999). However, wider adoption of Science-Space is dependent on advances in video-game technology before it becomes affordable. There are also a number of simulation tools that have been developed for job-related training, including VRML tutors for training power transformer operators, and CAD-based tutors for machine tool operators (Tam et al., 1999; Venner, 1999). Other science learning projects include NICE, an immersive environment that allows children to construct and maintain simple virtual ecosystems, collaborate virtually with children at remote sites, and form stories based on their interactions (Mahoney, 1998).

7   Conclusions

Other projects related to those described above include the Virtual Tools project which is designed to create software tools that will enable content experts to craft virtual worlds for instruction with a minimum of intervention or oversight by computing professionals. These tools include software for building abstraction hierarchies, concept frames, object interfaces, virtual maps, agent attitudes, and others.

Software agents are another of the continuing pursuits of WWWIC projects (Slator and Farooque, 1998). Several of the games implement a variety of agents from simple avatars providing atmosphere, to characters the contribute to game play, to tutors that visit players when they have made an error of certain types.

Assessment is another continuing research topic. WWWIC is developing a strategy and interfaces to a subjective evaluation of student progress that relies on player recall rather than objective recognition. These assessment instruments are being developed and incorporated into the pedagogical framework under which all the projects are working.

Future plans include the implementation of the "second generation" of virtual environments which seek to do two things:

- press the role-based elements in order to create more local player contexts that promote collaboration as well as competition.
- cross discipline boundaries by incorporating, for example, social science elements into a microeconomic context.

The Blackwood game is intended to be simulations of this second generation type.

Acknowledgments

The NDSU Worldwide Web Instructional Committee (WWWIC) research is currently supported by funding from the National Science Foundation under grants DUE-9981094 and EIA-0086142, and from the Department of Education under grant #P116B000734 and # P116B011528

References

Brown, J.S., Collins, A., and Duguid, P. (1989), "Situated cognition and the culture of learning," *Educational Researcher*, 18(1), pp. 32-42.

Bruckman, A. (1993), *MOOse-Crossing*, Thesis Proposal, Cambridge: MIT.

Carlstrom, E.-L. (1992), "Better living through language: the communicative implications of a text-only virtual environment," Student Paper, Grinnell College.

Clark, J.T., Bergstrom, A., Landrum III, J., Larson, F., and Slator, B. (2000), "Digital archiving network for anthropology," in Niccolucci, F. (ed.), *Proceedings of the Virtual Archaeology Between Scientific Research and Territorial Marketing Conference*, Arezzo, Italy, BAR International Series: Oxford.

Curtis, P. (1997), "Not just a game: how LambdaMOO came to exist and what it did to get back at me," in Haynes, C. and Holmevik, J.R. (eds.), *High Wired: on the Design, Use, and Theory of Educational MOOs*, Ann Arbor: University of Michigan Press.

Curtis, P. (1992), "Mudding: social phenomena in text-based virtual realities," *Proceedings of the Conference on Directions and Implications of Advanced Computing* (sponsored by Computer Professionals for Social Responsibility), Berkeley, April.

Curtis, P. and Nichols, D. (1993), "MUDs grow up: social virtual reality in the real world," *Third International Conference on Cyberspace*, May.

Dewey, J. (1900), *The School and Society*, Chicago, IL: The University of Chicago Press.

Duffy, T.M. and Jonassen, D.H. (1992), "Constructivism: new implications for instructional technology," in Duffy, T.M. and Jonassen, D.H. (eds.), *Constructivism and the Technology of Instruction*, Hillsdale: Lawrence Erlbaum.

Duffy, T.M., Lowyck, J., and Jonassen, D.H. (1983), *Designing Environments for Constructive Learning*, New York: Springer-Verlag.

Hartman, J. and Wernecke, J. (1996), *The VRML 2.0 Handbook: Building Moving Worlds on the Web*, Reading, MA: Addison-Wesley Publishing Co. Silicon Graphics, Inc.

Haynes, C. and Holmevik, J.R. (eds.) (1997), *High Wired: on the Design, Use and Theory of Educational MOOs*, University of Michigan.

Hill, C. and Slator, B.M. (1998), "Virtual Lecture, Virtual Laboratory, or Virtual Lesson," *Proceedings of the Small College Computing Symposium (SCCS98)*, Fargo-Moorhead, April, pp. 159-173.

Hooker, R. and Slator, B.M. (1996), "A model of consumer decision making for a MUD based game," *Proceedings of the Simulation-Based Learning Technology Workshop at the Third International Conference on Intelligent Tutoring Systems (ITS'96)*, Montréal, June 11, pp. 49-58.

Juell, P. (1999), "Educational opportunities using VRML in the AI classroom," *Proceedings of the International Conference on Mathematics/Science Education and Technology (M/SET-99)*, Association for the Advancement of Computing in Education, San Antonio, March 1-4.

Kass, A., Burke, R., Blevis, E., and Williamson, M. (1994), "The GuSS Project: integrating interaction and practice through guided simulation," Institute for the Learning Sciences, Technical Report #94-34, Northwestern University: Evanston, IL.

McClean, P.E., Schwert, D.P., Juell, P., Saini-Eidukat, B., Slator, B.M., White, A. (1999), "Cooperative development of visually-oriented, problem-solving science courseware," *International Conference on Mathematics/Science Education & Technology*, March 1-4, 1999, San Antonio, TX.

McClean, P., Saini-Eidukat, B., Schwert, D., Slator, B., and White, A. (2001), "Virtual worlds in large enrollment biology and geology classes significantly improve authentic learning," in Chambers, J.A. (ed.), *Selected Papers from the 12th International Conference on College Teaching and Learning (ICCTL-01)*, Jacksonville, FL: Center for the Advancement of Teaching and Learning. April 17-21, pp. 111-118.

McLellan, H. (1994), "Virtual reality goes to school," *Computers in Schools*, vol. 9, no. 4.

McLuhan, M. (1964), *Understanding Media*, New York: McGraw-Hill Book Co.

Poirer, J.R. (1995), "Interactive multiuser realities: MUDs, MOOs, MUCKs, and MUSHes," *The Internet Unleashed*, Indianapolis: Sam's Publishing, pp. 1126-1127.

Reid, T.A. (1994), "Perspectives on computers in education: the promise, the pain, the prospect," *Active Learning*, 1(1), Dec. CTI Support Service, Oxford, UK.

Saini-Eidukat, B., Schwert, D., and Slator, B.M. (1998), "Text-based implementation of the Geology Explorer, a multi-user role-playing virtual world to enhance learning of geological problem-solving," *GSA Abstracts with Programs*, vol. 30, no. 7, October 29, Toronto.

Saini-Eidukat, B., Schwert, D., and Slator, B.M. (1999), "Designing, building, and assessing a virtual world for science education," *Proceedings of the 14th International Conference on Computers and Their Applications (CATA-99)*, April 7-9, Cancun.

Schank, R.C. (1991), "Case-based teaching: four experiences in educational software design," ILS Technical Report #7, Northwestern University, Evanston, IL.

Schwert, D.P., Slator, B.M., Saini-Eidukat, B. (1999), "A virtual world for earth science education in secondary and postsecondary environments: The Geology Explorer," *International Conference on Mathematics/Science Education &Technology*, March 1-4, San Antonio, TX, pp. 519-525.

Shute, V.J. and Glaser, R. (1990), "A large-scale evaluation of an intelligent discovery world: Smithtown," *Interactive Learning Environments*, 1(1), 51-77.

Slator, B.M. and Hill, C. (1999), "Mixing media for distance learning: using IVN and Moo in Comp372," *World Conference on Educational Media, Hypermedia and Telecommunications (ED-MEDIA 99)*, June 19-24, Seattle, WA.

Slator, B.M. and Farooque, G. (1998), "The agents in an agent-based economic simulation model," *Proceedings of the 11th International Conference on Computer Applications in Industry And Engineering (CAINE-98)*, November 11-13, Las Vegas, Nevada USA, pp. 175-179. (International Society for Computers and Their Applications (ISCA)).

Slator, B.M. and Chaput, H. (1996), "Learning by learning roles: a virtual role-playing environment for tutoring," *Proceedings of the Third International Conference on Intelligent Tutoring Systems (ITS'96)*, Montreal: Springer-Verlag, June 12-14, pp. 668-676. (Lecture Notes in Computer Science, edited by Frasson, C., Gauthier, G., and Lesgold, A.)

Slator, B.M., Schwert, D., Saini-Eidukat, B., McClean, P., Abel, J., Bauer, J., Gietzen, B., Green, N., Kavli, T., Koehntop, L., Marthi, B., Nagareddy, V., Olson, A., Jia, Y., Peravali, K., Turany, D., Vender, B., and Walsh, J. (1998), "Planet Oit: a virtual environment and educational role-playing game to teach the geosciences," *Proceedings of the Small College Computing Symposium (SCCS98)*, Fargo-Moorhead, April, pp. 378-392.

Slator, B.M., Schwert, D., Saini-Eidukat, B. (1999), "Phased development of a multi-modal virtual educational world," *Proc. of the International Conference on Computers and Advanced Technology in Education (CATE'99)*, Cherry Hill, NJ, May 6-8.

Slator, B.M., Juell, P., McClean, P.E., Saini-Eidukat, B., Schwert, D.P., White, A.R., and Hill, C. (1999), "Virtual environments for education," *Journal of Network and Computer Applications*, 22(4), pp. 161-174.

Smith, G.H. (1972), *Like-A-Fishhook Village and Fort Berthold, Garrison Reservoir North Dakota*, Anthropological Papers 2, National Park Service, US Department of the Interior, Washington, D.C.

Suzie, J. (1994), "Donut: Starknet campus of the future," *The Journal of Virtual Reality in Education*, vol. 1, no.1, pp. 46-47.

TeleEducation NB (1995), *Is Distance Learning Any Good?* http://tenb.mta.ca/anygood/ .

Unkel, C. (1997), *WinMOO*, http://www-personal.engin.umich.edu /~cunkel .

White, A.R., McClean, P.E., and Slator, B.M. (1999), "The Virtual Cell: an interactive, virtual environment for cell biology," *World Conference on Educational Media, Hypermedia and Telecommunications (ED-MEDIA 99)*, June 19-24, Seattle, WA, pp. 1444-1445.

Chapter 2

Traditional vs. Technology-Integrated Distance Education

Z. Erlich, J. Gal-Ezer and D. Lupo

This chapter describes the transition to the integration of technology into traditional distance learning methods, at the Open University of Israel.

To exemplify this transition, we will present two case studies: One is a description of an innovative framework for integrating technology into a course called "Computer Applications for Social Science Students." It is based on traditional distance learning methods combined with e-learning tools. One of the main findings was that teaching the course using technological tools contributed greatly to the leaning process.

The second case study examined computer science students' attitudes towards the integration of technologies into their studies. The development process of a new mixed model for integrating technology, based on this study, will be presented. This mixed model can be adopted in other similar cases.

The conclusions obtained from our studies emphasize the advances pertaining to the use of Internet techniques in teaching and learning in general and especially in distance education. As new technologies are constantly being developed, there is a need to test them carefully and decide which and how they can be added to our mixed mode, described in this chapter.

1   Introduction

The conventional image of an academic course – a lecture hall with an instructor on the podium facing a group of students – does not apply to distance education. Distance education is traditionally based mainly on self-study of written materials, tutorials, submission of assignments and an examination at the end of the course. In the last decade, distance education has undergone rapid change due to the proliferation of new information and communication technologies, which has resulted in the evolution of novel approaches to teaching and learning. These developments have cultural implications on the habits of consumption of higher education by individuals and society.

In a world of rapidly-developing technologies, the Open University of Israel (OUI), a distance education institution that offers academic studies throughout Israel, set up the Center for Information Technology in Distance Education – *Shoham* – whose major focus is on research and development of teaching methods based on new information technologies and incorporating them into the course-development and teaching procedures at the Open University.

Since the pedagogical aspects of technology-mediated learning are not yet fully developed and since technological tools and their applications are in a state of constant flux, both in theory and in practice, and since where education is concerned, revolutions are not acceptable, educators and policy makers, separately and together, must carefully examine where the technology can help, and where it has little value. Hence the process of integrating technology in education must be evolutionary. As a result, at the OUI, we consider it very important to closely examine the process of integration of technologies into our distance education model, taking into consideration the specific needs of the various disciplines and the different study levels.

This chapter will describe traditional distance education at the Open University of Israel and the transition to the integration of technology into distance learning methods since the establishment of *Shoham*. To exemplify this transition, we will present two case studies: One is a description of an innovative framework for integrating technology into a course called "Computer Applications for Social Science Students." The course was developed to teach Social Science students computer literacy so as to enable them to utilize technologies and to take advantage of their growing potential in the distance learning environment. It is based on traditional distance learning methods combined with e-learning tools such as CD-ROM courseware, Web sites, and discussion forums, and is now a required course taken by more than 1,200 Social Science students each semester.

The second case study focuses on students specializing in Computer Science taking different courses on various levels. We assumed that these students did not need an introductory computer applications course, and that they would be capable of using the technologies with no prior training. However, we found that this was not as self-evident as we thought. After discovering that even CS students were reluctant to adopt CMC learning, we conducted a study to examine students' attitudes towards the integration of technologies into their studies in order to determine whether Internet activities can serve as a substitute for face-to-face activities.

Based on this study, we have developed a new model for integrating technology which can be adopted in other distance learning courses.

2 Traditional Distance Education at the OUI

The Open University of Israel (OUI) is a distance education institution which was established in 1976 to provide academic studies to students throughout the country. The University is open to all those who wish to study a single course or to pursue a full program of study toward a Bachelor's degree. Enrollment does not require matriculation or any other certificate from another educational institution. The various aspects of distance education developed by the Open University, along with its open admission policy, aim to open the world of higher education to all, irrespective of age, place of residence or occupation, in order to enable every individual to realize his or her academic ability. The method is not space- or time-dependent as it is not based on a central campus where lecturers and students gather, or on an established and uniform schedule.

The Open University is flexible in structure and organization. Applicants joining the Open University student body are not required to enroll in a faculty or department, but rather in specific courses. The students select the courses which comprise their program of study from a varied and wide-ranging selection. Those who wish to enhance their knowledge and understanding rather than pursue a degree may register for courses in all disciplines without any limitations. Students studying towards a degree are bound by rules which limit the multi-disciplinary flexibility of their personal program of study, such that their course list – which is the basis of their degree – has both internal logic and academic justification accepted in the general university community. The individual program may include a diverse array of disciplines (which in other universities belong to separate departments or faculties), or may be based on a more focused disciplinary format which resembles, to some extent, single-discipline or dual-discipline programs of study in other institutions.

Students at the Open University determine their own rate of progress which is not measured in units of time (years or semesters), but rather in the number of accumulated credits. Thus, the Open University does not compel its students to complete a uniform and prescribed program of study during a certain academic year. The individual rate of progress is determined by the students themselves – based on their diligence and determination as well as the amount of time available to them in light of their familial and work commitments. The only constraining time-frame is the semester, as the duration of most Open University courses is one semester of 15 weeks, and the students are required to meet the requirements of the course during the semester in which they are enrolled. Thus, there are students who study at a moderate rate, one course each semester, while others enroll in two or more courses simultaneously.

Thanks to its flexibility and in light of its academic vision, the OUI serves a wide range of students, from teenagers to pensioners, and from full-time students to working adults with families, including students with no formal high school education, high school graduates, and university graduates who are interested in expanding their knowledge in other fields.

The **Academic Counseling and Study Guidance System** bridges the Open University's open admissions policy and its academic requirements. It supplements the teaching system and accompanies the students throughout their studies by providing academic counseling and imparting and developing learning skills. Academic counseling is available in various frameworks including workshops and personal sessions. Special services are available for students with learning disabilities.

Academic counseling is intended to help the students choose a study track, select their first courses, plan and complete their program of study and transfer from one study track to another. Academic counselors provide information and updates concerning changes in courses and study tracks. The academic counselors hold office hours throughout the year on the main campus of the Open University and at study centers throughout the country.

Open University study centers function in effect as "campuses." These centers have several functions: they serve as a site for tutorial sessions in classrooms or laboratories and a meeting place for students. The centers also provide library and other services such as television broadcasts, movies, and so forth.

The OUI offers close to 500 courses in Life Sciences, Natural Sciences, Mathematics, Computer Science, Social Sciences, Management, Judaic Studies, Education, and Humanities, and serves more than 34,000 students. These courses are fundamentally different from courses offered at other universities. They are printed scholarly or scientific works, consisting of one or more volumes written by renowned specialists in their field and produced especially for OUI students. The coursebooks are adapted to self-study: they are usually divided into units, each of which deals with a specific topic and is studied within a fixed period of time. The material is explained with utmost clarity; guiding questions are integrated into the material, as are exercises and self-assessment questions. These enable students to test themselves on the material and to determine whether their level of understanding up to that point is satisfactory or whether they should consider rereading a specific section or unit.

Some of the courses are based on existing textbooks. These are accompanied by a detailed guide that contains the self-study tools characteristic of the Open University textbook and indicates which sections the student should read, expands, explains and clarifies sections or topics in the textbook if necessary, and provides questions and answers.

Each course includes face-to-face components: group tutorials, laboratory work or study excursions, in addition to periodic symposia. However, these components do not constitute the core of the course, and in most cases are not necessary for its successful completion. Students wishing to turn their studies into a personal campus can do so with utmost success based on the Open University's primary teaching method.

Students who choose to participate in the group tutorials can usually do so in one of two ways: regular or intensive. Regular tutorials meet once every two or three weeks; the intensive tutorials take place weekly. At the sessions, students discuss the course material studied up to that point, and have the opportunity to examine issues which they encountered during their self-study. While participation in these sessions is usually not mandatory, it is highly recommended, as the sessions contribute considerably to clarification of the study material, and also provide an opportunity to interact with other students enrolled in the same course. The sessions are held at the regional study centers.

Assignments are an additional component of Open University courses. Students submit assignments, exercises or other types of tasks during the semester by mail. Students must also pass the final exam of the course, held at study centers near their homes.

A student who registers for an Open University course receives the study materials designed specifically for the course, accompanied by the student's guide which describes the course syllabus and format in detail. It describes the topics covered, the dates of tutorials and topics to be discussed, as well as the course schedule and activities. It also includes the assignments and specifies their submission date. In most cases, the guide also contains a sample final exam which can serve as an additional learning aid and assist in preparing for the exam.

Each course has a teaching staff that consists of an academic supervisor, a course coordinator and a number of tutors. The course coordinator is responsible for supervising the tutoring, writing assignments and examinations and preparing answer keys. All students, regardless of study format, take the same final examination.

Tutors receive a ready-made self-study course, and their job is to support the students throughout their studies and help them perform their tasks. Contact between students and tutors is maintained through tutorial sessions, telephone conversations, assignments and correspondence.

The OUI carries out evaluation surveys of all its courses in order to help the academic staff identify problems and improve the courses. The **Evaluation and Academic Staff Development Department** is responsible for developing and carrying out these surveys and supplying the faculty with on-going feedback and statistical data, and training of the academic staff.

Open University courses have traditionally taken advantage of existing technologies for enrichment on a wide range of topics. Until the early 1990s, lectures by experts used to be broadcast daily on Israel radio; with the advent of cable TV, television broadcasts which accompany many OUI courses, have replaced the radio. Segments are aired several times a day, every day of the week. Telecourses, in which the video material is an integral part of the course rather than only for enrichment, have been developed or translated into Hebrew and adapted to the needs of OUI students, and others are being planned. With the rapid development of information and communication technologies in the 1990s, it was clear that the integration of state-of-the-art technology into OUI courses would have a significant impact on distance teaching at the OUI. The next section will describe the integration of such technology into OUI courses.

3   State-of-the-Art Technologies at the OUI

The Center for Information Technology in Distance Education (*Shoham*) was established in 1995 to help the Open University enter world-wide academic activity in the field of information technology in teaching and education. The major focus of the Center's activities is on research and development of teaching methods based on state-of-the-art information technologies and incorporating them into OUI courses.

The main reason for integrating technologies, and the Internet in particular, into OUI courses, was to provide a virtual campus as a substitute for a real campus, to compensate students for what they miss when learning at a distance. A second objective was to take advantage of additional educational resources, beyond what the university provides. These include all public domain educational resources and digital library services. The Open University's digital library allows students to access bibliographic and other databanks, electronic journals, computerized encyclopedias, as well as "Aleph", the computerized catalog of the university libraries network in Israel from their homes.

Another very important aim was to compensate for the lack of face-to-face tutorials for students whose nearest study center is far from their homes, or who are unable to attend tutorial sessions for various personal reasons, by providing virtual tutorials through electronic communication.

Since the pedagogical aspects of technology-mediated learning have not yet crystallized, technological tools and their applications are in a state of constant flux, both in theory and in practice. Through research, development and integration of new teaching methods that take into account pedagogical, social and technological aspects, the OUI makes use of advanced information and communication technologies for the mutual benefit of students and teachers (Jonassen *et al.* 1995). To ensure maximum fit between changing teaching methods and the needs of users, and in order to gradually and mindfully update the tools used, *Shoham* emphasizes two areas:

- Identifying promising technologies by, among others, carrying out pilot studies in cooperation with the industrial sector.
- Ongoing academic activity, in cooperation with faculty from the Open University and other academic institutions, both to develop a pedagogic infrastructure aided by state-of-the-art information technologies, and to promote research activities in the area of integrating these technologies into education.

A wide range of technological and media tools have been developed to supplement the written course material in accordance with the specific needs of each course. The new teaching methods do not replace the written study materials, but expand and enrich them and the incorporation of technological teaching methods is fully adapted to the written materials. Among the technologies used in different courses are the transmission of live interactive lessons through broadband communication, courseware and multimedia especially developed for specific courses, cable TV broadcasts, telecourses, digital library services and computer-mediated communication (CMC). These have been described elsewhere (Friedman and Beller 1997), and pedagogical and social issues arising from their integration have been examined (Beller 1996, Beller 1997).

It is likely that in the future, existing technologies will be transformed from a collection of separate tools or platforms into one system. Such an integrated teaching system will be flexible and better adapted to the pedagogical needs of its users – students and instructors – and to the demands of the different fields of knowledge and materials. Today *Shoham* is testing the feasibility of multi-disciplinary and inter-disciplinary projects which combine a number of information technologies within the teaching system of one course (e.g., satellite and Internet).

Shoham employs experts in the fields of computer science, software engineering, courseware and multimedia, education and oth-

ers. Each department focuses on the development of unique technological applications or platforms. These include *Ofek* (interactive
lessons through broadband communication), the Courseware and
Multimedia Development Unit, and *Telem* (computer-mediated distance education). These will be described below.

3.1 *Ofek* – Broadband Communication for Interactive Distance Education

The *Ofek* system uses broadband communication to transmit live
lectures or tutorial sessions broadcast from one of the studios located on the Open University campus to classrooms throughout the
country. The system affords voice and data communication and
students view the instructor on a television screen. They are able to
ask questions at any point during the session via telephone and can
respond to multiple-choice questions presented by the instructor
through data communication. Varied audio-visual aids such as
computer applications and video clips can be integrated into the
lectures, enhancing their quality.

Teaching via *Ofek* enables the University to bring the best and most
proficient lecturers and experts to teach any given subject. Through
Ofek, it is possible to combine the best teacher (whose expensive
services are usually not available for an unlimited number of ap-
pearances or in remote areas) with a fine lesson, thoroughly prepared with the help of experts and relying on the most advanced
audio-visual aids and technology.

The geographic dispersion of classes throughout the country saves
the students travel time and expenses, and provides for the same
quality of teaching in the center and in the periphery.

Ofek sessions can be integrated into the learning process as an alternative to regular and intensive tutorial sessions in existing
courses; in courses for which written materials are not yet avail-

able; to enhance courses, for example, through guest lectures; to meet specific course needs, such as introductory or practice sessions; as a supplement, for example, for updating materials in a course under revision; or as reinforcement for students taking regular or intensive tutorials.

3.2 The Courseware and Multimedia Development Unit

While Open University textbooks are the major teaching tool in most courses, the constant increase in the accessibility to students of personal computers, together with the high technical capabilities of the PC, provide the computer-user with an additional tool in the process of distance education. Among others, students studying independently can utilize interactive computer courseware which combines a range of multimedia including photographs, illustrations, animations, video clips, voice and text. In addition, the computer allows students to take advantage of hyperlinks between text and graphics and thus to study in a way that is not linear, unlike in textbooks. The use of courseware encourages independent construction of knowledge in various areas, allows for drilling and problem-solving, and replaces passive study with active learning through participation in the process of acquiring information. The courseware is produced on CD-ROM, which students can use in their homes, if they have a suitable PC, or in study centers near them.

The Unit produces various computerized aids including **interactive multimedia databases** that enable students to locate data efficiently and quickly through multimedia; **simulations** which allow students to control variables and actively participate in simulated laboratory experiments, research studies and processes described in textbooks; **computerized exercises** that allow students to utilize the computer's graphic elements to review and solve problems based on written materials; and multimedia **presentations** to help tutors present topics to students at tutorial sessions. The integration of photographs, illustrations, animations and video clips allow the tutor to present the topics clearly and reinforce students' knowledge and understanding.

3.3 *Telem* – Computer Mediated Distance Education

Telem is developing an interactive on-line learning environment on the Internet, which is part of the teaching/learning process and serves both students and faculty (Aviv 1999). In addition, *Telem* is involved in developing computer-mediated courses, which include learning materials and activities based on teaching/learning methods that suit a computerized learning environment.

For this purpose, *Telem* provides accessibility to computers and Internet communication for students throughout the country, trains development teams, instructors and students in the use of the interactive environment, and provides services and support to all users. What began seven years ago with five courses based on computer-mediated communication (CMC), has grown to close to 250 CMC courses, with state-of-the-art technologies incorporated into course development and teaching procedures.

3.3.1 Characteristics of the Computerized Teaching/Learning Environment

- *Interactive learning*: The computerized teaching/learning environment provides for one-on-one and group interaction among all participants in the course: students, instructors course coordinators and guest lecturers. The interaction may be asynchronous or synchronous.
- *Learning materials*: Learning materials are based on multimedia and hypertext and combine interaction between the student and the materials; technology-based learning aids that increase the

effectiveness of and enjoyment from the learning process, such as animations, simulations and multiple-choice exams with immediate feedback; and access to databases on the Internet.

- *Follow-up and evaluation*: Computerizing the learning environment allows for close, on-going follow-up and control to the benefit of the users: Students have access to the state of their studies, i.e., assignments submitted, chapters read; grades received; the teaching team has access to profiles of each student, and of the group; and on-line alternative assessment can suit assessment procedures to the new methods of study.

- *Administration*: On-line administrative services simplify processes such as registration, submission of assignments, notification about grades, distribution of notices and up-dates.

- *Change in the format of assignments*: The effortless access to sources of information, the search for information with the instructors' guidance, and the technology which affords interaction among the partners to the learning process can contribute to the creation of new types of assignments and projects which can augment or replace the traditional written assignments.

- *Combining the elements of the course*: The computerized learning environment merges the existing learning materials (textbooks and tutorial sessions) with the new computerized sources.

3.3.2 The Course Sites

Every CMC course has its own HTML and Java-based Web site that provides interactive learning materials through electronic asynchronous communication including discussion forums, e-mail, and materials that students can download (Lupo and Erlich 2001). The sites can be accessed by students in Israel or abroad through the Internet. Communication is currently mainly asynchronous; however, synchronous technologies are being examined, developed and adapted so as to supplement the CMC learning process with more interactive aspects (Moore 1989).

All course sites are graphically and functionally similar, and linked to administrative information drawn directly from the OUI's central database: the course schedule and description, the course tutors and the list of students. The academic aspect of the sites includes Hebrew-based applications that were specially developed to enable the course coordinator to easily and independently update the data, without the need for any knowledge of Web programming. After the students have taken one CMC course and become acquainted with the interface and organization of information, in subsequent courses, they find themselves in a familiar learning environment and feel they are veteran members of the virtual university created by the Web sites.

Generally, the Web activities can be divided into two different aspects: The Web as a *channel of communication* and the Web as a *study tool*.

The Web as a channel of communication: The Internet is used mainly to improve communication between the teaching staff and the students, using methods that have been examined in various ways by a number of scholars (Verdejo *et al.* 2000, Mason and Kaye 1989, Beuschel *et al.* 2000, Sandell *et al.* 1997, Brooks 1997). The traditional distance education method allows for only limited contact between the students and the course coordinator. At face-to-face meetings, a tutor provides additional explanations of the material and assignments, the examinations, etc. Because the tutorials are held throughout the country, the course coordinator can usually visit only one or two tutorial sessions for each group of students during a semester. Via the Internet, we attempted to augment communication between the students and the coordinator, making it more accessible, mutual and continuous throughout the semester.

There are a number of links at the top of each course home site; among these, links to discussion forums, relevant Web sites and file

downloads, where the course coordinator posts downloadable files
that include exercises, solutions to exercises, sample tests, etc. (see
Figure 1). A bulletin board is located on the course home page on
which the coordinator posts brief important messages such as
changes in meeting schedules, clarifications on deadlines for
submitting assignments, etc., and can also be used to provide links
on which students can click to reach more detailed information or
solutions to problems located elsewhere on the site.

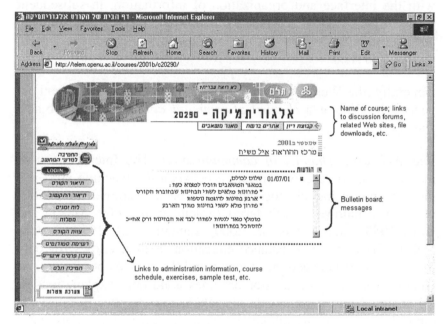

Figure 1. Typical course Web site.

In addition to serving as a source of learning materials, the Web
sites are intended to provide a virtual student campus where students can get to know each other, form study groups, and maintain
social contacts. To compensate for the lack of social life in a distance education institution, a special virtual meeting place called
"the course cafe" was opened, where students could discuss any
topic they wished, from culture to politics. Each site also includes a

list of students enrolled in the course linked to their e-mail addresses which enables students to communicate among themselves by e-mail beyond the framework of the course itself.

The Web as a study tool: Many studies have examined the effectiveness of the Web as a study tool in terms of the various options it offers: asynchronous discussion forums, synchronous discussions (text, voice and/or video) and animated illustrations and multimedia applications (Moore 1989, Beuschel *et al.* 2000, Sandell *et al.* 1997, Sajaniemi and Kuittinen 1999, Chan *et al.* 2001, Cookson 2000). All our course Web sites include discussion forums opened by the course coordinator for each topic depending on the structure of the course. They also provide useful links to other Web sites sorted by subject, including links to similar courses in other universities around the world, and to Java-based visualizations of various topics covered in each course and links to relevant sources in the OUI digital library. A description of each link tells students how and when to incorporate the materials into their studies.

4 Case Studies: Two Experiments

4.1 An Innovative Distance-Learning Computer Applications Course

To participate in a CMC course, students need to be computer-literate: they should have basic knowledge of computer applications, including the Internet. Many OUI students begin their academic studies with little or no computer literacy and therefore lack the know-how to participate in CMC courses and computer-aided activities. We would like all our students to understand the underlying concepts of computer science, to know how a computer works, and to be able to work with basic applications such as a word-processor and an electronic spreadsheet. They should also have the skills needed to take advantage of the Internet. The introductory course "Computer Applications for Social Science Students," developed at the OUI, provides students with such knowledge and enables them to cope with CMC courses in their studies.

In the fall of 1999 we ran the Computer Applications course for the first time. We developed a combined framework that integrated new technologies into traditional distance education methods and allows students with no prior knowledge to learn at a distance. In the first semester, we piloted the course with 26 students and in the following semester, with 219 students, on whom we performed the study described below. Today we teach the course to over 1,200 students each semester. The next section will briefly describe the course, its study method and the findings of the study. A detailed description of the course and the study can be found in (Lupo and Erlich 2001).

4.1.1 Course Description

"Computer Applications for Social Science Students" is a one-semester, two-credit course. It covers four main topics:

1. *Introduction to computers*: History of the computer and computer science; fundamentals of simple algorithms and their development; basic components of the computer; computer hardware; basic concepts of programming languages, data representation, information technologies and systems.
2. *Windows and Word processing*: Basic concepts of working with the Windows operating system; the desktop; files and folders; the Explorer; installing software; basic word processing concepts using MS-Word, and through Word, more about files, menus, hot-keys, etc.
3. *The Internet*: Using the Internet Explorer to browse the Web; locating and assessing academic information through various search engines; electronic mail, basic concepts of computer networks, history of the Internet and more.

4. *Electronic Spreadsheet (Excel)*: Basic and advanced topics relating to the electronic spreadsheet: functions; formulas; how to develop a spreadsheet for a specific problem; presenting data using charts and more.

Students are required to submit assignments via e-mail. Assignments include demonstrating word processing skills, creating electronic spreadsheets, participating in the course discussion groups, browsing the Web and searching for academic information. Students also submit a final project that reflects their ability to use all the applications studied, for which they search the Internet for academic information related to their major field of study, develop and process it using Excel, and present the results in a Word document which incorporates the spreadsheet. At the end of the semester, there is a final examination which tests the theoretical parts of the course.

4.1.2 Teaching Aids Incorporated into the Course

The Computer Applications course utilizes various teaching materials: a printed textbook, courseware, interactive Web-based technologies, and a study guide which steers the student in integrating the various materials. Each part of the course uses a different combination of teaching aids:

1. *Introduction to computers*: This part of the course rests only on written materials since the students are not yet familiar with computer use. The materials are periodically updated to reflect changes in the field.
2. *Windows and Word*: Courseware with step-by-step instructions, and short video clips for introducing the operating system and word processing is used for teaching this part of the course. The courseware is accompanied by a printed study guide with clear instructions for installing the courseware, guidelines for using it, and additional examples and explanations.

3. *The Internet*: This part of the course incorporates elements of various other technologies. Since we felt that hands-on experience is the best way to get used to the Internet, the teaching aids utilized in this part of the course were:
   - Courseware based on hyper-link navigation that includes the theoretical background, history and development of the Internet and its basic concepts, and practice in working with the Internet Explorer browser.
   - A book that contains all the information that a novice Internet user needs: instructions for connecting to the Internet, explanations about e-mail, chats, downloading files and specific multimedia aspects. The guide introduces both the Internet Explorer and Netscape, and different types of e-mail software that enable students to relate to information about software available on the Internet market.
   - A study guide that explains the basic concepts of computer networks, a brief historical overview, some basic theoretical issues concerning the Internet, and guidelines for studying.
   - A course Web-site: The students in the course are instructed in the use of the Web site and thus become accustomed to the concept of CMC. After the fourth week of the semester, the course Web-site becomes the main channel of communication between the university and the students.
4. *Electronic Spreadsheets (Excel)*: To teach this part of the course, we used
   - A book on Excel which includes a floppy-disk with a large number of examples.
   - Courseware with step-by-step instructions for performing basic and advanced Excel operations.
   - A detailed study guide that instructs the student in how to deal with the written material and the courseware.

4.1.3   The Courseware

The easy-to-install courseware was sent to the students on CD-ROMs. The installation program runs automatically and further steps are fully described in the study guide, along with screen snapshots of the installation process. The courseware for Windows, Word and Excel were all constructed using similar screen and navigation rules. The Windows and Word courseware also includes a short (2-5 minute) introductory video clip on each topic. The Internet courseware includes more multimedia features, such as hyperlinks, a larger number of video clips and on-line exercises. It is based on questions which are linked to answers, and sometimes accompanied by short video clips. The Internet courseware includes three main parts: (i) Theoretical aspects of the Internet; (ii) Navigating the Web; (iii) Dictionary of terms.

4.1.4   Tutorial Sessions

In this course we wished to have as few as possible face-to-face tutorial sessions so that the students would get used to electronic communication (e-mail, discussion groups, etc.) with the tutors. During the semester, students in the regular format met at five tutorial sessions while those in the intensive format mode had ten meetings, half of which were conducted in a classroom with the tutor using a computer connected to an LCD projector for illustrating the material, and half were held in a computer lab.

All the course tutors were connected to the Internet from their homes, and were thus able to take an active part in all the computer-mediated aspects of the course. Unlike tutors in other OUI courses, whose interaction with the students is limited to the tutorials and one hour per week phone-tutoring, there was on-going computerized interaction based on electronic communication, i.e., e-mail and discussion groups, between the students and the tutors of the course throughout the semester.

In addition to the face-to-face tutorials, towards the end of the semester, an optional interactive tutorial on advanced topics in Word and Power Point was broadcast live via *Ofek* to seven classrooms around the country.

4.1.5   The Study

We had doubts about the success of this innovation, since we had no prior experience in teaching computer applications through a novel framework that integrates new technologies into traditional distance education methods. After piloting the course with a group of 26 students, and following their progress closely throughout the semester, we found that the students were satisfied with the course. In order to get additional feedback on the course, we surveyed 219 students who took the course in the next semester. The major findings of the study are presented below; for a detailed description of the results, see (Lupo and Erlich 2001).

A questionnaire which related to various aspects of the course was sent to the students and included the following questions: (1) To what extent did you benefit from different parts of the course, and to what extent did your skills in each area improve? (2) Do you think that you will be able to independently move to future versions of the applications you learned about (e.g., upgrading Office97 to Office 2000) and other software packages? (3) How does studying from courseware compare with studying from books?

Most of the students had little knowledge of computer applications before the course, and those who had, knew only the basics of computer applications and/or the Internet. The survey indicated that an overwhelming majority of students felt that the course greatly improved their ability to use the Internet as an information resource in their academic studies. Most of the students felt that the course improved their ability to use word processing for academic needs, and that it improved their ability to use electronic spreadsheets. Although more than half of the students had some previous experience with the Internet, they didn't know how to use it as an academic tool; this was also true for the other topics studied. Also, most of them thought they would be able to keep up-to-date on new versions of software packages after taking the course.

When asked to compare studying from books with studying from courseware, we found that the majority preferred to study from courseware. Most also thought that the courseware was beneficial to the study process itself. Though initially we were not sure that students with no previous experience in navigating via hyper-links would be able to navigate the courseware, we found that they were able to do so with no special difficulty. The fact that the courseware is accompanied by voice explanations that describe exactly where and how to click to move on, seems to have helped students of different backgrounds to cope successfully with the courseware.

Regarding tutorial sessions, we know from past experience that OUI students like tutorial sessions and there is a great demand for extra tutorials in most courses. We were therefore quite surprised that only about half of the students of the course felt that more tutorial sessions were needed.

As to the interactive tutorial, where there is neither face-to-face interaction nor are students sitting at computers, we had no way of knowing what the students' reaction would be since we had no prior experience in teaching computer applications through this method. Although a relatively small number of students attended the tutorial which was given toward the end of the course and dealt with optional advanced topics that were not formally included in the course material, we were gratified to learn that most of the students who participated were very satisfied with the tutorial. Very few found the lack of face-to-face interaction problematic while most commented that a broadband communication tutorial was potentially a good tool for this course.

4.1.6 Conclusions

We believe that a university-level course in the use of the computer as an academic tool and of the Internet as an information resource, like the one described here, is of utmost importance. From our experience, we can conclude that computer literacy and applications can be studied via distance learning using a framework that integrates electronic learning tools with conventional distance learning methods.

Teaching the course using technological tools contributed greatly to the leaning process. The method itself afforded students active training in computer-based technologies, some of which were unfamiliar to them prior to the course. Students had the opportunity to get used to these technologies as well as to discover their advantages. Our doubt that students with no previous background in the use of computers would be able to cope with the technical problems involved proved to be completely unfounded.

Currently, the course is running with over 1,200 students each semester. We plan to continue experimenting with the framework in several directions: by reducing the number of tutoring sessions; expanding the learning technologies; and providing more broadband and other synchronous on-line tutorial sessions (chat, video-conferencing). In addition, we plan to adapt the course to students in fields other than the social sciences by changing the examples and exercises to fit specific fields of study.

4.2   Towards a New Mixed Study Format in Computer Science

Unlike the case of the Computer Applications course which targeted Social Science students, we assume that most Computer Science (CS) students are computer literate and would have no trouble using various technologies, including the Internet. Therefore, we were able to make a complete transition from traditional distance learning to CMC in all CS courses in the second semester of 1999. The department's CMC model includes a prescribed standard for every course, with a degree of flexibility that gives all course coordinators the freedom to use the Internet as they see fit, according to the specific needs of the course. The central guideline in introducing CMC into CS courses was to integrate the Web wherever it is beneficial and to avoid its integration in those cases when it becomes an impediment, as has been discussed in various studies (Boroni *et al.* 1998, Boroni *et al.* 1999, Byrne *et al.* 1999, Naps and Chan 1999, Trondle *et al.* 2000, Mester and Krumm 2000, Baker *et al.* 1999, Deaver and Resler 1999, Cordova 1999). For example, to avoid the disadvantages of screen-based reading, we decided not to place the written materials on our sites, but rather to continue to mail printed textbooks and other materials to our students.

At this stage, we did not make the CMC obligatory in any way. The Web sites were designed to help the students, and we left the decision of whether or not to take advantage of the Web up to them. No additional credit was given for participation in the discussion forums, and we did not rely on the Internet as a formal channel of communication. All information continued to be sent to students by "snail-mail" as had been the case before we introduced CMC into our courses.

In the same semester, we offered the option of a *pure* CMC format in an advanced CS course, "Computer Networks". Our intention was to open a study group which had no face-to-face tutorial sessions: all tutoring would be based on the course site and specifically on the discussion forums. We knew from previous experience that about 60% of the students in the course choose the regular distance format, and that about half of these do not participate in any of the tutorial sessions. These students were the target population for the CMC tutoring group since they had nothing to lose by enrolling in it. Yet, since very few of the students selected this option, the CMC group was never activated.

After integrating CMC into our courses for two semesters, we saw that only a small percentage of the students, including those in advanced courses, were taking advantage of this mode of communication. Thus, we decided to conduct a study to determine the students' attitudes towards the CMC model. The results of this study yielded a new study format based on a mix of traditional distance education methods and new technology-based ones. In the following section we will briefly describe the study and the process of developing the new framework. The full study is presented in a separate paper (Gal-Ezer and Lupo 2002).

4.2.1   A Brief Description of the Study

The study we conducted focused on the attitudes of students towards the integration of the Web as a channel of communication and a study tool in traditional distance education teaching of CS at the OUI. All CS students were divided into three groups: One included 700 students in our introductory course, who were new and still unaccustomed to our teaching method ("introductory" students). The second group included 150 students in an advanced elective, "Computer Networks", taken by students with rich experience in OUI courses ("advanced" students). The third group included the rest of the 3000 students in the department ("regular" students). Questionnaires were administered to all the students and a representative sample (20%) of the questionnaires for each group was examined.

The findings showed that when the use of the Web is voluntary, students do not take full advantage of it, even those who are advanced in their studies and have extensive experience in using computers and the Internet. An analysis of the questionnaires of "regular" students showed that although very few students took advantage of the CMC model, surprisingly, about 2/3 of the students did not reject the idea of studying in this format in the future. Some 30% responded that they would consider the option, and others stated that they would consider it under certain conditions. It should be noted that the question defined a CMC group as a group in which more advanced teaching tools – such as video-conferencing – would be incorporated. It is possible that students feel that CMC is still in its early stages, and expect it to develop further, and become more user-friendly and effective in the future. At present, the discussion forum interface poses problems in integrating Hebrew and English and in writing mathematical formulas, and while attachments are possible, these are less convenient and are time-consuming to open. This may be another factor that makes students wary of using the forums; however, students seem to be aware that this is merely a technical problem that will be resolved in the future. When this happens, it is likely that more students will opt for the CMC group.

Our findings showed that the use of the Web increases as students advance in their studies, although even in this case, the Web is not used as much as it could be, either as a channel of communication or as a study tool. Our findings support the following assumptions: The Web cannot substitute entirely for face-to-face learning, but it can serve as a reasonable alternative when the latter is unavailable; Using the Web to its full pedagogical potential requires a high level of self-study ability; The more distance-based the learning is, the more the Web is used and accepted by the students, and the more it serves them as a channel of communication and as a study tool.

As a result, we decided to try a new, mixed model of CMC and through it, to learn more about students' attitudes toward technology-based learning, and find the best ways to integrate these methods into the existing system.

4.2.2   The Mixed Study Format

The new CMC model utilizes the Internet to a greater extent in both the standard and the intensive formats by reducing the number of face-to-face tutorials, and defining the Internet as the sole channel of communication between the OUI, the teaching staff and the students. In the regular format, there are only three 3-hour face-to-face meetings (instead of seven meetings totaling 17.5 hours), and the intensive format has nine 3-hour face-to-face meetings (instead of 15 meetings totaling 30 hours), thereby making both formats more distance-based. The students were told at the beginning of the course about this CMC model, and of their responsibility to keep themselves up-to-date through the course Web site. All information regarding course activities and procedures is posted on the Web and no letters are sent by snail mail during the semester. Students are given the option to cancel their registration or to switch to another course if they find this mode of communication unsuitable for them, without having to give any explanation or to pay any fine (contrary to the usual procedures at the OUI).

The tutoring is based on the course Web site, where all students from all tutorial groups form one large virtual class tutored by the course coordinator through asynchronous communication. CMC tutoring includes posting guidelines for readings and additional questions, emphasizing certain teaching points and clarifying known problematic areas in the material, presenting visualizations and illustrations of specific topics, publishing video-based solutions to course assignments, etc. All on-line activity is asynchronous, while the synchronous activities take place during tutorial sessions. The tutors integrate the on-line activities into the meetings with the help of the course coordinator.

4.2.3   Findings

After running the new model for one semester, we arrived at two important conclusions, mainly based on interviews with students:

1. When on-line activities serve as the main teaching tool of the course, and the tutorial sessions are only supplementary (which is the case in regular format groups), it is important that the person who works with the students on the Web site is the one who meets them personally in class. In this way, there is personal communication between the tutor and the students, and the on-line activities are much more naturally connected to the tutorial sessions and, in time, the virtual class becomes a real class. Otherwise students tend to separate the on-line activities from the classroom activities and view the tutorial sessions as the basis of instruction (as occurs in the intensive format).
2. The students did not find video-based solutions to assignments helpful. Most of the students reported that they preferred the solution in a text file and not on video. The reason they gave was that the videos were not put on the site until a week after the assignment was submitted, by which time the students were already busy studying the next unit and did not have the time to spend on the previous one. In addition, students who succeeded in solving the assignments by themselves had no need for the correct solution.

Students also reported that the tutorial sessions were essential to the study process, and felt that four or five tutorial sessions would be optimal. We will therefore continue to run this mode of study with four face-to-face tutorials.

Students' achievements: Another important aspect examined was student achievement. One of our main concerns was that the change in the study format would have a negative effect on students' final grades. Examination of students' grades over two semesters as compared to previous semesters showed there was no need to worry. Students in the regular format with computer-mediation had slightly higher final grades than the average in previous semesters, while the grades of students in the intensive format were similar.

Upgrading the mixed study format: In the following semester, we changed the model for the regular format group. In addition to being in charge of all on-line activities, the course coordinator also acted as tutor of this group. Videos were presented to the students through the Web site to illustrate topics, rather than as solutions to assignments. The students now reported that the videos contributed to the learning process, and they found them much more useful than text. Still, there were some complaints about the quality of the video, which, to enable delivery through the Internet, had to be low. In the future we plan to change the video format to high-quality video files on a CD-ROM that will be delivered to the students with the other materials at the beginning of the semester. On-line videos will still be used when the course coordinator feels that text is not sufficient to clarify any points in an on-going discussion.

5 Integrating Technology into Distance Education: Conclusions

While many academic institutions began to teach off-campus students mainly because of the availability of the Internet and other technologies, at the OUI, where we have always taught off-campus students, we seek the best way to integrate these technologies into our traditional distance teaching methods.

Our aim is to compensate for the absence of a real campus, and the lack of close communication with the academic staff. We also want to offer a more motivating study method that exploits the potential of the new technologies, links up to additional educational resources, and encourages the use of digital libraries. We found that by cutting down the hours of face-to-face tutoring, and basing the tutoring on on-line activities, students are encouraged to take more responsibility for their learning, rather than depending on tutorial sessions. For this reason, the mixed format model described here suits advanced students who are used to independent study, and may need to be modified to fit less advanced students who as yet lack self-study abilities.

In describing the two different approaches we developed, we have related only to the academic-educational aspect and not to budgetary issues. We can very briefly mention that, clearly, as long as computer-mediated activities are used in *addition* to traditional methods, they add to the cost of running the course. If, in the future, CMC becomes the main tool, with other activities only supplementing the electronic activity, the financial aspect will have to be re-assessed.

The OUI is carefully considering how to move from traditional distance education methods to technology-based methods. From what we have learned to date, it seems that traditional distance methods will continue to serve as the basis for our teaching. We will, however, continue to expand our "tool box" of electronic elements to support various aspects of learning and teaching. Most of these tools are asynchronous, though some synchronous means, such as video-conferencing, are also being considered and will be piloted in the future. New technologies are constantly being developed and we will continue to test them and decide which can be added to our "tool box". At the moment, it seems that a mixed mode, like the ones we described, is preferable. Clearly, when no other means are available, electronic means, especially the Internet, are a reasonable solution. Through the Internet, students who are unable, for any reason, to participate in tutorials but who need the help of a tutor, can communicate via the Internet and feel that they are part of a large virtual class. The ability to use digital libraries and to follow links to other information sites becomes vital for the success of these students.

Since the jury is not yet in on the effect of technologies on the learning process, at present, we will proceed with our careful and promising approach.

References

Aviv, R. (1999), "Educational performance of ALN via content analysis," *Proceedings of the 1999 Sloan Summer Workshop on Asynchronous Learning Networks*, pp. 51-68.

Baker, R.S., Boilen, M., Goodrich, M.T., Tamassia, R., and Stibel, B.A. (1999), "Testers and visualizers for teaching data structures," *Proceedings of the 30th SIGCSE Technical Symposium on Computer Science Education*, pp. 261-265.

Beller, M. (1996), "Integrating new technologies in distance education: pedagogical, social and technological aspects," in Katz, J., Millin, D., and Offir, B. (eds.), *The Impact of Information Technology: from Practice to Curriculum*, London: Chapman & Hall, pp. 69-76.

Beller, M. (1997), "Integrating technology into distance teaching at the Open University of Israel," *ALN Magazine*, vol. 1, http://www.aln.org/alnweb/magazine/issue1/beller.htm .

Beuschel, W., Bork, A., Hughes, C., McMahon, T.G., Serdiukov, P., and Stacey, E. (2000), "Better learning online?" in Franklin, S.D. and Strenski, E. (eds.), *Building University Electronic Educational Environments*, Boston: Kluwer, pp. 233-252.

Boroni, C.M., Goosey, F.W., Grinder, M.T., and Ross, R.J. (1998), "A paradigm shift: the Internet, the Web, browsers, Java, and the future of computer science education," *Proc. of the 12th SIGCSE Techn. Symp. on Comp. Sc. Education*, pp. 145-152.

Boroni, C.M., Goosey, F.W., Grinder, M.T., Lambert, J.L., and Ross, R.J. (1999), "Tying it all together: creating self-contained, animated, interactive, Web-based resources for computer science education," *Proceedings of the 30th SIGCSE Technical Symposium on Computer Science Education*, pp. 7-11.

Brooks, D.W. (1997), *Web-Teaching: a Guide to Designing Interactive Teaching for the World Wide Web*, New York: Plenum, pp. 87-184.

Byrne, D.M., Catrambone, R., and Stasko, T.J. (1999), "Evaluating animations as student aids in learning computer algorithms," *Computers and Education*, 33: 253-278.

Chan, T., Hue, C., Chou, C., and Tzeng, O.J.L. (2001), "Four spaces of network learning models," *Computers and Education*, 37: 141-161.

Cookson, P.S. (2000), "Implications of Internet technologies for higher education: North American perspectives," *Open Learning*, vol. 15, no. 1, pp. 71-80.

Cordova, J.A. (1999), "Comparative evaluation of Web-based algorithm visualization systems for computer science education," *Proc. of the 10th CCSC South Central Conference*, pp. 72-77.

Deaver, D.M. and Resler, R.D. (1999), "VCOCO: a visualization tool for teaching compilers," *Proc. of the 30th SIGCSE Technical Symposium on Computer Science Education*, pp. 7-11.

Friedman, B. and Beller, M. (1997), "Integrating Internet technology into distance teaching at the Open University of Israel," *WebNet '97*, Toronto.

Gal-Ezer, J. and Lupo, D. (2002), "Integrating Internet tools into traditional CS distance education: students' attitudes," *Computers and Education*. (To be published.)

Jonassen, D., Davidson, M., Collins, M., Campbell, J., and Bannan Hag, B. (1995), "Constructivism and computer-mediated communication in distance education," *The American Journal of Distance Education*, vol. 9, no. 2, pp. 7-26.

Lupo, D. and Erlich, Z. (2001), "Computer literacy and applications via distance e-learning," *Computers and Education*, 36: 333-345.

Mason, R. and Kaye, A. (eds.) (1989), *Mindweave, Communication, Computers and Distance Education*, New York: Pergamon.

Mester, A. and Krumm, H. (2000), "Animation of protocols and distributed algorithms," *Computer Science Education*, vol. 10, no. 3, pp. 243-265.

Moore, M.G. (1989), "Three types of interaction," *The American Journal of Distance Education*, vol. 3, no. 2, pp. 1-7.

Naps, L.T. and Chan, E.E. (1999), "Using visualization to teach parallel algorithms," *Proceedings of the 30th SIGCSE Technical Symposium on Computer Science Education*, pp. 232-236.

Sajaniemi, J. and Kuittinen, M. (1999), "Three-level teaching material for computer-aided lecturing," *Computers and Education*, 33 (1999): 269-284.

Sandell, K., Stewart, R., and Stewart, C. (1997), "Computer-mediated communication in the classroom: models for enhancing student learning," *To Improve the Academy*, 15: 59-74.

Trondle, P., Mandl, H., Fischer, F., Koch, J.H., Schlichter, J., and Teege, G. (2000), "Multimedia for problem-based learning in computer science," in Franklin, S.D. and Strenski, E. (eds.), *Building University Electronic Educational Environments*, Boston: Kluwer, pp. 37-50.

Verdejo, M.F., Rodriguez-Artacho, M, Mayorga, J.I., and Calero, M.Y. (2000), "Creating Web-based scenarios to support distance learners," in Franklin, S.D. and Strenski, E. (eds.), *Building University Electronic Educational Environments*, Boston: Kluwer, pp. 141-154.

Chapter 3

Facilitators and Inhibitors of e-Learning

J. Liu, S. Chan, A. Hung and R. Lee

E-learning, or Internet-based online learning, has become the main stream of modern distance education. It uses Internet to deliver learning resources and to provide an effective virtual meeting place for e-learners and coaches to interact. It is a formal way of learning without the traditional restraints of the classroom. It can be defined as technology-enabled distance learning, where the learners are no longer classroom-bound. The personal computer is the main tool, and the Internet is the main channel used to deliver interactive learning experiences. As part of their learning activities, students receive learning materials through medium rich environment like interactive Web-based courses and multimedia channels which influence the effectiveness of online delivery and providing rapid, compelling interaction and feedback to students, making the learning process an active one.

This chapter presents the driving factors underpinning the adoption of the new model of learning as well as factors that might hinder its acceptance. We try to analyze the behavior of postgraduate students in Hong Kong towards e-Learning, and exploit possible factors that contribute to its successful development and delivery. We also look into the perceptions and benefits of such Internet-based learning, which may differ from others elsewhere as mentioned in literature.

1 Introduction

The intention is to examine the use of the Internet to support and encourage the revolution which has been taking place in the education sector (Jefferies and Hussain, 1998). New learning environments have been developed which are based on principles of active learning thus reflecting the change in the culture of education from teacher-centered to learner-centered (Butler, 2000). E-learning, or Internet-based online learning, has become the main stream of modern distance education. It uses the Internet to deliver learning resources and to provide an effective virtual meeting place for e-learners and coaches to interact. It is a formal way of learning without the traditional restraints of the classroom. It can be defined as technology-enabled distance learning, where the learners are no longer classroom-bound. The personal computer is the main tool, and the Internet is the main channel used to deliver interactive learning experiences. As such, e-Learning is anything that delivers learning materials via the World Wide Web and this encompasses new but fully-fledged degree-awarding institutions to distance education initiatives within existing traditional institutions (Whittington 2000). E-Learning model is based on blending a choice of technologies with aspects of campus-based delivery and distance learning (Volery and Lord, 2000) (pull learning model complemented by push model with emphasis of the first). The involved pull technology allows us to pull information from the Web or receive information from a Web server upon our explicit request. Other than that, push technology is involved to provide an automated delivery of specific and current information from a Web server to our specific hard drive. Students received learning materials through medium rich environment such as interactive Web-based courses and multimedia channels which influence the effectiveness of online delivery and provide rapid, compelling interaction and feedback to students, makes the learning process an active one.

The B2C (business-to-consumer) learning institutions are not the only organizations that offer online courses to the public since the 1990's as the implementation of e-Learning has also been extended to corporations that use it to deliver company training to their employees and customers. Cisco Systems, a leader in developing Internet technologies that change the way people work, live, play, and learn, is now focusing its efforts on e-Learning. It has a large e-Learning initiative that will significantly change the way the company educates and trains its employees, deliver information automatically to partners, and customers. A $19.1-billion company in the USA has already had over 80,000 students enrolled in its 5,352 Networking Academies in over 84 countries. According to a 1999 study by the International Data Corporation (IDC), the on-line learning market is currently generating US$600 million in annual receipts and will exceed US$10 billion by 2002. For the US market alone, IDC has estimated the size of online learning to be US$2 billion. It is projected to grow to US$5.5 billion by 2002. In Asia, the biggest growth in IT training will come from the e-Learning segment, which will grow at a massive 93.7 per cent a year between now and 2004, to reach US$235 million. A study by Training Magazine concludes that corporations can save 50-60 percent of their training cost by using e-Learning. As a result of the advantages, the corporate e-Learning market is expected to explode in the coming years, with IDC predicting a global market worth US$23 billion in 2004. The potential development of e-Learning is therefore very great. This chapter will examine the issues and trends of e-Learning in Hong Kong. It focuses on investigating the implications of facilitators and inhibitors for Internet-based learning, finding its perceptions and benefits, which may differ from others mentioned in the literature.

2   Literature Review

2.1   Traditional Learning vs e-Learning

In traditional classroom teaching, students can pose questions or comments to the instructor, interact by verbal discussion, or work in small groups. Such training is teacher centered and information tends to flow from the teacher to students (Figure 1). It is mainly a one-to-many learning process. Today, the forms of activities that are frequently suggested as necessary and sufficient conditions for effective learning, particularly for university courses, are those with a high degree of interactivity. Online learning focuses more on the students as information often flows to the students from the system. It appears to be a one-to-one learning environment. Figure 1 indicates a shift from teacher centered learning to student centered learning. For e-Learning, the student receives knowledge from the lectures provided by the lecturer and also searches for his/her own information on the Internet. He/She will have interactions with fellow students through electronic forums, bulletin boards and group projects. He/She can also interact with the lecturer through email and during limited on-campus tutorials if any. The student is continuously evaluated through examinations and his/her participation in activities such as forum discussions, online quizzes, exercises or Q&A. The server computer monitors and records the time spent and the activities done while the student logs in the course.

Since the e-Learning process requires the learner to become the center of focus, the role of the lecturer, becomes that of a facilitator and a mentor, rather than an instructor or a teacher. The mentor stimulates the learners online, updates the materials, and answers questions posed by the learners through various channels. Once in a while, the mentor may meet all learners for discussions when they will benefit from face-to-face interaction. This approach emphasizes user-friendliness, and interactivity. Courseware, instructional design, and all learning resources are tailored to fit the needs and constraints of a client or user's specific requirements, with enhanced human interaction rather than dehumanizing the training and learning processes.

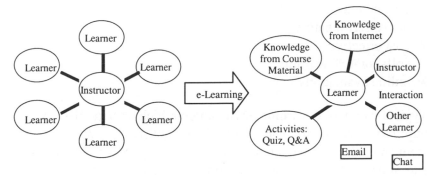

**Shifts from teacher-centered learning to
student-centered learning**

Figure 1. Moving towards learner centric.

2.2   Review of e-Learning

Due to the emergence of a knowledge-based economy, more people are interested in higher education (Chaudhury and Chew, 2000). A shortage of qualified teachers in critical areas/college preparatory courses and resource limitation of class offerings in small schools, are the common rationale used when initiating the distance learning courses. They have become an important field where Web-based technology is very quickly adopted and used for course delivery and knowledge sharing. To cope with the changes in the educational environment resulting from IT evolution, universities are enhancing their technology infrastructure and teaching environment by using the Web. The key features of such Internet-based learning environments include (Khan, 1997; Liu and Chan, 2001):
➢ interactive

➢ device-distant-time independent
➢ globally accessible
➢ online resources, distributed
➢ learner-controlled
➢ convenient
➢ non-discriminatory
➢ cost effective
➢ collaborative learning
➢ online evaluations

Typical web-based learning environments such as Virtual-U (VLEI: http://www.vlei.com) and WebCT (WebCT: http://www.webct .com) include course content delivery tools, synchronous and asynchronous conferencing systems, polling and quiz modules, virtual workspaces for sharing resources, white boards, grade reporting systems, logbooks, assignment submission components and so on. Several prestigious schools, such as Standford, Berkley and MIT, have developed their own systems to deliver course material online. Standford Online (http://standford-online.standford.edu/) offers course notes for download, and videos of lectures that can be viewed live or downloaded. There are substantial costs involved in the development of e-Learning. These include hardware / software, system maintenance / upgrading, telecommunications / transmission charges, technical support, faculty / program development and evaluation, student support, and a myriad of personnel and infrastructure costs associated with these vital components and services. The importance of these critical and continuing costs and constant technological change usually necessitate the reinvestment of virtually all income generated by the enterprise. Typically those who take profits do at the risk of losing the market share they won in the first place.

IDC indicates that there will be a significant shift in training channels between now and 2004. Currently, ILT (instructor-led training) accounts for 87 per cent of the total delivery media in the Asia Pacific region. IDC is expecting that by 2004, ILT will drop to 74 per cent due to the challenge from the Internet, LANs and CD-ROMs as alternative mediums of delivery. Typical institutions that offer e-Learning education include ICUS of Singapore (www.icus.net), Yapster of the Philippines (www.2StudyIT.com), and MIS Technologies Centre of Asia (www.misasia.com) which has launched the first MIS e-Learning Network system to support the Asia IT projects: Hong Kong – Cyberport, Singapore – Infocomm21, and Malaysia – Multimedia Super Corridor initiative.

In general, we need to devise a pedagogy that would facilitate Web-based content delivery and also provide adequate support for students who must take more responsibility for their learning than they would have done in the conventional mode of delivery. The biggest challenge, however, for implementing e-Learning in Asia is poor bandwidth and high telecom charges for Internet access. Each country has its own unique issues in this area. The second most common problem identified is the creation of quality software to deliver and enable the e-Learning infrastructure. These two concerns are also equally applicable in Hong Kong. However, following the recent advert of broadband Internet access by several major Internet Service Providers, the business potential of e-Learning has been realized by a number of entrepreneurs, and several e-Learning web sites are beginning in Hong Kong starting from the later part of year 2000. These include:

- CyberU from Hong Kong Polytechnic University (www.hkcyberu.com)
- iMBA from City University (www.imba.cityu.edu.hk)
- College of Lifelong Learning from Hong Kong University of Science and Technology (www.eedvision.com)
- TeachOnNet (www.teachonnet.com)
- Eschool (www.teachonnet.com)

Hong Kong CyberU (PolyU) is an e-Learning institution on the Internet co-founded by The Hong Kong Polytechnic University and Pacific Century CyberWorks (PCCW). They target students from different regions including Hong Kong, Mainland China and the South East Asian region. The Interactive Master of Business Administration (iMBA) of City University is offered in partnership with Hong Kong's dominant phone company, HKT. It has been ranked as the best Asia distance MBA program by Asiaweek in 2000. The HKUST's College of Lifelong Learning has collaborated with eEd Vision Ltd to offer an Online Executive Certificate in eBusiness. The program is supported by ESDlife (www.esdlife .com), IBM, Lotus, i-STT Hong Kong Ltd with the objective of keeping participants abreast of the key issues and latest development in the new network economy. TeachOnNet.com has launched a vast variety of professional multi-media on-line education courses since July 2000. The courses include diploma/non-diploma courses, degree courses and multi-media materials and resources tailored for primary and secondary students. eSchool.com has formed partnership with the Hong Kong Productivity Council (HKPC) in providing e-Learning programs for local companies. They have since offered over 250 offline courses and mixed-module courses with local learning institutes such as City College, Hong Kong Productivity Council, Hong Kong College of Technology and so on. Table 1 shows the system requirements by institutions in taking those e-courses.

2.3   Operation Models of e-Learning

E-Learning courses are operated under three operations models:

1. Pure Cyber university or institutions – these are learning institutions set up mostly from scratch and as a distinct entity providing solely e-Learning courses for the public. Examples of these are Jones University in the US, Clyde Virtual University in Europe and eSchool_World.com in HK.

Table 1. Minimum system requirements by different institutions.

	PC	Internet Access	Web Browser
Poly-technic University – CyberU	• Pentium III 500Mhz processor • 128MB memory • 4GB hard disk • CD ROM drive • Display card to support 32-bit true color • Sound card to support 16-bit sound • 15" color Monitor • Speakers / headphones • Microsoft Windows 98	Broadband Internet connection required	Netscape 4.7 with the following plug-ins: • RealPlayer 7 • Adobe Acrobat v.4.05 • Shockwave 8 and Flash 4.0 Players • Windows Media Player
City University – iMBA	• Pentium II 400 Mhz or better processor desktop or notebook • 128MB memory • multi-media hardware including microphone and loudspeakers	Broadband Internet Access from the business partner, HKT, is preferred.	Not mentioned
HKUST – College of Longlife Learning	• Pentium II class processor • 64MB memory • 5MB free disk space • 256 color video card • 16-bit sound card • 4x CD Rom drive • 56 kbps modem • Microsoft Windows 95, 98 or NT	Internet access through an Internet Service Provider or LAN connection. Broadband Internet connection strongly recommended for best online viewing quality.	A Java enabled web browser, such as Internet Explorer 4.01 (or later) or Netscape Navigator 4.08 (or later).
TeachOn Net.com	• Pentium 100 Mhz or about (200Mhz or above recommended) • 64MB memory • 10MB free disk space • Sound card, speakers, microphone (headset with microphone recommended) • Microsoft Windows 95, 98, 2000, NT • Powerpoint 97 • Winzip	56k modem broadband or LAN (any one of the connections)	Internet Explorer 4.0 or above and Netscape 4.08 or above (IE recommended), with these plug-ins: • Windows Media Player • Hear Me Plug-in • Authorware Player
eSchool .com	• Pentium 133 Mhz processor • 16MB memory • Sound card and speaker • 33.6 kbps modem • Microsoft Windows 95 or above	Broadband Internet access is not required	Internet Explorer 4.0 or above and Netscape 4.0 or above, with following plug-ins: • Flash 4 • Real Player 4.0

2. Spin-offs from existing traditional institutions – the spin-off entity is an extension of traditional brick and mortar institutions and is set up perhaps with other business partners. Example of such is the HK CyberU.
3. Traditional institutions offering online courses themselves on the Internet. Examples include City University in HK and Curtin University of Technology in Australia.

2.4   Drivers of e-Learning

E-Learning in Hong Kong is considered to be in its infancy stage with just a few higher education institutions currently beginning to offer such a mode of studies. The Hong Kong Polytechnic University, with the backing of Pacific Century Cyber Works, launched the Hong Kong CyberU in 2000 offering Master degree courses in E-Commerce, Project Management and Professional Accounting. City University of Hong Kong also launched its only online course in 1999, i-MBA. As the operation began not long ago, the lack of course choices is understandable.

It is a culture in this region where much emphasis is placed on certificates of formal education and training of all sorts. The number of day and evening schools providing sundry training; like accounting, computing and languages to just name a few; are mushrooming and cater for different groups of people of different age groups and backgrounds. In addition, various e-Learning sites have emerged in the territory offering various short courses for personal development and enhancement:

- www.campusonline-hk.com
- www.oe21.com
- www.netbig.com
- www.eschoolworld.com
- www.britishcouncil.org.hk

The following are the driving forces for e-Learning development, particularly in Hong Kong:

◆ Increased complexity and rate of change of the working environment due to technological changes;
◆ High cost of the traditional training methods;
◆ Life-long learning requirements;
◆ Trade off between self-development and work productivity.

3 Critical Consideration Factors for e-Learning

Various factors such as personal preference, organizational support, and skill may influence the adoption of the Web technologies as teaching complements or supplements. Researchers have exploited the Internet as an excellent model when distance, time, space, cost, diversity of cognitive capabilities and scheduling are taken into account. Internet-based learning is not only a matter of navigation through a browser or searching for slide show presentations, it is a more advanced process. Also, western expectations of the benefits of e-Learning may also differ significantly from the Asian ones, due to the differences in the academic systems. These factors could affect the acceptance of the new learning method within the learning community. Typical examples of considering factors are:

◆ Technology (Volery and Lord, 2000; Whittington, 2000)
◆ Personal attitude (Johnson et al., 2000)
◆ Personal characteristic (Angulo and Bruce, 1999)
◆ Limited course offering (Johnson et al., 2000)

Most of these factors are inherent to distance learning in general and e-Learning in particular. We need to identify the various factors having cultural, technological or environmental influences that will facilitate or hinder the acceptance of e-Learning and to perhaps point out those that are unique to HK.

3.1   Facilitators

The critical success factors in e-Learning can be classified as: environment, culture, technology, personal attitude and business driven.

Environment and Culture

♦ **Convenience of access**
   The convenience brought about by e-Learning in that one can study anywhere at anytime provides a great relief and flexibility to the time-starved people.

♦ **Alleviating capacity constraints**
   This factor is most obvious in Hong Kong because of its geographical constraints and the locations of most of its universities. The campuses of most western universities are so large that room for expansion is available. In contrast, the campuses of local universities are generally difficult to expand. Any expansion program is limited to within the confines of the campus as nearby sites are not available. It would be very expensive to operate a remote site as supporting facilities and amenities have to be built resulting in redundant facilities and personnel. Some institutions are hoping to use online education to avoid enlarging their bricks and mortar capacities. This is seen as one driving factor for these institutions to adopt the e-Learning mode of teaching.

♦ **Capitalizing on emerging market opportunities**
   The growing acceptance by public of the value of lifelong learning has fuelled an increased demand for higher education services among people outside the traditional 18-24 age range. According to statistics from Census Department and the HK 1999 Annual report, the age group between 15-64 years old accounted for about 72.4% of total HK population as of 1999 with the median age at 36. This age group makes up the majority of people

taking various courses in different learning centers in HK resulting in the flourishing of training schools in the territory. In addition, HK people are investing in further education to better equip themselves and prepare for future opportunities.

♦ **Decline in public funding**
Public funding for the Universities and other higher learning institutions has been declining in recent years. By capitalizing on emerging market opportunities, many educational institutions hope to generate significant revenue through e-Learning courses. These are often operated with a higher expectation for cost recovery than on-campus counterparts. Aside from targeting local student populations, these institutions often have a broader aim of reaching clients previously outside their geographical locations. HK CyberU aims to target student populations in China and nearby Asian countries. It becomes a phenomenon as the Institute of Academic Technology (1994) calls "the periphery maintaining the core", where deficit reduction targets to support core on-campus programs arc under financial pressure and are met by demanding increased "profitability" of their non-traditional counterparts.

Technology

♦ **Maturity of Web based e-Learning technologies**
Technologies for online chatting, e-mailing, bulletin board, video conferencing and work collaborations with multimedia effects are being used widely nowadays. The maturity of Internet libraries is a big enabling factor for the e-Learning process. Digital libraries are the combination of digitized information resources plus the information technology that support the acquisition, storage, indexing, retrieval, presentation and delivery of desired information (Lang and Zhao, 2000). Network-based resources provide students with enhanced opportunities for learn-

ing to which they would not otherwise have had access. The flexible, open-ended availability of online course materials provides students with an expanded range of instructional opportunities for acquiring, exchanging and reflecting on the significance of information.

♦ **Internet accessibility**
A highly developed telecommunications infrastructure is one of the major requirements for e-Learning. HK is probably the most deregulated telecom market in the world and one of the few countries that meets this requirement. The city has a fully digitised telecommunications network and various local telecom companies are currently developing the broadband Internet access capability to meet the increasing demands. According to a research report from Salomon Smith Barney, the broadband subscriber growth in the Asia Pacific region is expected to grow at a terrific pace, reaching 18 million by 2005. Hong Kong, Taiwan, Korea and Singapore account for 75 percent of all broadband users in the region (Computerworld 8/9/2000). On the local scene, International Data Corporation Asia Pacific Ltd.(IDC), expects the number of Internet users to grow rapidly at a 5-year compound annual growth rate of 26.9 per cent by 2003. The penetration of broadband service and its adoption pose another great factor for the success of e-Learning which will ensure an effective and efficient online learning environment, and study materials consist of files, film clips and other multimedia materials must flow smoothly and efficiently to and from the student.

There is also the exciting possibility of broadband access via satellite. This holds the promise of low-cost and high-speed data services that bypass congested terrestrial systems. Countries such as China and India with large rural populations and low telephone penetration rates will benefit most from such technology.

Personal Attitude

♦ **Computer literacy and experience on using Internet**
As e-Learning courses are all delivered to the students through the Internet, the student is expected to be computer literate and be able to get around the World Wide Web with ease and comfort. Learners must develop core skills for distributed learning. These would include basic PC familiarity, word processing, telecommunications knowledge including dial-in procedures, online tools including FTP, Telnet, email and web browser familiarity, online library searches, download routines, and system software with all these functions. It is crucial that the instructors have a good control of the technology, exhibit interactive teaching styles, and encourage interaction between the students and the instructor.

In order for students to successfully learn a particular content from a virtual classroom learning environment, they must first learn how to use the system. Until learners master this skill, they run the risk of spending inordinate amounts of time simply trying to get to the area of the system they are interested in. They may become frustrated with the system to the point where they abandon it. Aside from student's technical orientation, the quality of web page interface is also crucial - ease of use, navigation, cognitive load, mapping, screen design, information presentation, aesthetics and overall functionality pose either as aid or hindrance to the study. Navigation within the web pages refers to moving between web pages. If the web pages of the course are designed using the more complicated structures like empirical or web structure instead of the more simple linear or sequence design, the chances that students will get lost would be greater resulting in a less satisfactory experience.

As e-Learning is student-centered using the pull model of learning, students are required to be properly motivated and disciplined. To properly motivate a student, the student has to be motivated. One of the powers of interactivity in a web environment is the capability of rapid, compelling interaction and feedback to students. Motivation is also enhanced by problem-based presentation of educational materials. If properly motivated, students will avail themselves of additional learning opportunities, and they should, generally, benefit from using well-designed online instructional resources. As e-Learning uses the Pull mode of learning, students can specify individual learning needs, goals and outcomes, plan and organize the learning task, evaluate its worth and construct meaning from it. Bright and motivated students may prefer learning in the individual environment that e-Learning creates. The instructor's characteristic can greatly influence the student's learning attitude. Students attending a class with an instructor who has a positive attitude towards distributed learning and who promotes the technology are likely to experience a more positive learning outcome. In a distributed learning environment, students often feel isolated since they do not have the classroom environment in which to interact with the instructor. The instructor should exhibit interactive teaching styles, encouraging interaction between students and with the instructor (Volery and Lord, 2000).

Business Driven

♦ **Telecommunication providers create demand**
Telecommunications companies have been competing fiercely in the Internet market recently by setting up Internet access sites for locals to connect to the net. Some provide access to the Internet at a small monthly fee; others offer free connections with certain conditions attached. The focus of these companies has been shifted to the broadband market as this is the high growth sector

and this is where real revenues will come from. Internet software contents and applications like Internet games, video conferencing and phone over the internet are creating demands for more and more bandwidth. These telcos are trying hard to add more and more contents and applications that would require the use of broadband and encourage its subscription. Besides that, the major broadband providers in the territory start to have outfits offering online courses to create the need for broadband.

The phenomenon of telecoms providers creating broadband application like e-Learning in particular is not common and we think it is a unique facilitator in HK.

3.2   Inhibitors

There are many barriers to computer-based education. The inhibiting factors for e-Learning can be classified as: environment, technology and infrastructure, personal characteristic, cost and resources.

Environment

- **Geographical factor**
  For a relatively small city such as Hong Kong with a livable land area of 1098 square kilometers and a high people/sq m ratio of 6480, the traveling distance to attend a campus course is not forbidding. This is in sharp contrast to western world where physically attending a campus course might be impractical. With the sophisticated public transportation system in the territory, going from one end to the other would still be bearable. Another factor is universities in HK are geographically dispersed around the territory, making access to one of them quite convenient.

- **Crowded living environment**
  Hong Kong residential units are well known for being small and crowded. A typical family of 4 often lives in a 500 square foot

unit. The environment within the home unit would not be conducive to studying, considering the noise and distraction at home like television, voices, telephones and traffic noise from street and so on.

As HK has a very high population density and is notorious for crowded living quarters, the 2 inhibiting factors listed above are somehow unique to HK.

Technology and Infrastructure

♦ **Telecommunication infrastructure**
  Current bandwidth does not support fast enough delivery, particularly for multimedia communication. This is a serious concern and the one that is most often cited by students as difficulty in the use of the Internet. A high-speed connection is required to provide a rich medium for effective online course delivery. A rich medium allows for both synchronous and asynchronous communications and supports a variety of elements like text, graphics, audio and video messages. A rich medium would relate to interactivity and in turn create motivation in students. On the other hand, there is a need to optimize the use of the Internet to prevent information overload. Current search engines do not appear to be sophisticated enough to relieve the problem.

Personal Characteristic

♦ **Old habits are hard to change**
  Using the Internet to support learning and teaching requires a culture change in both the teaching staff and the students. Both staff and students would probably need to perceive an "added value" to using the Internet as opposed to other resources for course related work. The degree of acceptance of the Web as a

teaching tool, however, varies from professor to professor even in the same university environment (Leidner and Jarvenpaa, 1995). HK people are accustomed to the traditional style of learning and teaching. Faculty members, particularly those who have been in their teaching career for a long time are likely to resist the change. In most cases the senior members of the academic institution hold the decision-making power, and as a result, most institutions have been cautious and slow to embrace new models.

Cost and Resources

+ **Unequal income in the region**
  Tuition fees for online courses are in general cheaper than the corresponding on campus courses. But if the institution is targeting students from other regions (e.g. China, Thailand), tuition fees would pose as hindrance. The people in China have a per capita income of RMB5,854, the tuition fee of something like US$200/credit would be quite burdensome to many not to mention their relatively high Internet access cost. The situation is the same in other countries in the region like Thailand and the Philippines. For those who can afford the tuition fees in these countries, they have more choices from reputable institutions offering e-Learning courses elsewhere.

+ **High course development cost**
  The cost of developing the online course material is very expensive as compared to developing course materials for the traditional mode of learning. More time and effort as well as various multimedia resources are required for the production. The maintenance cost is also expensive particularly for IT subjects which keep changing rapidly. Hong Kong's case is further worsened by the fact that it adopts British professional standards which hinder the institutions from purchasing ready-made materials from the

US which is considered the fore-runner in e-Learning. A reduction in cost and the production of high quality materials are needed to ensure the wide spread adoption of the Internet as a viable medium.

♦ **Limited course offering**
It is understandable that not all the courses offered in the traditional brick and mortar institutions are suitable for online delivery. Consequently, there are very few e-Learning courses currently offered by local institutions and the scope is quite narrow. This will discourage e-learners from taking these limited courses and they will therefore search for other substitutes elsewhere.

In view of the number of factors that could facilitate or inhibit the development of e-Learning, we would like to investigate the impact of a couple of factors: personal attitude, and computer skills of students. These two factors though mentioned in literature, have not been closely looked into within the problem domain here. We are interested in identifying and finding out the relevant impact of factors that pose as inhibitors and facilitators of one's behavior towards e-Learning. The study is based on a combination of first-hand and second-hand interviews as well as empirical analysis.

4   Research Analysis

4.1   Interviews

We have made the following observations:

1. The potential market for e-Learning is huge
An interview conducted by Apple Daily with Ms Wu, CEO of Global University Alliance (GUA) revealed that the potential annual turnover of e-Learning at master level or above in Asia would be estimated as around US$50 to 100 millions.

2. Hindrance of narrow-band

An interview conducted by the Hong Kong Economic Times with Mr. Zin, Marketing Executive of **eSchool** revealed that one of the major hindrances for the development of e-Learning was the low penetration rate of broadband at present. Most of the students are still using narrow–band or unreliable connections to attend the classes, which results in unsatisfactory and unpredictable video quality leading to learner frustration and greatly reduced learning efficiency. In addition, learners desire the flexibility of obtaining course materials using various new forms of low-bandwidth Internet access such as wireless LANs and cellular access or even with no Internet access at all.

3. Resistance to accepting non-traditional learning methods

Mr Zin of **eSchool** also said that the major obstacle to the development of e-Learning was the human factor. Most of the students still resist non-traditional learning methods. They prefer face-to-face teaching methodology and building up a human relationship with the tutor.

4. Brand-name of university and recognition of award granted

According to an interview carried out by the Hong Kong Economic Times with Ms Lee, Manager of Marketing Development Department of **Informatics** (holding company of an e-Learning portal site: www.purpletrain.com operating in Singapore) on 25th October, 2000, Ms Lee said that 700 students attended the e-Learning courses provided by **PurpleTrain.com** in 1999 and the number of students attending the e-Learning courses increased by 30 times to 23,000 last year. She concluded that the major reason for the success of **PurpleTrain.com** was that all its courses were provided by famous universities in the UK, the USA and Australia such as Cambridge, Portsmouth and the like. With the famous brand-name of these universities and the degrees or certificates granted being internationally recognized, the students have more confidence and incentive to those e-courses offered by these universities.

In addition, based on recent interviews associated with some of these e-Learning institutions, further observations are as follows:

1. **A strategic joint-venture business model**
   The set-up of this sort of e-Learning institution is through a strategic joint venture between a traditional university and a telecommunications company in the region. The university provides all the teaching materials and tutors whilst the telecommunication company provides all the necessary hardware, software and telecommunication systems. The merit of this joint venture is that both parties can benefit from it. The university does not need to invest a large amount in technology and hardware and the telecommunications company can in turn boost the demand for broadband and expand their market share.

2. **Target market for e-Learning institution is high-end post-graduates**
   The major target market for this e-Learning institution is the local postgraduate students and the university only concentrates on providing courses for Master Degrees. It is believed this kind of students are more mature, self-motivated, self-financed and can manage their time more efficiently. The undergraduate students are not their target market since this batch of students requires more face-to-face teaching and benefits from campus life.

3. **Push teaching model vs pull teaching model**
   Traditional university is the push teaching model in that a tutor pushes the teaching materials to the students. However, the e-Learning institution is totally different. It is a pull teaching model in that all teaching materials are stored in a database and the students are required to retrieve or download the teaching materials through the Internet by themselves.

4. Adopting on-line teaching methods to replace face-to-face teaching methods

An e-Learning institution has adopted various on-line teaching methods like electronic bulletin boards, online chat, lecture film strips, online exercises, quizzes and on-line study materials to replace the traditional face-to-face teaching methods. However, students are still required to attend the examinations on-campus.

5. Major problem in developing e-Learning institution

An e-Learning institution operates in a similar way as other e-commerce businesses. The development cycle is relatively short due to the fact that the market changes very rapidly, even every six months. Thus, the time constraint is the major problem in developing the e-Learning institution. The situation is exacerbated by the pressure to deliver quickly, staff inexperienced in distance education and in learning environments, and the widening of the cultural settings in which students are to be located.

6. Course materials are fully self-developed by the institution

Course materials are fully developed by the institution itself and the ownership of the course materials is the major issue. The whole process of developing course materials needs to pass through a rigid validation and control process. This makes buying a package course developed outside very inconvenient. Also the development time and cost many times higher than those required in developing conventional course materials.

4.2   Empirical Analysis

Survey method is used in this research. We focus on two hypotheses:

H1: Students with better computer skills will be more willing to accept e-Learning.

H2: Students who are accustomed to old ways of learning are not willing to accept e-Learning.

A questionnaire which contains 10 questions on factors affecting
students' decision to take a course is designed. They are Likert-type
5-point scale questions. Pilot test of the questionnaire was conducted using several individuals, which resulted in some re-
sequencing of the questions for clarity. The sample size of the survey was 250 and questionnaires were distributed to students taking
on-campus courses at local universities. Participants are asked to
rate the factors from "strongly disagree" to "strongly agree". The
questionnaires also ask the students to express their opinions on
some attributes of cyber course. Demographic data and Internet
online experience of students are also collected for analyzing the
profile of the students. 105 questionnaires were returned and 85
were found to be usable. The effective response rate was therefore
about 34%.

Simple correlation (Pearson) analysis is used to determine any significant relationships between variables. T-tests are used to determine the nominal variables with other variables. A SPSS package is
used for the statistical analysis.

4.2.1   Testing of Hypothesis 1

The students that agreed to use WebCT with no class in their institutions would be considered as willing to accept e-Learning. Computer experience and Internet experience were measured in terms of
the number of years in using computer and Internet. Students were
also asked to rate their computer skill from beginner to professional
level. The correlation result is shown in Table 2.

Correlation analysis shows that there is no direct relationship between computer skills and acceptance of e-Learning. However,
there are some points worth noting.

Table 2. Statistical test for computer skill and acceptance of e-Learning.

		Q1	Q2	Q3	Q4	Q5	Q6
Only WebCT with no class (Q1)	Pearson Correlation	1.000	.388**	.210	.120	.044	.027
	Sig. (2-tailed)		.000	.054	.281	.694	.815
	N	85	85	85	83	83	80
WebCT is useful to me (Q2)	Pearson Correlation	.388**	1.000	.117	.222*	-.118	.015
	Sig. (2-tailed)	.000		.287	.043	.288	.896
	N	85	85	85	83	83	80
Computer Skill not affecting e-Learning (Q3)	Pearson Correlation	.210	.117	1.000	.213	.049	-.010
	Sig. (2-tailed)	.054	.287		.053	.657	.928
	N	85	85	85	83	83	80
Computer experience (Q4)	Pearson Correlation	.120	.222*	.213	1.000	.240*	.276*
	Sig. (2-tailed)	.281	.043	.053		.029	.014
	N	83	83	83	83	83	79
Internet experience (Q5)	Pearson Correlation	.044	-.118	.049	.240*	1.000	.290**
	Sig. (2-tailed)	.694	.288	.657	.029		.010
	N	83	83	83	83	83	79
Computer skill (Q6)	Pearson Correlation	.027	.015	-.010	.276*	.290**	1.000
	Sig. (2-tailed)	.815	.896	.928	.014	.010	
	N	80	80	80	79	79	80

* Correlation is significant at the 0.05 level (2-tailed)
** Correlation is significant at the 0.01 level (2-tailed)

1. The validity of claiming using WebCT to substitute classroom teaching is debatable. Although that is the mode of e-Learning of some institutions (e.g. PolyU), it may not be the exact perception of students. A supplementary question, WebCT is useful or not, was set to cross test this. There is also no direct relationship between computer skills and their opinions on the usefulness of WebCT. In view of both results, it would be more appropriate to claim that there is no direct relationship between computer skills and the acceptance of e-Learning.
2. There is a close correlation between those who find WebCT useful and those who accept e-Learning. At first glance, as the definition of e-Learning is WebCT with no class, it should be natural that there is a close relationship. However, the no class dimension of e-Learning definition should make a great difference.

Those who find the interface of WebCT intuitive but still treasure interaction with classmates and professors will still reject e-Learning. The existence of a close relationship between the acceptance of the WebCT and e-Learning indicates that e-Learning acceptance greatly depends on the interface of the Web system. A good design of the system greatly enhances the acceptance of e-Learning, just like Window95 greatly enhance the acceptance of PC both at home and in office.

3. However, in the absence of relationship between the acceptance of e-Learning and computer skills, we did find correlation between the acceptance of WBI and computer skills. If the deduction of point 2 above is valid, there should be an indirect relationship between computer skills and e-Learning.

4. Although the students are asked to rank their computer skills from beginner to professional level, the self-evaluation may not be a true and fair description of their skill. If the measure of skills is not valid, the correlation analysis between skills and the acceptance of e-Learning would be meaningless. Questions have been set to enhance the creditability of the evaluation. In Table 2, we can see that there is a significant correlation between the self- evaluated skill level and the use of computer and the Internet. This relationship in some way has validated the self-evaluated skill level.

4.2.2   Testing of Hypothesis 2

Using the same measure in determining the acceptance of e-Learning, students were asked about their learning habit to see if they were accustomed to the old way of learning. The factors considered include:

1. Acceptance of Internet searching as learning tools
2. Acceptance of multimedia in learning
3. Acceptance of Internet communication, such as chat room and email, in interaction in learning

4. Preference of notes and lecture type of learning
5. Preference of passive way of learning

Table 3. Statistical test for learning habit and acceptance of e-Learning.

		Q1	Q2	Q3	Q4	Q5	Q6	Q7
Only WebCT with no class (Q1)	Pearson correlation	1.000	.087	.095	.029	-.011	.567**	.170
	Sig. (2-tailed)	.	.430	.389	.789	.918	.000	.120
	N	85	85	85	85	85	85	85
Often use Internet to search (Q2)	Pearson correlation	.087	1.000	-.001	.025	-.094	-.048	.314**
	Sig. (2-tailed)	.430	.	.996	.822	.392	.662	.003
	N	85	85	85	85	85	85	85
Print material and read (Q3)	Pearson correlation	.095	-.001	1.000	.328**	.104	-.061	-.044
	Sig. (2-tailed)	.389	.996	.	.002	.343	.579	.687
	N	85	85	85	85	85	85	85
Notes and lectures are best (Q4)	Pearson correlation	.029	.025	.328**	1.000	.267*	-.101	-.030
	Sig. (2-tailed)	.789	.822	.002	.	.013	.357	.786
	N	85	85	85	85	85	85	85
On-campus can learn passively (Q5)	Pearson correlation	-.011	-.094	.104	.267*	1.000	-.090	-.091
	Sig. (2-tailed)	.918	.392	.343	.013	.	.412	.406
	N	85	85	85	85	85	85	85
Internet still good interaction (Q6)	Pearson correlation	.567**	-.048	-.061	-.101	-.090	1.000	.243*
	Sig. (2-tailed)	.000	.662	.579	.357	.412	.	.025
	N	85	85	85	85	85	85	85
Multimedia is more effective (Q7)	Pearson correlation	.170	.314**	-.044	-.030	-.091	.243*	1.000
	Sig. (2-tailed)	.120	.003	.687	.786	.406	.025	.
	N	85	85	85	85	85	85	85

* *Correlation is significant at the 0.05 level (2-tailed)*
** *Correlation is significant at the 0.01 level (2-tailed)*

As shown in Table 3, the learning habits do not have direct correlation with the acceptance of e-Learning. The only exception is the interaction factor that is highly correlated with the acceptance of e-Learning. This implies that interaction will be a very important factor in the learning process. Similar observation was obtained by Dede (1996) who claimed that collaboration and interaction provide a social context which reinforces and motivates learning. The students at the remote site were appreciative of the opportunity to take a course via distance learning that would not have otherwise been available. Only those found that chat room, and email could replace face-to-face communication would accept e-Learning.

To test the relationship between those accustomed to the old way of learning and their willingness to accept e-Learning. We ask the question from students who are accustomed to notes and lectures and students who are not accustomed. The result is shown in Table 4 below.

Table 4. Statistical test for the old way of learning and acceptance of e-Learning.

	Notes and lectures are best	N	Mean	Std. Deviation	Std. Error Mean
Only WebCT with no class	>= 4	61	2.28	1.03	.13
	< 4	24	1.96	1.04	.21

Table 5. Independent sample test.

	Case	Levene's Test for Equality of Variances		t-test for Equality of Means						
		F	Sig	t	df	Sig. (2-tailed)	Mean diff.	Std. error diff.	95% Confidence Interval of the Difference	
									Lower	Upper
Only WebCT with no class	1	.942	.335	1.282	83	.203	.32	.25	-.18	.82
	2			1.279	41.909	.208	.32	.25	-.19	.83

Remarks:

Case 1- Equal variance assumed

Case 2- Equal variance not assumed

We can see that over 70% of the respondents either agree or strongly agree that notes and lectures are the most effective way of learning. We then tried to divide the students into two groups. The ones who agreed or strongly agreed that notes and lectures were the most effective were classified as students that were accustomed to the old way of learning. Others were put in another group that was open to learning in the new way. We then came to analyze these two groups' level of acceptance the concept of e-Learning. As shown in Table 5, the value of t is 1.282 with two-tailed significance of 0.203. Even when one-tailed significance is assumed, the value is 0.101 which is still over 0.05 significance. Therefore there is no significant difference in the acceptance of e-Learning between those that are accustomed to notes and lectures and those that are not.

4.2.3 Ranking of Facilitators and Inhibitors

Students were asked to rank 5 given facilitators or inhibitors. If they chose to take an Internet course they were asked to rank facilitators. If they chose not to take any Internet course, they were asked to rank inhibitors.

Facilitators were ranked as follows, with the first one being the most chosen:
1. Flexible study schedule
2. Cheaper tuition fee
3. Course not available elsewhere
4. Multimedia base teaching
5. No need to attend class physically
6. Possessing the required computer skills

The ranking of computer skill as the last facilitator confirmed the result we found in correlation analysis. The logistic factor of traveling was not an issue in Hong Kong, as the city is small. However, it may be quite different if the survey data was collected in other countries.

Flexibility and cheaper tuition fee are more personal factors and they topped the list. The need for flexibility may be accounted by long working hours, heavy family commitments or tight time working schedule. The personal finance resource limitation of students may explain why cheaper tuition fee was the second ranked facilitator. However, the value for money consideration would also be valid. In this case it would be a more course-related facilitator.

The other two factors: uniqueness and innovative nature of course are also course related facilitators. They would be good selling points for students looking for such courses to study. Interestingly, there are not many such innovative courses offered by institutions here. It seems that the success of e-Learning may be enhanced by studying the needs of students and offering subjects that cannot be found elsewhere. Multimedia based materials are a unique feature of e-Learning. This should be a natural facilitator and unique selling point. Surprisingly, it was only ranked third.

Inhibitors were ranked as follows:
1. I prefer face-to-face interaction
2. I like the traditional mode of teaching
3. Home environment not suitable to study
4. Do not trust quality of web courses
5. Do not have broadband access
6. Computer skill set not suitable

As can be seen from the list, computer skill set was ranked last. This confirmed with the above findings. Interaction and change of mindset are two issues that e-Learning needs to address before it could be a big success.

5   Conclusion and Future Work

Based on interview results, we have observed that low broadband penetration rate, minimal time to market and to develop courses, human factors, and the lack of sufficient and quality course materials that are reasonably priced are some of the inhibiting factors that e-Learning operators are now facing. On the other hand, providing or guaranteeing the quality of a course program is a must for course operators as students tend to go for brand-names. Local e-Learning operators could seek the cooperation of popular foreign institutions to boost the brand-name effect.

The two hypotheses are not supported, based on our empirical research. However, the findings in different parts of the questionnaires are in line with each other. For example, we found that there is no correlation between the computer skill set and the acceptance of e-Learning. At the same time, this factor was also ranked the lowest in both the facilitator and the inhibitor listings. This has the implication that computer skill set does not affect people's decision on taking e-Learning courses. We have also found from the analysis that interaction is a prime factor when people consider taking e-Learning courses. As such, we believe this is a critical success factor for doing e-Learning business, particularly in Hong Kong.

For further studies, we would recommend the following:
- Increase the sampling population size
- Expand the research to include students from multi-disciplines
- Further drill down on e-Learning web site features that would enhance the degree of interaction.

In our opinion some of the inhibitors that we presented in the chapter are going to disappear in the long run. More and more software vendors are coming up with new technologies and software packages, which are enablers for this sector of e-commerce. Lotus and IBM have this e-Learning site-software called Lotus Learning Spare 4.0. Cisco recently has announced its solution package for e-Learning which according to them would greatly enhance the distribution of learning materials to the students. A local software company Prime Sino Limited is promoting itself as an e-Learning service and solutions provider. All these new software and technologies will drive the cost of setting up an e-Learning site down dramatically and also cut its time to market. As our younger, more technically savvy generation, who have practically grown up in the Internet world, go into their career phase in life, sooner or later they will find the need to further enhance themselves, and their mindset is more inclined to accept this mode of learning. Higher educational institutions will also revolutionize its old model of operating as an individual. Groups of institutions will form alliances and offer programs and courses to students where students would be able to tailor the program according to their own need. A student will be able to finish a program by taking courses that are offered in different schools thus creating a customized degree for each student. As the Chinese economy is growing at a remarkable rate, the disposable income of its people will also increase in the future, making e-courses more affordable. Telecommunication infrastructure inhibitors would also vanish as the less developed countries get wired up and the cost of access drops. This provides a strong indication that e-Learning should have a great potential for further development. Much effort should be spent on enriching the design, construction and presentation of course materials (Thomas, 2000) and allowing for more interaction and feedback in the e-Learning system.

In addition, e-Learning recognizes that learning is a complex process and that people learn in different ways. The process cannot simply be automated; rather, there has to be a right balance and integration of pedagogy, technology and innovation. The implementation must be careful and professional, and aimed at creating a vibrant learning community in cyberspace. In general, we need to (Murphy et al., 2001):

- adopt a clear pedagogy for our core Web-based materials
- commit to a learning environment that supports Web delivery and learner-managed study
- manage the transformation to the distance mode by taking essentially an incremental approach which allows academics and students to gradually change their practices.

Besides, advanced technology including mobile agents (Kotz and Gray, 1999) and data mining (Cooley et al., 1997; Zaiane and Luo, 2001) provides a comprehensive web usage tool for enhancing the e-Learning environments and personalizing lecture requirements. Only then can e-Learning succeed in producing the optimum learning outcomes. This is the subject for future work.

Acknowledgment

The authors would like to acknowledge the partial support of the Departmental Teaching and Learning grant (1.480W) from The Hong Kong Polytechnic University.

References

Angulo, A.J. and Bruce, M. (1999), "Student perceptions of supplemental Web-based instruction," *Innovative Higher Education*, 24(2), pp. 105-125.

Butler, J. (2000), " Is the Internet helping to create learning environments?" *Campus-Wide Information Systems*, 17(2), pp. 44-48.

Chaudhury, A.S. and Chew, L.M. (2000) "Assessing the preparedness of information institutions for the knowledge-based economy," *Proceedings of 28th Annual Conference by Canadian Association for Information Science, CAIS 2000:Dimension of a Global Information Science*, Edmonton, Alberta, Canada, May 28-30.

Cooley, R., Mobasher, B., and Srivastava, J. (1997) "Web mining: information and pattern discovery on the World Wide Web,"

Proceedings of the 9th IEEE International Conference on Tools with AI, pp. 558-567.

Dede, C. (1996) "The evolution of distance education: emerging technologies and distributed learning," *The American Journal of Distance Education*, 10(2), pp. 4-36.

Liu, J.N.K. and Chan, S.C.F. (2001), "Facilitators and inhibitors for adaptation of e-Learning in Hong Kong," *Proceedings of IASTED International Conference on Computers and Advanced Technology in Education*, June 27-29, Banff, Vancouver Canada, pp. 71-76.

Jefferies, P. and Hussain, F. (1998), "Using the Internet as a teaching resource," *Education + Training*, 40(8), pp. 359-365.

Johnson, S.D., Aragon, S.R., Shaik, N., and Palma-Rivas, N. (2000), "Comparative analysis of learner satisfaction and learning outcomes in online and face-to-face learning environments," *Journal of Interactive Learning Research*, 11(1), pp. 29-49.

Lang, K.R. and Zhao, J.L. (2000), "The role of electronic commerce in the transformation of distance learning," *Journal of Organizational Computing and Electronic Commerce*, 10(2), pp. 103-127.

Khan, B.H. (1987), *Web-Based Instruction (WBI): What Is It and Why Is It? Web-Based Instruction*, Educational Technology Publications Inc., Englewood Cliffs, NJ, pp. 5-18.

Kotz, D. and Gray, R. (1999), "Mobile agents and the future of the Internet," *ACM Operating Systems Review*, 33(3), pp. 7-13.

Leidner, D.E. and Jarvenpaa, S.L. (1995) "The use of information technology to enhance management school education; a theoretical view," *MIS Quarterly*, 19(3), pp. 265-291.

Murphy, A., Bakry, W., Milankovic-Atkinson, M., Sadler, C. and Woodman, M. (2001), "Choosing pedagogy and technology for an international Web-based Masters degree," *Proceedings of the IASTED International Conference on Computers and Advanced Technology in Education*, June 27-29, Banff, Canada, pp. 47-53.

Thomas, R. (2000), "Evaluating the effectiveness of the Internet for the delivery of an MBA programme," *Innovations in Education and Training International*, 37-2, pp. 97-102.

Volery, T. and Lord, D. (2000), "Critical success factors in online education," *International Journal of Educational Management*, pp. 216-223.

Whittington, D. (2000) "Evaluating three years' use of virtual university," *Quality Assurance in Education*, 8(1), pp. 48-52.

Zaiane, O.R. and Luo, J. (2001) "Towards evaluating learners' behaviour in a Web-based distance learning environment," *Proceedings of IEEE International Conference on Advanced Learning Technologies (ICALT 2001)*, Madison, WI, USA, 6-8 August, pp. 357-360.

Chapter 4

Developing and Accessing Adaptive Internet-Based Courses

R.M. Carro, E. Pulido and P. Rodríguez

In their most simple form, Internet-based courses consist of a set of plain HTML pages which are linked into a more or less complicated structure. Several approaches have been developed which extend these basic courses by providing additional features. This chapter deals with an approach that can increase the teaching and learning possibilities of other existing techniques: the automatic adaptation of a given course to different student models. With this adaptive approach students are provided with the most suitable course instance, by selecting the most appropriate contents and concept sequencing for each of them. Specifically, the chapter presents a design methodology for adaptive courses that facilitates the creation and maintenance of this kind of courses.

The structure of the chapter is as follows. Section 1 introduces the subject of web-based educational applications. General problems and needs related to the design of adaptive courses are discussed in Section 2. Sections 3 and 4 describe the key points of the proposed methodology: the separation between course structure and contents, and the dynamic generation of the pages presented to the student. The TANGOW (Task-based Adaptive Guidance On the Web) system is presented in Section 5 as an example of an educational Internet-based adaptive system. This system allows accessing to courses developed by using the proposed methodology. Finally, some conclusions are discussed in Section 6.

1   Introduction

Since its origins, the use of the Internet is continuously creating new opportunities for teaching and learning. At its earliest stage, Internet and WWW services made it possible to distribute through the net the existing educational applications which, at that time, were mainly based on the CD technology. Later, not only application downloading was possible, but also the execution of some of these applications directly through the net, by connecting to a WWW server that delivers the educational material.

At present, educational web-based applications are becoming more and more powerful. They are able not only to deliver educational materials, but also to offer help to the students who wish to learn about a specific subject. In fact, this is the main goal of most of the current educational environments. With this purpose, researchers are actively working on web-based teaching and learning environments that provide students with some kind of guidance during their learning sessions. The facilities included in most of these environments fall into two main categories: administration and Internet-based curriculum development. *Administration facilities* can include online registration, time-tabling and assessment management (WebCT 2001). *Curriculum development facilities* have to do with the creation and organization of the materials that will be presented to students. Although both categories can be considered equally important, this chapter will center mainly on the curriculum sequencing aspects of the Internet-based teaching and learning environments.

In their most simple form, Internet-based courses consist of a set of plain HTML pages which are linked into a more or less complicated structure. Several approaches have been developed which extend these basic courses by providing additional features. They make use of a model of both the teaching and the learning processes and contribute to complete different Internet-based learning and teaching models, depending on which aspect of the process is emphasized.

One of these approaches aims directly at the creation of the so-called "virtual environments." In this case, the emphasis is put on the co-operation activities among the students that attend a course and/or among the students and the tutor. These virtual environments integrate different communication facilities such as bulletin boards, e-mail, interactive chat and any other tools for group management. The previous applications directly fall into the area of Computer Support Co-operative Work (CSCW), a very interesting research area from the educational point of view (CSCW 2001).

Another interesting initiative, which is much more domain dependent than the previous one, has to do with the creation of "virtual laboratories." In this case, the objective is to help students to make their own experiments about some subjects that could be difficult to understand if only theoretical materials were offered (Rowe and Galvin 1998). In principle, there exist two possibilities: remote control of equipment and simulation. The first option works on the remote performance of experiments that make use of real equipment: the students can give value to the experiment parameters and see what results are obtained (Cervera *et al.* 2000). As for simulations, the idea is to make it possible for the students to simulate real experiments in a controlled virtual framework (Alfonseca and de Lara 2001).

A completely different area in which a lot of work is being carried out is the re-use of existing educational material. In this case, the objective is to build distributed environments which integrate Internet resources for teaching and learning. Most of the work in this direction points at the definition and categorization of standard learning objects that could be directly used by standard applications. In this sense, it is worth mentioning the Dublin Core Metadata Initiative (DublinCore 2001) and the work being done by the IMS Global Learning Consortium (IMS 2001).

Finally, with respect to the curriculum development facilities, a last approach exists that can increase the teaching and learning possibilities of all the above-mentioned techniques: the automatic adaptation of a given course to different student models (Nill 1997, Eklund and Brusilovsky 1996, Brusilovsky 2001). In general terms, adaptivity driven approaches try to provide students with the most suitable course instance, by selecting the most appropriate contents and concept sequencing for each of them. Different aspects of adaptation will be dealt with in detail in the following sections.

1.1 Internet-Based Courses and Adaptivity

To provide individual support to each student, it is necessary to determine student needs. In addition, it is important to decide how educational systems can be adapted to these needs, that is, which aspects of educational systems are amenable to be personalized, and how guidance can be implemented. The goal of this adaptation is to present students with the most suitable contents in the most appropriate way and at the right moment.

According to (Brusilovsky *et al.* 1998), in Internet-based education systems, there are two main aspects that can be adapted depending on the student profile. The first possibility is to adapt the page appearance, that is, to customize the contents and/or the navigational options offered to each student while taking a course. A second alternative is to adapt the curriculum sequencing. Adaptation can refer to either one of them, or both simultaneously.

In both cases, the adaptation performed is based on the underlying student models which include the students personal features (static student modeling) as well as the actions performed by the students during their learning process (dynamic student modeling). The students may have different goals and preferences when accessing a course. Moreover, their background, experience and previous knowledge are different. This static student model is completed with the conclusions derived from the student actions when interacting with the system.

To summarize, the underlying student model determines how the adapted course is generated. If only static features are taken into account, the whole adapted course is generated at the beginning of the session by instantiating the general course pattern. Arthur (Gilbert and Han 1999) and CAMELEON (Laroussi and Ben 1998) are examples of this kind of systems. On the contrary, if the student actions stored in the dynamic model are also considered, it is possible to offer guidance at every step by selecting at runtime the best learning itinerary and the most appropriate materials to be presented to the student. DCG (Vassileva 1998), ISIS-Tutor (Brusilovsky and Pesin 1994), ELM-ART (Brusilovsky *et al.* 1996), SHIVA (Zeiliger 1993) and HyperTutor (Pérez *et al.* 1995) are examples of systems that perform some adaptation based on the student actions at every step.

2 Adaptive Hypermedia Development

Apart from the aspects discussed in the previous sections, it is important to emphasize that although adaptivity centers on the students, the adaptation process should be transparent for them. For students, a course should appear just a set of HTML pages in which they should concentrate in order to learn what they are expected to. Thus, the responsibility of managing the adaptation process must rely on the educational system, which should be able to generate the successive HTML pages the students will interact with, by taking their models as input.

If the educational system is to be able to manage the complexity of the adaptation process, it is evident that a good design methodology is required. This methodology should take into account all the actors present at the educational scenario (Ausserhofer 1999), which mainly fall into one of the following three groups: the students with their corresponding student models, the course creators, and the tutors. It should be noted that, for a given course, the later two roles could be played by different people.

In addition, the design methodology should also take into consideration the whole life cycle of the adaptive Internet-based teaching and learning process, which basically consists of five elements:
• The basic course creation
• The student modeling
• The projections of the student models on the course
• The customized course instantiation, including the course testing procedure
• The maintenance procedures

The course creation process must end up with the raw material that makes up the course. This material must be flexible, allowing the adaptation process to be followed afterwards. As for the student modeling process, it must conclude with the set of static features and/or dynamic actions that will determine the student models space. These two elements are closely related, and determine which course instance is selected for each student from the set of all possible projections of the student models on the course pattern. With respect to the procedure followed to generate every customized course, it is important for course designers to be able to test the state of the course at the generation stage. And last but not least, the maintenance procedures should allow, among other things, to modify existing courses and to make changes to the student models in use.

With respect to the whole process, one of the main problems that arises while developing web-based adaptive courses lies at the design phase. Generally, it is not easy for course designers to achieve this task which can be seen as the formalization of a multidimensional space. In this space, course designers are required to determine not only the conceptual representation of the course structure, but also every possible curriculum sequencing for each student (depending on their personal features and their interaction with the course) and every different way of explaining a given subject. This situation makes it necessary to define a formalism able to represent the course structure for each student model, as well as to describe the curriculum sequencing and the relations between course structure and contents as easily as possible. It is also desirable for designers to rely on a tool that facilitates this process, because usually they are experts in the course domain but not in the required technologies.

Additional problems and needs emerge when designing a course, inherent to the fact that the courses are adaptive. As stated by Nanard and Nanard (1995), it is convenient to have the possibility of reviewing the design choices and testing the final aspect of a course while developing it. This is especially important because of the adaptive nature of the courses. There will be n different final courses, one per student in the richest case, and it is very important to check that the individual versions of the course will be appropriate and run correctly for each of them.

The possibility or impossibility of offering complete information to the students at runtime about the whole course is directly related to the previously stated need. Moreover, when the student profile and actions are taken into account, the course structure is not prefixed in advance but decided while the student is interacting with the course. For this reason, it is necessary to find out alternative methods to help students to find their bearings around the course hyperspace during the learning process.

The life cycle of the Internet-based courses is illustrated below.

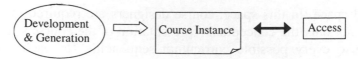

Figure 1. The basic course creation process.

Figure 1 represents the classical course creation process, where the development and the generation phases cannot be distinguished separately. Figure 2 depicts the deployment of adaptive course instances that take into account the static student models.

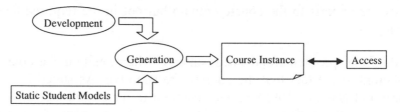

Figure 2. The course creation process when static student models are taken into account.

Finally, Figure 3 includes the student actions in the process, which allows the generation of a piece of the course at each step and, consequently, a much more personalized guidance process. Maintenance procedures should be foreseen in every case.

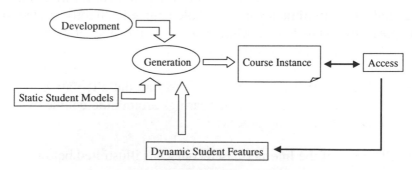

Figure 3. Dynamic course instantiation.

3   Relationship between the Course Structure and Contents

In general, two different approaches might be followed when developing an adaptive Internet-based course. The main difference lies in the relationship between the conceptual structure and the contents. In the first approach, each concept to be presented is directly mapped to an HTML page. In this case, the work to be done is to identify those nodes or concepts that need to be explained and to develop the corresponding HTML pages. Then, the concepts are mapped directly to the documents presented to the students, and there exists a perfect correspondence between the course structure and the hyperspace structure (the set of pages and the links established among them).

A second approach establishes a separation between the conceptual structure and the page fragments to be presented to the students. In this case, it is necessary to identify the nodes or concepts related to the subjects and to associate each of them to the pages or materials that could be used for explaining them to the students. Therefore, the course structure is described separately from the materials that will be used for explaining each concept.

Both approaches present advantages and disadvantages. In the first case, where the conceptual structure is directly associated to the documents, the development process is much easier. Nonetheless, the updating of the structure will always affect the contents presentation, and vice versa.

The main advantage of keeping the course structure and contents independent comes from its adaptive possibilities. It is possible to associate different materials to the same concept, so that the most suitable ones for each student are selected during the course execution. In this way, not only the most appropriate curriculum is selected for each student, but also the most suitable multimedia elements that should be presented for explaining the concepts. On the other hand, the course representation formalism must be powerful enough to allow the description of all the course components: concepts, materials, and relationships among concepts, or between concepts and materials.

As important as the design of adaptive web-based courses is their maintenance. The information, in general, is susceptible of being modified at any time. That is the reason why every system that offers information to students should include the possibility of making changes related to the course structure and contents. But these are not the only possible changes that authors might want to make. They may come up with other changes related to the kind of adaptation carried out, or to the refinement of the student model (i.e. the user features that should be taken into account to adapt the course).

The course structure is easier to maintain if it has been designed in a modular way, so that a structural change results in a change of the relations among these modules. Note that this is related with an aspect that has not been considered by most of the existing systems: link maintenance. In a given unit, there might be links that allow students to access other units. If these links are manually generated by the authors, and a structural change takes place, they will have to locate the pages affected by this change, and make the appropriate link adjustments. In contrast, a dynamic link generation makes the maintenance of coherence and consistency into the course easier.

Content updating is not difficult in those systems that store them independently from the course structure and the navigation options. When contents are mixed with other kind of information about the course structure or the navigational options, the maintenance task can be harder because it might be difficult to locate the places where changes should be made, and avoid inconsistencies, especially if the course is large.

4 Dynamic Hypermedia Generation

With independence of the existing relationship between the course structure and contents, the students attending an adaptive course will be presented with an HTML page at each step. At the generation phase, there are different possibilities which depend on the granularity of the contents fragments managed by the system:

- To directly present the page(s) associated to each concept.
- To present the more suitable pages for each student, among all the available pages associated to each concept.
- To dynamically generate the pages that will be presented, by using the most appropriate materials associated to a concept.

The two last possibilities allow the adaptation of the generated page to the characteristics of the student models, whilst the first forces the presentation of the same pages to every student, still allowing curriculum sequencing adaptation.

In any case, and whenever possible, the final pages should offer the students some kind of information about their location with respect to the global course. The objective of these complementary data is to avoid student disorientation or overloading, as well as to inform students about their learning progress.

4.1 Creating the Final Pages

When the page presented to the students is adapted, the main factors usually taken into account are closely related to the characteristics of the static student models. Most of these fall into the following categories: student profile, student preferences, and student learning style.

The student profile includes all the features inherent to each person that cannot be changed. One of these is the student age. If the course provides a variety of text fragments associated to the same concept, written for different vocabulary grades, the student age can be used to choose the most appropriate one for each student. This would be the case if a course were to be used for both adults and children. It is clear that the vocabulary and multimedia elements used for children should be different than those used for adults, because children are supposed to know fewer words. On the other hand, a richer vocabulary can be used for adults. In addition, children usually get tired sooner while studying, making it necessary to include more graphics, animations and funny elements to catch their attention. These elements can be tiring for adults, who usually want to "learn more quickly."

The special characteristics of disabled persons, if taken into account, are also included in this category: persons with visual problems will benefit from the inclusion of spoken texts in the course, and so on.

Another feature that can be included in the student profile is the language. If multilinguality is one of the objectives, the same contents can be made available in different languages.

Other group of adaptive features is associated to the student preferences. These are not inherent to each student, and can vary if the same student is taking different courses. One of them could be the student background about the subject. Novice students usually need more explanations, which are superfluous for experts. It is also possible to design a course adapted to several depth levels, allowing students to glance at the subject or to learn it in depth. What to do in each case depends on the student preferences.

Finally, the student learning style relates to how a student reacts while learning. Some students are preferentially visual or textual. In the first case, the use of images makes learning easier. Also, students can be individualist or co-operative according to their tendency to work on their own. For any student, an initial test will make it clear what their learning style is. However, it is not always easy to decide what the system should do, given that reinforcing the extreme learning styles is not necessarily the best solution. For instance, it is not obvious that a completely visual student should not be presented with text, or that a student prone to individual learning should not be invited to co-operate with others.

4.2   Providing Feedback to Students

In any learning environment, it is advisable to provide students with information about their situation in the course. This information has to allow them to easily know where they are from several perspectives and take the place of the feedback mechanisms used to when following non-adaptive courses.

From the course structure viewpoint, the problem is that each student can eventually follow different learning itineraries. This means that there is no pre-established table of contents to be accessed, given that the course instances are continuously updated. At the same time, the underlying guidance process implies that only a limited number of concepts is accessible at a given moment. Moreover, the list of accessible concepts can vary at each step.

The most commonly adopted solution is based on the dynamic creation of an "annotated table of contents," as proposed by Schwarz *et al.* (1996), based on the traffic light metaphor. The table of contents should include information about the state of the different sections that make up the course (available/unavailable, learned/not learned) with respect to the student. In this annotated table, each item is colored according to the following code:

- Green: items/concepts available at this moment
- Red: items/concepts unavailable at this moment
- Black: items/concepts already learned
- Blue: current item/concept

Though very useful, this kind of table of contents does not completely answer the question about how much is left, quite important from the students perspective. It is as though the student is provided with a table of contents, but the whole "book" is not accessible. It is still necessary to provide some hint about the percentage of the course that has already been taken. This information is important, because students can then infer how much is left.

Both the generation of the table of contents and the portion of the course already performed are difficult tasks. This is due to the fact that, if the course is dynamically generated, at runtime neither the course structure nor the total course size are available. In these cases, the table of contents usually shows only the portion of the course structure that is already known, which is incremented at every step, and the percentage shown is estimated rather than exactly calculated.

Apart from this, the student has to receive additional feedback. For instance, if some exercises are proposed, it is necessary to provide the students with the right answer in every case. This feedback can be provided after doing the exercise, so that the student can know whether it has been correctly answered or not. In addition, it is also convenient to inform the students about the (partial) results of each learning session, presenting them with data such as the number of items visited, or the total number of exercises correctly solved.

Finally, it is also important to fix the layout of the generated pages, so that the position of every element on the screen is the same after every click made by students. This avoids students disconcert while taking a course. The page elements include the information about topics, the navigation buttons, the table of contents, the progress indications and every additional element that could be considered as necessary.

5   The TANGOW System

In this section, the TANGOW system (Carro *et al.* 1999, TANGOW 2001) is presented as an example of an educational Internet-based adaptive system. The procedures used for developing and accessing a TANGOW course are explained, as well as the underlying formalism.

TANGOW (Task-based Adaptive learNer Guidance on the Web) allows students to access Internet courses that adapt themselves to the student specific needs during their learning processes. The system and the associated methodology are the results of a project called InterEdu (Internet in Education), which started in 1997[1]. Its main goal was to design and implement a system for the development and access of adaptive Web-based courses. The requirements to be satisfied by the system were twofold. On the one hand, the framework and formalisms provided should be as intuitive as possible so as to allow designers to create adaptive courses, as well as to debug them in an easy way. On the other hand, the system should provide students with a standard web-based interface and a guidance procedure along the course.

The designer should decide on the balance between the portions of the course for which guidance is provided and those that could be freely accessed by the students. In addition, the courses should adapt both to the student static models and to the student actions (dynamic modeling).

In the rest of this section the underlying formalism as well as the course deployment process are described. All the examples presented belong to a course on number base conversion.

---

[1] The work started in InterEdu, continued in the EnCiTec project, which began in 1999.

5.1   The Underlying Formalism

From the knowledge representation viewpoint, educational adaptive systems are complex systems that need to represent both course and student models. Moreover, both models have to be related, making it possible that the curriculum sequencing adapts to each student.

As already mentioned, the main goal in adaptive courses is to help students during their particular learning processes so that they can receive the required information in the most suitable way. Therefore, the representation formalism has to support multiple itineraries in a consistent way. In that sense, educational adaptive systems are strongly characterized by the formalism used for knowledge representation. In this section, a formalism is presented that allows designers to describe adaptive hypermedia courses. This formalism establishes a clear separation between the course structure and the contents of the documents presented to the students. At the design stage, course authors must describe, first, the course structure, then, provide the multimedia elements that will appear in the HTML pages presented to the students.

The course structure is defined by:
1. specifying a set of nodes which represent the subjects, concepts or pieces of knowledge included in the course, and
2. establishing the relationships among these concepts.

Nodes are referred to as **teaching tasks**, since they represent tasks that the students have to perform in order to achieve a learning goal. These tasks may correspond to a theoretical explanation, an example, a simulation or an exercise.

A teaching task is described by giving values to the following attributes:

- Name: it uniquely identifies a teaching task within a given course.
- Description: it is an explanation about the task goal. If the course is to be available in different languages, one description per language must be supplied.
- Type (theory/practice/example): a teaching task can be either a theoretical explanation, an example or an exercise.
- Atomicity (atomic/composite): it distinguishes between atomic and composite tasks.
- Ending requirements: it is a method associated to each atomic task. It is evaluated to decide, at runtime, whether the task can be considered finished. The method parameters are related to the student actions during the task execution, such as the number of pages visited, the number of exercises solved, or the percentage of exercises correctly solved.
- Fragments: a task may have a list of fragment identifiers. Each fragment contains the multimedia elements that will be presented to the students while performing a task. The specific fragments to be displayed are selected according to the student personal features.

While teachings tasks are the basic units in a course, **teaching rules** describe the relationships among them. A teaching rule specifies the way a composite task is divided into subtasks. In other words, it indicates which subtasks the student must perform so that the composite task can be considered as done. It also indicates the order in which the subtasks must be performed, and the conditions that are necessary for the activation of the rule. A teaching rule is made up of the following attributes:

- Name: it identifies the teaching rule.
- Left-hand side: the composite task.
- Right-hand side: the list of subtasks.
- Sequencing: it indicates how subtasks have to be performed. AND indicates that all the subtasks have to be performed in the

order in which they appear in the rule. ANY means that all of them must be performed in the order preferred by the student. OR indicates that at least one of them has to be performed. And XOR means that exactly one of them can and must be done.

- Activation condition: a rule may have some conditions associated which have to be satisfied for the rule to be active. These activation conditions can be related to the student profile and/or actions performed while taking the course. When the conditions associated to a teaching rule are satisfied for a student at a given moment, the rule will be active and the subtasks that appear in the right-hand side of the rule will be available for this student at that very moment.

By using activation conditions, it is possible to describe different decompositions for the same composite task depending on the student profile. It is also possible to include dependencies among teaching tasks so that a set of subtasks is not available for a student unless certain results have been obtained while performing other subtasks.

In such a way it is possible to describe different structures for the same course by taking into account the student profile and their previous actions, so that the course can be presented to each of them in the most suitable way.

5.2   The Adaptation Mechanisms

As it has been stated before, the proposed formalism allows the creation of hypermedia educational courses that can be adapted to every student so that all of them can be guided during their learning processes. Adaptation can be implemented in two different ways:

- Adapting the navigational options that are available for a student in a concrete moment and lead to the teaching tasks that can be performed at every moment.

- Adapting the contents that compose the pages presented to a student in a concrete moment.

The methods that are used for adapting the navigational options are, basically, a global guidance that helps the students to find the path to their personal goals and a local guidance that suggests them the most relevant links at every moment, facilitating the selection of the next navigational option. Both methods can be implemented by using teaching tasks and rules for describing the course structure.

The guidance process can range from direct guidance to free navigation. When defining the teaching rules that compose a course it is possible to implement the different kinds of guidance by using different sequencing modes: AND sequencing will guide the students directly, while OR will let them choose the tasks they perform and the order they do them. In the former case students do not need to select the next concept to study, because it is automatically selected by the system: the link to this task is removed and the student is taken directly to this task. In the latter, students have all the possibilities available so that they can select from a list the next topic to be studied. Between both approaches, there exists the possibility of selecting automatically, from the whole set of navigational options, those that are considered more appropriate for the student at a particular moment. In this case, only the links that lead to those tasks are presented, while the other ones are hidden (the options are presented with no active links).

These adaptation techniques can be implemented, thanks to the use of teaching tasks and rules. On the one hand, activation conditions in teaching rules indicate which tasks are available for every student depending on their profile and their actions while taking the course. On the other hand, the sequencing field in these rules indicates the order in which tasks have to be performed and the necessity of doing each of them.

As important as adapting the navigational options available for every student is the adaptation of the contents that appear in the pages presented to them. When different students are taking a course, it is convenient to present the information in the most suitable way for each of them, so that they can understand it easily and feel comfortable while interacting with it.

The way this adaptation is included in a hypermedia course is by creating different versions of each contents fragment associated to a teaching task. Each of these versions corresponds to a different student profile. In this way, it is possible to offer contents in the most appropriate way for each specific student since displayed pages are constructed by selecting the most appropriate fragment version for each student.

5.3 Some Examples of Teaching Tasks and Rules

The course on number base conversion contains several conceptual units. Let us consider one of them whose goal is for students to learn how to perform the conversion from decimal to binary notations. The conversion procedure consists of two stages:

- An iterative process in which the number to be converted and the resulting quotients are successively divided by 2 until a quotient equal to 1 is obtained.
- The construction of the binary result by taking the final quotient and the remainders in an inverse order to that in which they were obtained.

After this procedure has been explained to students, it would be convenient to present some exercises for them to solve. In the case of novice students some illustrative examples would also be useful.

In summary we will have a composite unit which could be referred to as "Decimal to binary conversion." This unit could be decomposed into four smaller units: "Iterative process," "Result construction," "Examples," and "Exercises." These four units would be atomic. The previous decomposition could be applied to novice students. An alternative decomposition for expert students would omit the "Examples" unit.

As mentioned in the previous section, in the TANGOW environment, each conceptual unit corresponds to a task, and each decomposition corresponds to a rule. This means that, for our example, we will need to define five tasks ("Dec_to_bin," "Iterative_proc," "Result_const," "Binary_exam," and "Binary_exer") and two rules.

Table 1. Description of the "Iterative_proc" teaching task.

Slot Name	Slot Content
Task Name	Iterative_proc
Type	Theory
Atomic	Yes
English Description	Iterative Process
End Method	F_TEO
Parameters	tot_pag, pags_visited
HTML fragments	BIN5

As shown in Table 1, the "Iterative_proc" task is a theoretical and atomic task. The method to be executed to check whether the student has successfully performed this task is named "F_TEO" and has two input parameters: "tot_pag" (total number of pages associated to the task) and "pags_visited" (number of pages visited by the student). The finalization method checks whether the values for both parameters are the same, which means that the student has visited all the pages related to the task. It is not necessary to specify such method for composite tasks since they finish when all the corresponding subtasks are finished.

Finally, the HTML slot contains a list with identifiers corresponding to the contents fragments needed to build the HTML page. In our case this list contains a single element: "BIN5."

The definition of the "Binary_exer" task is done in a similar way. In this case, the finalization requirement is given by the "F_PRAC" method, which calculates the ratio between the number of exercises correctly solved by the student with respect to the total number of exercises. This ratio is used to decide whether the task can be considered as finished. In this case, in the HTML slot, in addition to the exercise contents, it is necessary to include the correct answer for each of them. In this case, it is assumed that the exercises are test like, though there are other possibilities. The description of the "Binary_exer" task is shown in Table 2.

Table 2. Description of the "Binary_exer" teaching task.

Slot Name	Slot Content
Task Name	Binary_exer
Type	Practical
Atomic	Yes
English Description	Decimal to binary. Exercises
End Method	F_PRAC
Parameters	exer_ok, exer_done, tot_exer
HTML fragments	EXE1 a
	EXE2 d
	EXE3 c
	EXE4 a
	EXE5 b

One of the composite tasks in our example is "Dec_to_bin." As mentioned earlier, there are two different decompositions for this task, which means that two rules are to be defined. Table 3 shows one of them, the "R1" rule, which describes how the "Dec_to_bin" task is decomposed into four subtasks: "Iterative_proc," "Result_const," "Binary_exam," and "Binary_exer." The sequencing mode chosen is AND, which indicates that the listed subtasks must be performed in the specified order. This rule should be activated only for novice students. This is indicated with the "c_novice" value in the "Act_condition" slot.

Table 3. Description of rule "R1."

Slot Name	Slot Content
Rule Name	R1
Sequencing	AND
LHS	Dec_to_bin
RHS	Iterative_proc, Result_const, Binary_exam, Binary_exer
Act_Condition	C_novice
Parameters	None
Calc_Parameters	add_time_in(Iterative_proc, Result_const, Binary_exam, Binary_exer)
	add_tot_pag(Iterative_proc, Result_const, Binary_exam, Binary_exer)
	add_exer_ok(Iterative_proc, Result_const, Binary_exam, Binary_exer)
	add_exer_done(Iterative_proc, Result_const, Binary_exam, Binary_exer)
	add_tot_exer(Iterative_proc, Result_const, Binary_exam, Binary_exer)
	add_pag_visited(Iterative_proc, Result_const, Binary_exam, Binary_exer)

The alternative decomposition for the "Dec_to_bin" task is expressed by means of the rule "R2" (Table 4). In this case, the "Binary_exam" task is omitted at the right-hand side of the rule and the activation condition will be satisfied for advanced students.

Apart from defining different task decompositions (i.e., rules) for a specific task, adaptivity can be implemented in TANGOW in other ways. One of them is to provide different versions of a specific content fragment, each of which applies to a different student model. It is also possible that students are given access to a specific task only if they have obtained a satisfactory performance for a related task. Other options are available depending on the author's criteria.

Table 4. Description of rule "R2."

Slot Name	Slot Content
Rule Name	R2
Sequencing	AND
LHS	Dec_to_bin,
RHS	Iterative_proc, Result_const, Binary_exer
Act_Condition	C_advanced
Parameters	None
Calc_Parameters	add_time_in(Iterative_proc, Result_const, Binary_exer)
	add_tot_pag(Iterative_proc, Result_const, Binary_exer)
	add_exer_ok(Iterative_proc, Result_const, Binary_exer)
	add_exer_done(Iterative_proc, Result_const, Binary_exer)
	add_tot_exer(Iterative_proc, Result_const, Binary_exer)
	add_pag_visited(Iterative_proc, Result_const, Binary_exer)

5.4   The Course Creation Procedure

Figure 4 illustrates the whole process, as implemented in the TANGOW environment, from the moment authors start designing a course until the course is made available to the students, including also the maintenance work. A previous step before starting with the design process is to decide what the student model will be, i.e., what student features will be considered as important when interacting with the course.

The testing stage is a process in which the author first uses the TANGOW-D tools to create the structure and contents of the course, taking into account the previously defined student models. This tool loads the required databases with the course definition.

As a second step, the author uses TANGOW-R, the runtime tool, to access the course as it is at that moment and adds, removes or changes if necessary. The author can repeat these steps as many times as needed until the course is ready to be deployed. An important aspect to point out about this testing stage is the fact that there is no delay between the design and the execution time. This means that, as soon as the authors make a change, they can test how this change will be seen by a student accessing the course.

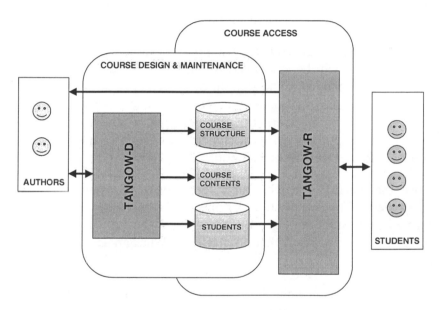

Figure 4. The authoring and deployment processes in the TANGOW environment.

If the course creation stage is analyzed in a more detailed way, when an author is faced with the task of constructing a course, a two-step procedure has to be followed. First, the structure of the course must be designed; i.e., the required tasks and rules have to be defined. In this respect, the author has to decide, first, what conceptual units will be presented to the student and, for each of them, whether the unit is atomic or it must be divided into smaller units.

Different decompositions can be associated to a specific unit, each corresponding to different student models.

In the case of composite units, a decision has to be made about the relation between these smaller units. In general, these decisions have to do with the answer to three questions: (i) are all the units compulsory?, (ii) must they be presented in a specific order or will the student be given the chance to choose which unit to study next?, and (iii) does the access to a unit by the students depend on their mastering of another conceptually related unit?

The second step in the construction process is to create the contents fragments that will be associated to each conceptual unit. A single unit can be explained to the student by means of several fragments. Different versions of a fragment can be built, each corresponding to different student characteristics. For example, if students of different ages are supposed to follow the same adaptive course, the lexicon used for defining a concept could vary.

Once the creation stage has been completed, the course will be "compiled." This means that a consistency checking will be performed to be sure, among other things, that the tasks appearing in rules have been defined, that no atomic task has an associated rule, etc.

When the consistency check succeeds, the task and rule definitions are stored in the corresponding database. At this moment, the course is available, and can be accessed from the standard Web navigator.

As an intermediate format, each task and rule definition is stored as an HTML page. Once designers are familiarized with the use of the authoring tools, they might prefer to give the task and rule definition directly as HTML pages instead of using the tool interface.

An additional stage in the authoring process is the maintenance task. This should be a permanent process in which the tutor takes into account the feedback provided by students, and updates the structure, the contents, or both. Besides the student feedback there might be other reasons for updating the course, such as the inclusion of new materials which should replace existing ones that might have become obsolete or whose addition is considered necessary. As with the testing stage, the TANGOW-D tool facilitates the modification of the structure as well as the contents of an existing course.

A last point to be mentioned about the facilities provided by the design tool has to do with the collaboration between different authors in the course construction process. The author who creates a course has the possibility of giving access to additional authors who will collaborate in the design of the course.

5.5   The Course Instantiation and the Dynamic Hypermedia Generation

When accessing a course, the concept to be presented to a student at a given moment is determined by taking into account the specific student profile and actions. All the characteristics included in the student models are suitable to be considered in the rule definitions.

An adaptation mechanism has been developed based on the representation formalism described previously. The goal of this mechanism is to select, at each step, the teaching tasks that a specific student is allowed to perform. Initially the only task that can be performed is the main task of the course. At each learning step, the system must decide which are the most appropriate tasks for each student among the available ones. A task is considered to be available if it satisfies any of the following conditions:
- It is an atomic task

- It is a composite task described by rules with no activation conditions
- It is a composite task described by rules whose activation conditions are satisfied.

After obtaining the set of available tasks, a menu is generated so that the students can select the task they wish to perform. If there is a single available task it will be offered directly to the students for them to perform it.

The contents that will appear in the generated HTML pages are inserted into a course as hypermedia fragments, including the multimedia elements necessary for explaining the different parts of the course. The idea is to provide little fragments containing, each of them, just the materials necessary for explaining a concept, procedure, example, and so on. In such a way, these materials can be reused in different parts of a course if convenient.

In order to present the information in the most suitable way for every particular student that is taking a course, teachers can provide different versions of the same hypermedia fragments. These versions will be different depending on student features.

When including a hypermedia fragment, designers can provide different versions in the cases that they consider useful, while keeping a unique version in the other cases. In the first case, designers must associate the same identifier to all the versions, so that the most suitable one for each student can be selected during the course execution.

The above-mentioned student features are not the only ones that can be considered for content adaptation. The formalism presented allows the definition of the student features that should be taken into account in every course to personalize the contents, facilitating the inclusion of different fragment versions according to these features.

The contents presented in every page depend on the task that the student is performing. If the task being performed is an atomic task, an html page is constructed by concatenating the various content fragments associated to the task in question. On the contrary, if the task is composite, a page is constructed with the corresponding content fragments together with a menu containing the description of the available tasks.

The content fragments are classified according to certain features such as the language in which they are written, the age of the students they are addressed to or the level of detail in which they are written. When a page is being constructed, the most appropriate fragments are selected among the distinct versions that are available, by taking into account the student profile.

In addition to the content fragments and the task menu, a set of navigation buttons are included in the displayed page, that allow students to continue their learning process or to exit the system.

Besides the elements strictly needed for the fulfillment of a course, additional help elements are included in the generated pages. One of these elements is the table of contents which allows students to know, at every moment, where they are situated with respect to the whole course. The entries of this table are annotated by using the traffic light metaphor proposed by Schwarz *et al.* (1996). These annotations offer students information about their situation with respect to the whole course, how much of the course they have already performed and how much is left, and about the sections which are available at each moment.

Due to the dynamic nature of adaptive courses, students do not know the amount of material that remains to be reviewed. With the purpose of solving this problem, at least partially, a progress bar is built which shows an estimation of the percentage of the course yet to be done before finalizing it. This estimation is calculated as a ratio of the fragments already presented to the student with respect to the total number of fragments available for the course.

It is also possible for the designer to define a common pattern for all the pages to be generated. The general aspect of a final page including all the elements just described is shown in Figure 5. It can be observed that pages are organized in three different frames: table of contents on the left, navigational buttons on the bottom right and contents and menu on the center.

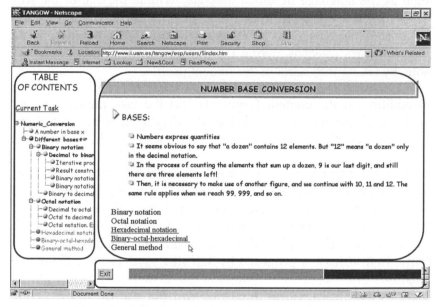

Figure 5. A final page in the number conversion course.

There are two special classes of pages that do not follow the schema just described. One of them are the pages displayed after a student solves an exercise, which contain feedback about the solution. Another special page is the one presented at the end of a session, with information about the results obtained by the student, such as the number of pages visited, the number of exercises solved and the success percentage obtained.

5.6 Accessing a Course on TANGOW

The architecture of the TANGOW system is described next. A Student Process is created for each student connected to the system. This process consists of two programs, the Task Manager and the Page Generator, and a data area, the Dynamic Workspace. There is also a program that maintains information about each of the Student Processes in execution. This program is the Task Manager.

Students connect to the system through their browsers and submit requests. These requests are transmitted to the Process Manager, which sends the request to the corresponding Student Process. Within this process, the Task Manager is in charge of guiding the student during his/her learning session. It keeps information about each session in the Dynamic Workspace. This information relates to the student profiles as well as to the actions they perform during their learning processes. By taking into account this information and the teaching tasks and rules that compose the course, it selects the available tasks and sends the relevant information to the Page Generator, so that the pages to be presented to the student can be generated.

At the end of a session, the information about all the actions that the students performed is stored at the Student database in order to restore the situation in subsequent sessions.

5.7 The Number Conversion Course

The whole course on number conversion mentioned in the previous sections is described in detail in this section as implemented with the TANGOW system. The subject of the course is how to convert a number in a specific base to a number in a different base. The course consists of six parts: (i) what is a number in base x?, (ii) binary notation, (iii) octal notation, (iv) hexadecimal notation, (v) binary/octal/hexadecimal conversions, and (vi) general conversion method.

A general schema of the whole course is shown in Figure 6. The concepts that compose the course are shown, by using a description of each of them. The discontinuous line indicates a dependency between concepts and an asterisk preceding a word shows the necessary conditions to decompose a concept into a set of them in a certain way.

Table 5 shows all the tasks in the course. As it can be observed, the attributes that appear are the task name, type (T: theory, E: example, P: practice), atomicity, description in English, and the contents fragments associated to each task.

The finalization methods have been omitted in Table 5 because the default ones are used. In the case of theoretical tasks these default methods check that all the associated pages have been visited. If the task is practical, they check that all the exercises have been solved.

Table 6 presents the teaching rules that specify the relations between the corresponding tasks.

Figures 7 and 8 show the learning itineraries followed by two students taking the course on number conversion. Both students have different personal features and preferences. As it can be observed in the figures, both students have performed the definition task first since it is the first subtask within a rule with AND sequencing. In addition, in both cases the "General" task (which corresponds to the generalization method) has been performed after the "Bin_Oct_Hex" task. This is because there is a theoretical dependence between both tasks (i.e., "General" should not be available until "Bin_Oct_Hex" has been performed).

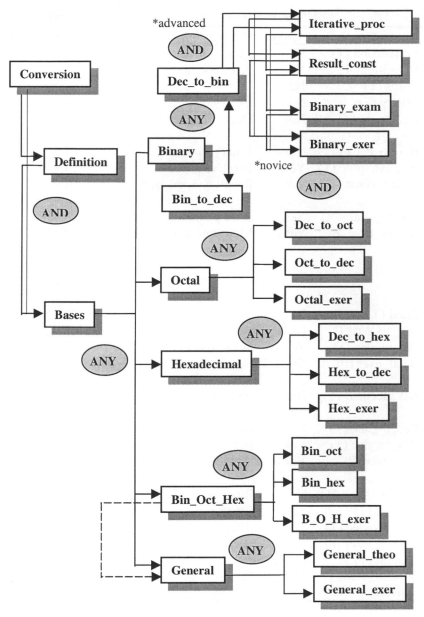

Figure 6. A sample course on number conversion.

Table 5. Teaching tasks of the course on conversion between bases.

Name & type	Atomic	Description	Fragments
Conversion (T)	No	Base conversion	CONV
Definition (T)	Yes	A number in base x	DEF
Bases (T)	No	Different bases	BASES
Binary (T)	No	Binary notation	BIN1
Dec_to_bin (T)	No	Decimal to binary	BIN2, BIN3
Bin_to_dec (T)	Yes	Binary to decimal	BIN4
Iterative_proc (T)	Yes	Iterative process	BIN5
Result_const (T)	Yes	Result construction	BIN6, BIN7
Binary_exam (E)	Yes	Binary notation. Examples	BIN8
Binary_exer (P)	Yes	Binary notation. Exercises	EXE1 a, EXE2 d, EXE3 c, EXE4 a, EXE5 b
Octal (T)	No	Octal notation	OCT1
Dec_to_oct (T)	Yes	Decimal to octal	OCT2
Oct_to_dec (T)	Yes	Octal to decimal	OCT3
Octal_exer (P)	Yes	Octal notation. Exercises	EXE6 a, EXE7 c
Hexadecimal (T)	No	Hexadecimal notation	HEX1, HEX2
Dec_to_hex (T)	Yes	Decimal to hexadecimal	HEX3
Hex_to_dec (T)	Yes	Hexadecimal to decimal	HEX4
Hex_exer (P)	Yes	Hexadecimal not. Exercises	EXE8 b, EXE9 d
Bin_Oct_Hex (T)	No	Binary-octal-hexadecimal	BOH1
Bin_oct (T)	Yes	Binary/octal conversions	BOH2
Bin_hexadec (T)	Yes	Binary/hexadecimal	BOH3
B_O_H_exer (P)	Yes	Bin-oct-hex. Exercises	EXE10 a
General (T)	No	General method	GEN1
General_theo (T)	Yes	General method. Theory	GEN2
General_exer (P)	Yes	General method. Exercises	EXE11 c

Table 6. Teaching rules of the course on conversion between bases.

Rule	Main task & sequencing	Subtasks	Act_Cond
R0	Conversion (AND)	Definition	
		Bases	
R1	Bases (ANY)	Binary	
		Octal	
		Hexadecimal	
		Bin_Oct_Hex	
		General	
R2	Binary (ANY)	Dec_to_bin	
		Bin_to_dec	
R3	Dec_to_bin (AND)	Iterative_proc	C_novice
		Result_const	
		Binary_exam	
		Binary_exer	
R4	Dec_to_bin (AND)	Iterative_proc	C_advanced
		Result_const	
		Binary_exer	
R5	Octal (ANY)	Dec_to_oct	
		Oct_to_dec	
		Octal_exer	
R6	Hexadecimal (ANY)	Dec_to_hex	
		Hex_to_dec	
		Hex_exer	
R7	Bin_Oct_Hex (ANY)	Bin_oct	
		Bin_hex	
		B_O_H_exer	
R8	General (ANY)	General_theo	C_theo Bin_Oct_Hex
		General_exer	

The differences between both itineraries are, firstly, the order in which the tasks in the second level of the tree have been performed. Each student is allowed to choose the preferred order since they appear on the left-hand side of a rule with ANY sequencing (see rule "R1" in Table 6). Another difference has to do with the fact that both students have different level of knowledge about the number conversion subject. As a consequence, only the novice student will be presented with examples about the decimal to binary conversion ("Binary_exam" task in Figure 7).

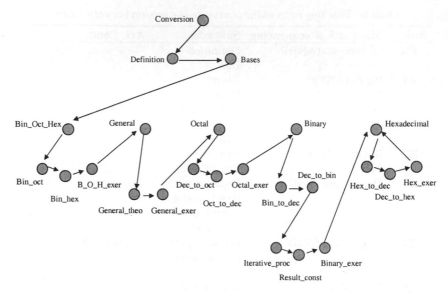

Figure 7. The itinerary followed by student A.

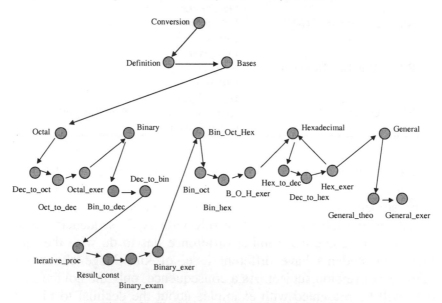

Figure 8. The itinerary followed by student B.

The learning itinerary followed by students affects the final page displayed to them. For example, the page shown in Figure 5 will be presented to student B just before starting the "Binary_octal_hexadecimal" task. For this reason, the "Binary notation" and the "Octal" tasks are not clickable at the central frame, although they are accessible from the table of contents. The "General" task is not accessible, even from the table of contents, because the student has not performed the "Binary-octal-hexadecimal" task yet.

6   Conclusions

In this chapter we have presented the development and access to internet-based courses. In order for these courses to be useful for a wide range of students, it is becoming generally accepted that they need to include some adaptive features.

In the area of Internet-based education, adaptivity is understood to mean that both the contents and the navigational options offered to each student while taking a course can vary. These variations depend on the students personal features as well as on the actions they perform during their learning process. Moreover, adaptivity also applies to the curriculum sequencing for each student. Adaptation techniques allow course designers to provide students with a personalized guidance in contrast with the impersonal approach that is customary in the Internet.

Although the advantages of adaptive hypermedia systems are numerous, the process of developing this kind of systems has proved to be a complex task. However, this complexity should not have an effect from the student's point of view. That is, adaptation should be a transparent process for the students: the pages they are presented with should be standard HTML pages, although they have been dynamically generated at each learning step. Consequently, the responsibility of managing the complexity of the adaptivity process relies on a good design work. This calls for a design methodology suitable for this kind of courses. As a result of the design phase, this methodology should produce a formal structure easily understandable by a course server. The development of a methodology that facilitates the creation and maintenance work to course designers, is the main motivation of the work presented in this chapter.

The proposed methodology makes use of a formalism based on establishing a clear separation between the structure and the contents of a course. The course structure is described by identifying the main conceptual units (referred to as teaching tasks) and by establishing different relationships among them (by means of teaching rules). By associating activation conditions to these rules, it is possible to adapt the navigational options offered to the student. The pages presented to the students are dynamically generated, and may include several content fragments, as well as adaptive navigational options. Contents adaptation is achieved by providing different versions of these fragments and selecting the most appropriate for each student.

On the other hand, the course structure described by using the proposed formalism bears a similarity with context-free grammars, as in Computational Linguistics applications, where teaching tasks would play the role of lexical units, and teaching rules would establish the relations among them. The main task of the course represents the grammar axiom. All this makes the formalism very easy to grasp even by non-technology experts. In addition, the above-mentioned separation between structure and contents, and the modular description of the structure, facilitates the reuse of components and the course maintenance. The dynamic generation of navigational options from task and rule descriptions guarantees the consistency of the links included in the course.

A design tool that allows the creation of adaptive courses described by means of the proposed formalism has been implemented. Several courses have been developed using this tool. We believe that the described formalism is easy to understand by designers, who are able to create and maintain such adaptive courses. These courses can be accessed by students through Internet by using a runtime system called TANGOW (Task-based Adaptive Guidance On the Web). TANGOW runs on the server side, whereas students only require a standard browser.

References

Alfonseca, M. and de Lara, J. (2001), "Constructing simulation-based Web documents," *IEEE Multimedia*, http://www.computer.org/multimedia/mu2001/u1toc.htm, vol. 8, no. 1, pp. 42-49.

Ausserhofer, A. (1999), "Web-based teaching and learning: a panacea?" *IEEE Communications*, vol. 37, no. 3, pp. 92-96.

Brusilovsky, P. (2001), "Adaptive hypermedia," *User Modeling and User-Adaptive Interaction*, 11, Kluwer Academic Publishers, pp. 87-110.

Brusilovsky, P. and Pesin, L. (1994), "ISIS-Tutor: an adaptive hypertext learning environment," in Ueno, H. and Stefanuk, V. (eds.), *Proceedings of JCKBSE'94, Japanese-CIS Symposium on Knowledge-Based Software Engineering*, Pereslavl-Zalesski, Russia, pp. 83-87.

Brusilovsky, P., Schwarz, E., and Weber, G. (1996), "ELM-ART: an intelligent tutoring system on World Wide Web," in Frasson, C., Gauthier, G., and Lesgold, A. (eds.), *Proceedings of the Third International Conference on Intelligent Tutoring Systems, ITS-96*, Berlin: Springer, pp. 261-269.

Brusilovsky, P., Kobsa, A., and Vassileva, J. (eds.) (1998), *Adaptive Hypertext and Hypermedia*, Dordrecht. Kluwer Academic Publishers, pp. 1-43.

Carro, R.M., Pulido, E., and Rodríguez, P. (1999), "TANGOW: Task-based Adaptive learNer Guidance On the WWW," *Proceedings of the Second Workshop on Adaptive Systems and User Modeling on the World Wide Web*, Toronto and Banff, Canada, Computer Science Report 99-07, Eindhoven University of Technology (1999) 49-57.

Cervera, M., Gómez, F., and Martínez, J. (2000), "A World Wide Web based architecture for the implementation of a virtual laboratory," *Proceedings of the 26th Euromicro Workshop on Multimedia and Telecommunications*, vol. 2, pp. 56-62.

CSCW (2001), CSCW@Technische Universität München, http:// www.telekooperation.de/cscw/cscw-links.html .

DublinCore (2001), The Dublin Core Metadata Initiative homepage, http://dublincore.org/ .

Eklund, J. and Brusilovsky, P. (1996), "The value of adaptivity in hypermedia learning environments: a short review of empirical evidence," *Second Workshop on Adaptive Hypertext and Hypermedia. Ninth ACM Conference on Hypertext and Hypermedia*, Pittsburgh, USA, pp. 13-19.

Gilbert, J.E. and Han, C.Y. (1999), "Adapting instruction in search of 'a significant difference,'" *Journal of Network and Computer Applications*, 22.

IMS (2001), The IMS Global Learning Consortium homepage, http://www.imsproject.org/ .

Laroussi, M. and Ben, A.M. (1998), "Providing an adaptive learning through the WEB case of CAMELEON: computer aided medium for learning on networks," *Proceedings of the 4th International Conference on Computer-Aided Learning and Instruction in Science and Engineering (CALISCE'98)*, Göteborg, Sweden, June.

Nanard, J. and Nanard, M. (1995), "Hypertext design environments and the hypertext design process," *Communications of the ACM*, vol. 28, no. 8, pp. 49-56.

Nill, A. (1997), "Providing useable and useful information by adaptivity and adaptability," GMD-German National Research Center for Information Technology, Sankt Augustin, Germany, http://zeus.gmd.de/~nill/flexht97.html .

Pérez, T.A., Gutiérrez, J., and Lopistéguy, P. (1995), "An adaptive hypermedia system," *Artificial Intelligence in Education, AIED'95*, Charlottesville: AACE, EE.UU.

Rowe, N. and Galvin, T. (1998), "An authoring system for intelligent procedural-skill tutors," *IEEE Intelligent Systems*, pp. 61-69.

Schwarz, E., Brusilovsky, P., and Weber, G. (1996), "World-wide intelligent textbooks," in Carlson, P. and Makedon, F. (eds.), *Proceedings of ED-TELEKOM 96 – World Conference on Educational Telecommunications*, Charlottesville, VA: AACE, pp. 302-307.

TANGOW (2001), TANGOW homepage, http://www.ii.uam.es /esp/investigacion/tangow/present.html .

Vassileva, J. (1998), "A task-centred approach for user modeling in a hypermedia office documentation system," in Brusilovsky, P., Kobsa, A., and Vassileva J. (eds.) *Adaptive Hypertext and Hy-*

permedia, Kluwer Academic Publ. Dordrecht, chapter 8, pp. 209-247.

WebCT (2001), The WebCT homepage, http://www.webct.com .

Zeiliger, R. (1993), "Adaptive testing: contribution of the SHIVA model," in Leclercq, D. and Bruno, J. (eds.), *Item Banking: Interactive Testing and Self-assessment*, NATO ASI Serie F, vol. 112, Springer-Verlag, Berlin, pp. 54-65.

Chapter 5

Towards Intelligent Media-Oriented e-Learning Environments

M. Kayama and T. Okamoto

In this chapter, we propose a Distance Educational Model (DEM) and describe the structure, function, mechanism and the educational meaning of this model. To develop the model, it is necessary to construct an individual learning environment as well as a collaborative one, which supports learners' self learning/training by using Internet distributed environments and multimedia technologies. Our project proceeds towards an intelligent media-oriented e-learning environment under the concept of DEM. We have built a free and flexible, self learning/training environment, called RAPSODY. This learning environment is superior to a simple rule-based instructional plan, as it allows a better and more natural overview of the global structure as well as a quick identification of missing parts. The system is therefore a good example of how to integrate various media and intelligent adaptation techniques with e-Learning in a hybrid and goal oriented manner. Further on, we need to extend our functions by accumulating various kinds of teaching expertise. In such a way, the concept of "knowledge-sharing" and "knowledge-reusing" can be brought to life. The extended version of the RAPSODY (RAPSODY-EX) has an educational knowledge management function for both students and faculties. RAPSODY-EX can effectively carry out the collaborative learning support in asynchronous/synchronous learning modes. Various information in the educational context is referred and re-used as knowledge which oneself and others can practically utilize.

1   Introduction

The educational field has gradually migrated towards the World Wide Web, mostly under the slogan of free, accessible from/to anyplace, and at anytime (Chan *et al.* 1997). This development triggered, among other effects, the important shifting from the teaching paradigm to the learning paradigm (Kuhn 1962, Fischer 1999). In fact, to obtain learner-oriented and customized learning environments, Artificial Intelligence in Education (AI in ED) techniques are adapted and developed for the Web (Johnson and Shaw 1997, Kaplan 1998). These advances of technology promise revolutionary changes in the whole educational system of the new millennium (Okamoto *et al.* 2000a).

Recently, with the development of information and communication technologies, various teaching methods using Internet and multimedia are being introduced (Cumming *et al.* 1998). Most of these methods emphasize, in particular, on the aspect of collaborative communication between students and teachers during interactive teaching/learning activities (Brna 1997, Dillenbourg 1999, Frasson and Aimeur 1996, Woods and Warren 1996). Therefore, nowadays it is extremely important for not only the teacher but also the student to acquire computer communication literacy (Nishinosono 1998).

The utilization of Internet spreads out worldwide. Hence, a new learning environment called "e-learning" has risen in the educational area. This e-learning environment is expected to be more flexible modality of learning than traditional classroom environments. We can regard the Internet environment as a huge depository, which connects distributed information and knowledge logically. Therefore, it is natural for people to use this huge resource for their various educational needs. However, this technological resource needs a new conceptual framework for the construction of the learning environment at the same time. It may need new learning ways/forms, curriculum development, digital contents, learning tools/applications and management of educational data, and others. Hopefully, people would have closer communication in this environment and exchange idea/opinions each other. Moreover acquire meaningful knowledge from far sites to satisfy their learning/working needs.

Here, in this study, we defined two aspects of the meaning of e-Learning. The first aspect is an ordinary concept, concerning with a distance educational system adopting the information and communication technologies, such as networking, digital media, and so on (Hara and Kling 2000, Meissner 1999, Nkambou *et al.* 1998, Schneider and Godard 1996, Synnes *et al.* 1999). So far, people have developed many educational/learning support systems such as CAI (Computer Assisted Instruction), ITS (intelligent Tutoring Systems), ILE (Interactive Learning Environment) WBL (Web Based Learning), and CSCL (Computer Supported Collaborative Learning) for improving learners' competency/skills. Especially, those systems could deliver many contents and functions to the different far sites synchronously and asynchronously. The second aspect is an artificial intelligence oriented concept, concerning with technological methodology to activate/enhance human learning activity regarding highly cognitive behaviors. In such case, we need to provide an environment to support human learning behaviors with sophisticated technologies to activate human internal competency such as visualization, knowledge discovery, and knowledge acquisition.

This study aims to explore the fusion of the second technical concept into the first practical concept. Thereby, our ultimate research goal is "Towards Intelligent Media-Oriented e-Learning Environment." The concept, "Intelligent Media Oriented," does not only mean intelligence of media, but also intelligence of digital learning environment. We would like to emphasize the latter to warrant collaborative knowledge communication/guidance/discover/refinement among learners. Moreover, we expect the interoperability for co/re-use of the various resources in this environment to realize more effective and smooth usage of media. The various kinds of intelligent tools to support human learning that will be developed, will be provided to many users in e-learning world.

Therefore, we have tackled to build the open e-Learning environment (collaborative platform for knowledge managing) in order to share the rich meaningful media, which will be developed in the near future.

Based on such a background, it is necessary to construct an individual, as well as a collaborative learning environment, which supports learners' self-learning/training, by using Internet distributed environments and multimedia technologies. A learner can choose the most convenient learning media (learning form) to learn the contents (subject units) that he/she desires.

The new information and communication technologies provide rich and useful opportunities for the self-development of people. Knowledge concerning the teaching contents and methods can be stored as multimedia information, in the form of pictures, videos and sound tracks. Moreover, by using the network environment, it is possible to make use of all resources over the net, without any constraints or restrictions of time and/or geographical location.

With this goal in mind, we are developing the integrated distance education/training system for supporting learners' self-learning/ training, called RAPSODY (Remote and AdaPtive educational System Offering DYnamic communicative environment).

2   Related Studies about Distance Learning Systems

In general, there are two classes of systems that support distance education. One represents seamless systems for smooth communication among remote sites. The other represents collaborative systems that positively support users' various learning activities related to distance education.

An example of the first class, is the learning environment of the Open University in Britain, where they have implemented a Teleconference system with multimedia under the concept of "Electronic Campus," working since 1980 (Kaye 1994). Furthermore, systems of the "virtual university," providing educational services via distance educational facilities, are in actual use at the University of Phoenix (www.uophx.edu) and the Jones International University (www.jonesinternational.edu), etc. Then, in Britain, there is the National Grid Plan for Learning, which will provide the environment for distance education with distance self-learning and is based on huge resources for building a life-long educational system (UK Government 1997). One of the aims of this project is to integrate and totally manage (one step access) the various kinds of on-line learning materials.

In Japan, the Tokyo Institute of Technology, developed ANDES (Academic Network for Distance Education by Satellite), a distance educational system using a communication satellite of sending/passing digital movies interactively (Shimizu 1999). In addition, IBM Japan, a Web-Collaboration system that is a type of synchronous distance educational system that makes use of the sharing technology of Web-browsers, has been developed (Kobayashi *et al.* 1998).

An example of the second class, is the TeleTOP project (teletop .edte.utwente.nl), at the University of Twente (Collis 1999). This project has started as a CBT project since 1980. At the present, further amelioration are made to be a more flexible distance educational system, under the name of C@mpus+, which emphasizes functions such as course designing/authoring/delivering curriculum development/management and educational evaluation of the distance system itself. The University of Trento is developing a Webfree system for distance learning (Colazzo and Molinari 1996). This system allows a user to manage the lesson in a way that guarantees coherence in the exposition of the arguments without using CGI (Common Gateway Interface), Java or HTML (Hyper Text Markup Language), and without the need of having a Web-Browser available. The prototype provides a cooperative environment, which uses the Internet as a means of transmission, where teachers and learners can interact in a non-hierarchized manner with dynamic didactic materials that may or may not be pre-constructed. Moreover, we can mention the "Electronic Learning" (Elisabeth *et al.* 1997) of CARTE (The Center for Advanced Research in Technology for Education), at the University of Southern California, in which the intelligent functions for course design and authoring are incorporated as a distance education supporting system.

In Japan, some distance educational systems that integrate both the synchronous and asynchronous learning modes have been developed by several research organizations and utilized in some educational institutes (Aoki and Nakajima 1999, Okamoto and Cristea 2001). The features of those systems are aimed at embedding the functions of pasting information of annotation/illustration and linking freely to other Web pages during the student's learning activities.

3   Distance Ecological Model

3.1   Concept of Distance Ecological Model

In this section, we will define our Distance Ecological Model, which is based on the concept of Educational Organization Based Curriculum Development and Training System (Okamoto and Cristea 2001), advocated by UNESCO (1998) and OECD/CERI, and we will describe the structure, function, mechanism and the educational meaning of this model. To develop the model, it is necessary to construct an individual learning environment as well as a collaborative one, which supports learners' self-learning/training by using Internet distributed environments and multimedia technologies. In such an environment, a learner can choose the most convenient learning media to learn the contents that s/he desires.

Our Distance Ecological Model is built on three aspects (Okamoto and Cristea 2001). The first aspect represents the learning goals, which are:
1. The study of subject-contents,
2. The study of teaching ways (knowledge and skills), and
3. The study of evaluation methods of the students' learning activities.

The second one stands for the aspect of the curriculum (subject-the The second one stands for the aspect of the curriculum (subject contents) that represents what the learners want to learn. The the third aspect concerns the favorite learning media (form) that can be chosen, e.g., VOD (Video on Demand) (Acharya *et al.* 2000, Hui 2001, Peltoniemi 1995), CBR (Case Based Reasoning) (Kolodner and Riesbeck 1993), etc.

By selecting a position on each of the three aspects, a certain CELL is determined. A CELL consists of several slots, which represent the features/characteristics of the learning Object. Especially, the most important slot in the CELL is "Script," which describes the instruction guidelines of the learning contents, the self-learning procedure. Figure 1 depicts the structure of this model. The concept of the CELL in Distance Ecological Model is quite important, because it generates the training scenario, including the information to satisfy the learner's needs, the learning-flow of subject materials and the guidelines for self-learning navigation. The frame representation of a CELL is shown in Table 1. These slots are referred when RAPSODY guides the process of the learner's self-learning. Table 2 shows an example of the CELL definition.

In the following, we will explain the meaning of each aspect in more details.

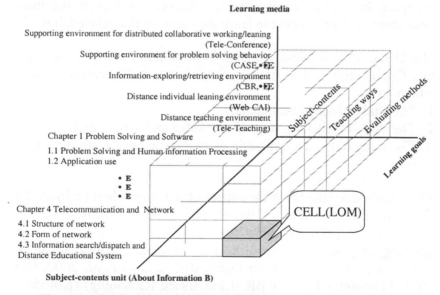

Figure 1. The Conceptual Structure of the Distance Ecological Model.

Table 1. The Frame Representation of the CELL.

	Frame-name:	*Slot-value*
Slot-name	Learning objectives for a student	Subjects which should be understood Subjects which should be mastered
	Subject-contents	The unit topic
	Teaching method	The students' supervision method and instructional strategies
	Evaluating method	The students' evaluation method
	Useful tools	The software used for the training activity
	Operational manual of tools	The software operation method used for the training activity
	Prepared media	The learning media which can be selected
	Guide-Script	The file which specifies the dialog between the trainee and the system

Table 2. An Example of the CELL.

101	
Learning objectives for a student	Learn the fundamentals of modeling
Subject-contents	• Theory of system dynamics • Method of modeling • Model description • Model components • Building model • Simulation
Teaching method	NULL
Evaluating method	NULL
Useful tools	Modeling tool: STELLA, Spread sheet: MS-Excel
Operational manual of tools	STELLA user's guide book, MS-Excel user's guide book
Prepared media	Tele-teaching, Tele-conference
Guide-Script	"file:c\aaa\Product_PSS.script"

3.2   Learning Goals Aspect

For the learning goal aspect, we have already proposed three sub goals, which are:
1. Subject-contents,
2. Teaching ways, and
3. Evaluating methods.

It is extremely important for learners to achieve those sub goals for understanding how to use and apply information technologies in order to enhance their problem solving abilities (Okamoto *et al.* 2000b). This involves comprehensive learning activities, such as problem recognition, investigation and analysis, planning and design, implementation and execution, evaluation, reporting and presentation. We expect that learners acquire the proper respective skills for evaluating students' achievements, as well as understanding of the subject-content itself, according to each of the above activities. Those components are the necessary learning objectives that the learner must acquire in order to carry out the educational process of "information." This aspect is an essential competency/skill for self_training/learning. However, at the moment, the knowledge/content bases (learning units) about Teaching ways and evaluating methods are not incorporated in our system yet.

3.3   Subject-Contents Aspect

For the subject-content aspect, we focus on the subject called "Information," which is due to be established as a new obligatory subject in the regular courses of the academic high school system, in Japan. The subject "Information" is composed of three sub-subjects, "Information A," "Information B" and "Information C." The contents of each sub-subject are as follows.

Information A: This sub-subject places importance on raising the fundamental skills and abilities to collect, process and transmit "information" using computers, the Internet and multimedia.

Information B: This sub-subject places importance on understanding the fundamental scientific aspects and the practical usage methods of "information."

Information C: This sub-subject places importance on fostering the desirable and sound behavior regarding participation, involvement and contribution in an information society. It focuses on understanding people's roles, and the influence and impact of technology, in the new information society.

3.4   Learning Media Aspect

This aspect represents five different learning environments, defined as follows:

- Distance teaching environment (Tele-Teaching) based on the one-to-multi-sites telecommunications.
- Distance individual learning environment (Web-CAI) based on CAI using WWW facilities.
- Information-exploring and retrieving environment using VOD, CBR.
- Supporting environment for problem solving, by providing various effective learning tools.
- Supporting environment for distributed collaborative working/learning based on the multi-sites telecommunications.

Brief explanations for each environment are given in the following.

- Distance teaching environment (Tele-Teaching):
  This environment delivers the instructor's lecture image and voice information through the Internet, by using the real-time information dispatching function via VOD.
- Distance individual learning environment (Web-CAI)
  This environment provides CAI courseware with WWW facilities on the Internet.
- Information-exploring and retrieving environment
  This environment delivers, according to the learner's demand, the instructor's lecture image and voice information, which was

previously stored on the VOD server. For delivery, the function of dispatching information accumulated on the VOD server is used. In addition to it, this environment provides a CBR system with short movies about classroom teaching practices.

- Supporting environment for problem solving
  This environment provides a tool library for performance support, based on CAD (Computer Aided Design), Modeling tools, Spreadsheets, Authoring tools, and so on.
- Supporting environment for distributed collaborative working and learning
  This environment provides a groupware with a shared memory window, using text, voice and image information for the trainees.

In the following, we describe the concept of the learning media. The learning media stand for instruction forms using synchronous and the asynchronous modes. The asynchronous media are time-free delivery environments of lecture video/audio information and activities. Information exploring and retrieving environments can deliver the previous stored lectures media resources from the VOD server (Inoue and Okamoto 1999), CBR module with short movies about classroom teaching practices (Kayama *et al.* 2000), navigation system (Abou-Jaoude and Frasson 1998), and so on. Supporting environments for problem solving provide a tool library for performance support based on modeling tools, authoring tools, etc. The synchronous media are live lectures using audio/video media resources. The intelligent media software handles adaptive linkage between learning support software and the media resources. They are capable of inferring relationships between the content of different resources. They tackle problems of knowledge sharing, knowledge-retrieval and various types of collaboration in the learning environment (Paiva 1996, IEEE-LTSC 2000). When the learners explore the available resources, they are offered opportunities to analyze the needed information. The heart of our project is the exploration of how we can effectively make use of the learning media to support learners who have a range of different needs.

4   An Intelligent Media-Oriented e-Learning Environment: RAPSODY

The system configuration of the self learning/training environment is composed of two subsystems based on the Distance Ecological Model. One of the subsystems is the training system, where a trainee can select and learn the subject adequate for him/her guided by the script in the CELL. Another subsystem is an authoring system with creating and editing functions for CELL description. The users of the second environment are the authors who can design lecture-plans in this environment.

4.1   RAPSODY with Distance Ecological Model

Figure 2 shows the RAPSODY usage image. RAPSODY is an integrated guide system that can logically connect individual learning unit (CELL)s. The CELL corresponds to the Learning Object Metadata (LOM) proposed by IEEE-LTSC (2000) and IMS (1998), and is intentionally focused on three primary aspects in order to represent educational meaning within the distance learning environment: learning goals, learning contents and learning media We call this conceptual scheme the Distance Ecological Model. Each of the CELLs has also the other several attributes (slots) such as features of the material, available tools, a related CELL, Guide-Script, besides those three primary aspects. From a user's (a learner's) point of view, this model seems to be quite transparent in order to identify/select his/her leaning conditions, and the system can easily guide towards an adequate learning object, according to his/her requirements. The word of "Ecological Model" in distance learning means multi-modal "learning gestalt" reflecting learning goals, learning contents and learning media/environment including any situation of individual/self and group/collaborative learning. We use the Distance Ecological Model in the wider sense of ecology, as a closed, perpetual mobile system, which functions without interference from the outside, once the actors (such as designer, author, and learner) and their interactions are defined.

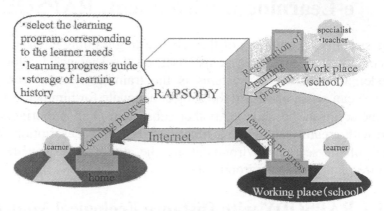

Figure 2. RAPSODY usage image.

In this system, in one hand, the word "designer" means a person who designs/describes each value of a LOM and a Guide-Script. On the other hand, the word "author" means a person who produces digital course materials such as Web-based contents, movies and sound of VOD, etc., by means of any authoring tools.

A Learning Object Metadata for any learning course-material would be defined, modified and registered from far sites by designers or authors according to a certain educational goal. At the same time, authors such as schoolteachers, university professors, etc., would produce and store their digital learning contents in their local server machines individually. Of course, each of contributors may play any of the two parts. This system can logically link the CELLs based on the Distance Ecological Model of RAPSODY, which provides the learning guide environment by taking into consideration each user's individual learning needs/conditions.

4.2   Primary Functions of RAPSODY

Our project proceeds towards an intelligent media-oriented e-Learning environment under the concept of education, but life-long learning, in-service training and career development. We have built a free and flexible, self-training environment: RAPSODY. We have realized the foundation of the integrated distance education. This learning environment is superior to a simple rule-based instructional plan, as it allows a better and more natural overview of the global structure as well as a quick identification of missing parts. The system is therefore a good example of how to integrate various media and intelligent adaptation techniques with e-Learning in a hybrid and goal oriented manner. RAPSODY already encompasses other distance education projects in our laboratory and is constantly growing. Further on, we need to extend our databases by accumulating various kinds of teaching expertise. In such a way, the concept of "knowledge-sharing" and "knowledge-reusing" can be brought to life.

4.2.1   Learning Guide Mechanism of RAPSODY

The training system aims to support learners' self-training. The configuration of this system is shown in Figure 3. The role of this system is first to identify a CELL in the model, according to the learners' needs. Then, the system tries to set up an effective learning environment, by retrieving the proper materials for the learner, along with the Guide-Script defined in the corresponding CELL. Therefore, the system offers programs for both Retrieving and Interpreting. The training system works as shown in the following:
1. Record the learner's needs.
2. Select a CELL in the Distance Ecological Model according to the learner's needs.
3. Interpret the CELL in the guide WM (Working Memory).
4. Develop the interactive training with the learner according to the Guide-Script in the guide WM.

5. Store the log-data of the dialog. The log-data collects information on the learning histories and learners' needs and behaviors.
6. Provide the needed and useful applications for the user's learning activities and set up an effective training environment.
7. Give guidance-information, according to the CELL script guidelines, and decide on the proper CELL for the next learning step.

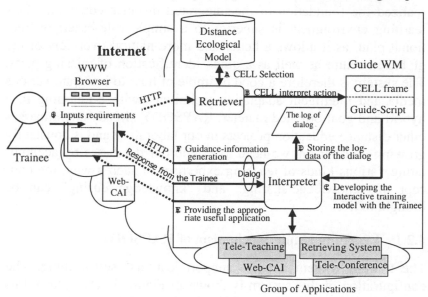

Figure 3. The System Configuration of RAPSODY.

Here, it is necessary to explain the dialog mechanism (algorithm) between the user and the system. The interpreter controls and develops the dialog process between the user and the machine according to the information defined in our Guide-Script description language. This Guide-Script description language (GSDL) consists of some tags and a simple grammar for interpreting a document, similar to the HTML on the WWW. The interpreter understands the meanings of the tags, and interprets the contents. An example of GSDL is shown below.

<free>   Definition: description of the text (instruction)
<slot >   Definition: a link to a slot value in the CELL
<question>   Definition: questions to a trainee
<choice>   Definition: branching control according to a
            trainee's response
<exe>   Call: to relevant CELLs
<app>   Definition: applications used for training activities
            (e.g., Tele-Teaching, etc.)

A. Training course selection

B. Guidance Information_1

C. Lesson(Tele-Teaching)

D. Guidance Information_2

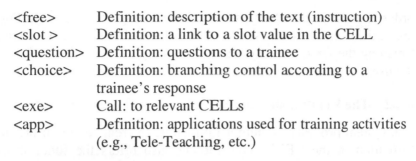
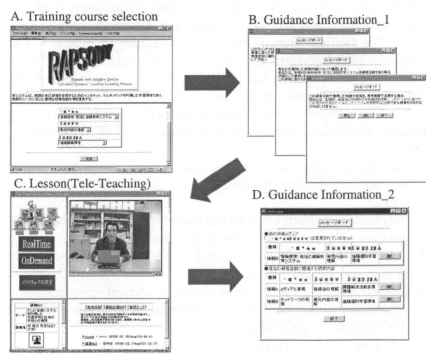

Figure 4. The screen shots of the Training System.

Figure 4 shows some screen shots of RAPSODY. Firstly, a user inputs his/her needs or requests for self-training (A). Then, RAPSODY computes the appropriate training course based on the user's request, and gives the user some consulting information in order to confirm the contents of his/her training course (B). In Figure 3, the user takes a lesson under a Tele-teaching mode (C). After finishing the lesson, the system shows the guidance information to the user for going on to the next step of his/her training (D).

4.2.2   The Relationship between CELL and Guide-Script

The system provides an authoring module to create and edit the information in the CELL. This module also offers the function of adding new CELLs, in order to allow a designer (supervisor/experienced teacher) to construct the learners' training program. The configuration of this system is shown in Figure 5. The tasks that can be performed by this system are: adding new CELLs, editing the existing CELLs, receiving calls for tele-teaching lectures and managing the lectures schedule. This system is composed of the CELL frame creating module, and the Guide-Script creating module. A CELL design can be performed as shown in the following:

1. Get the slot-values of "learning goals," "subject-contents/teaching ways/evaluating methods," and "useful tools" from the CELL.
2. Substitute the return value of the slot of the prepared media with the training-contents corresponding to the user's needs.
3. Substitute the slot-value in the CELL for the corresponding tag in the Guide-Script template.
4. If "Tele-teaching" as learning media is selected, then get some information about the lecture, by referring to the lecture-DB and the VOD short movie-DB.
5. Add new CELL to the Distance Ecological Model.

The lecture-database consists of "lesson managing files" containing user-profile data, lecture schedules, trainees learning records, lecture abstracts, and so on. The Guide-Script template file contains tag-information, written in the GSDL, for all subject-contents items in the Distance Ecological Model.

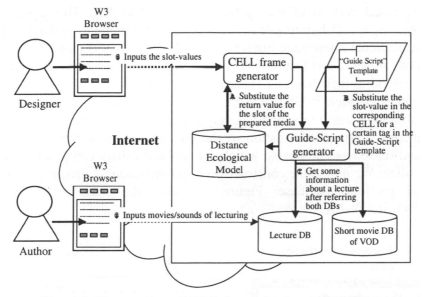

Figure 5. The procedure of CELL description for creating/editing.

Figure 6 shows the screen shots related to the authoring system. If a certain designer/author wants to register a new training course into RAPSODY, he/she has to describe the values of its course characteristics, which are: a learning objectives, an abstract of the course, a recommended learning environment (learning tool), Guide-Scripts of this course, and so on (A). This Guide-Script is a kind of short scenario about the lessons in the course (B). A designer/author inputs the subject-contents, its learning objective for a student and the learning media (form) as the attributes of related lessons (C).

4.3   Collaborative Learning Environment: RAPSODY-EX

Moreover, we can implement various kinds of learning forms and design interactive and collaborative activities among learners. The extended version of the system is RAPSODY-EX. This system handles a collaborative learning support environment, and has an educational knowledge management (Davenport 1997) function for both students and faculties. This function works for promoting and facilitating their learning tasks based on the collaborative learning process model. RAPSODY-EX can effectively carry out the collaborative learning support in asynchronous/synchronous learning modes. Various information in the educational context is referred and reused as knowledge which oneself and others can practically utilize. We aim at the construction of an increasingly growing digital portfolio database. Figure 7 shows the usage image of PARSODY-EX.

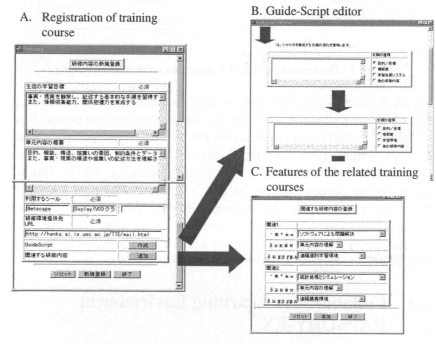

Figure 6. The screen shots of the authoring system.

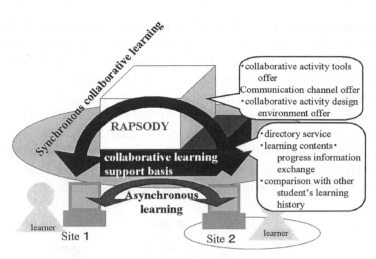

Figure 7. RAPSODY-EX usage image.

A learner group, which guarantees the smooth transmission of knowledge, can form a community (the knowledge community) by sharing and reusing common knowledge learning activities that occur within this group are as follows: the achievement of learning objectives as a group; the achievement of the learning objectives of each learner; the achievement of the learning objectives of the learner group that consists of multiple learners. RAPSODY-EX supports the transmission of knowledge in the learner group and the promotion of the learning activity. Figure 8 shows an example of the collaborative learning with RAPSODY-EX. It is indispensable that RAPSODY-EX has the following functions:

- the function which controls learning information for the individual learner and the group.
- the function which manages learning information of the learner for mediation.

RAPSODY-EX is a collaborative learning environment which extends the functions of RAPSODY, in consideration of the concept "Intelligent Media Oriented." RAPSODY selects assignment of the learning media to a student. The examples of the learning media are shown in Figure 9. One of the learning media for individual learning is the CBR system with short movies about classroom teaching process about "information." The learning medias for collaborative learning are an object_model editor, an action simulation tool and a communication tool. The student advances his/her study about "information," using these tools with RAPSODY and RAPSODY-EX. Based on the Guide-Script defined by the mentor, the learning media considered to be suitable for the learning state of a student are reasoned. At this time, RAPSODY use a student's needs, a learning history of a student, the mentor's expertise and so on.

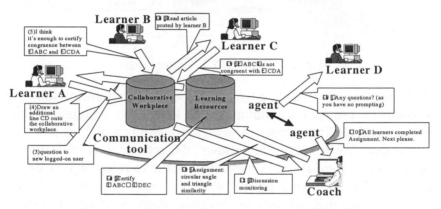

Figure 8. Collaborative Learning with RAPSODY-EX.

At first, the learning mode for a student is determined. RAPSODY has two learning mode, an individual learning mode and a collaborative learning mode.

In the individual learning mode, the learning process within the given learning media is not dependent on RAPSODY. Only the result of learning is recorded by RAPSODY, and serves as his/her learning history. The results of learning are the study media, the learning date, the learning time, the result of the pretest and/or posttest, degree of comprehension, and so on. They are depended on the learning media that registered with RAPSODY.

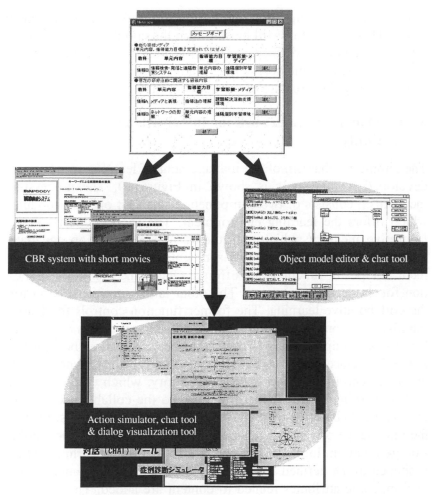

Figure 9. Examples of the learning media in RAPSODY.

In the collaborative learning mode, the learning process within the given learning media is preceded in RAPSODY-EX. RAPSODY-EX provides the communication tool between learners/mentors, and the tool/application for collaborative and/or cooperative work. A learning history while using these tools is stored and managed by RAPSODY-EX.

The learner and group information are produced from the learning space. This information will be stored in the collaborative memory. This information is defined as the information of learning entity. We also define the method of information management of such information and the structure of the collaborative memory.

4.3.1   Managing Framework for Information of Learning Entity

The simple mechanism of the management of learning information developed in this study is shown in Figure 10. The processing mechanism consists of two components. The first one is a module, which offers the learning environment. The second one is a collaborative memory, which controls various information and data produced from the learning environment. In the learning environment, 2 types of functions are offered. One is the monitoring function for the learning progress. The other is the tool/application for the collaborative learning. The former function controls the learning history/record of individual learners and the progress of the collaborative group learning. The latter tool/application becomes a space/workplace for collaborative synchronous/asynchronous learning. The information of learning entity, which emerged from such a learning environment, is handed to the collaborative memory. The collaborative memory offers 2 types of functions. One is the knowledge processing function, and the other is the knowledge storage function. In the former, input information of learning entity is shaped to the defined form. In the latter, for the formatted information, some attributes related to content are added. The complex information processing takes place in the collaborative memory.

4.3.2   The Collaborative Memory

In the collaborative memory, information generation / arrangement / housing / reference / visualization are the management processes of expressive knowledge in the learning space. RAPSODY-EX is a learning environment, which possesses a knowledge management mechanism. In this environment, following objects are realized during the learning by a group.

- the review of the learning process,
- the summarization of the problem solving process and
- the reference of other learners' problem solving method.

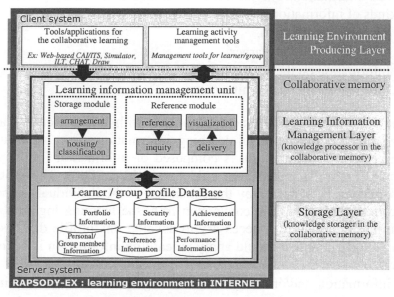

Figure 10. Management Framework of the RAPSODY-EX.

Learning information is expressed by an unified format. Then, that information is accumulated in the collaborative memory. This information becomes the reference object of the learner. The generation and the management of the information on the learning performance and the portfolio of the learner and group are main objects of the knowledge management. In this study, learning information is obtained from the application tools for the collaborative learning. It is necessary to control the learning record, the reference log of the others' learning information and the log of problem solving and learning progress. To realize this control not only techniques based on symbolic knowledge processing approach, but also techniques based on sub-symbolic knowledge processing approach are used.

The collaborative memory consists of two parts. One is the information storage unit. The other one is the management unit of the stored information. The information storage unit mainly processes 4 kinds of information.

- Learning information,
- Information on the learner,
- Information on the setting of the learning environment and
- Information on the learning result.

The information management unit deals with the reference / arrangement / integration of learning information. The Individual learner profile information is composed of information following the IEEE Profile information guidelines (IEEE 2000). The group information is expressed by the expansion of the individual learner profile information. The conversion from the learning log data to learning information is necessary to develop this profile database. The information that should apply in learning information is as follows:

- information and/or data on its learning context and/or learning situation
- information about the sender and the sendee of the information
- significance and/or outline in the educational context
- information on the relation structure of the information of learning entity
- the reference pointer to individual learner and group who proposed or produced the information
- the relation with other material

By adding these information, the information of learning entity is arranged into a unique form. If a learner requires some information related to his/her current learning, RAPSODY-EX shows the (estimated) desired information to the learner.

4.4   The Knowledge Management in RAPSODY-EX

In this study, the processing described in Section 4.3 is considered as a process of the knowledge management in the learning context. The concept of the Knowledge Management is defined by Davenport (1997). The knowledge management is "the systematic process of finding, selecting, organizing, distilling and presenting information in a way that improves an employee's comprehension in a specific area of interest."

Nonaka (1995) arranged the process of knowledge management as a SECI model. The SECI model is expressed as a conversion cycle between tacit knowledge and expressive knowledge. Tacit knowledge has a non-linguistic representation form. Expressive knowledge is a result of putting tacit knowledge into linguistic form. Tacit knowledge is shared with others by converting it into expressive knowledge. In the SECI model, socialization (S) / externalization (E) / combination (C) / internalization (I) of knowledge is expressed.

The knowledge management in educational context is defined as follows: "the systematic process of finding, selecting, organizing, distilling and presenting information in a way that improves a learner's comprehension and/or ability to fulfill his/her current learning objectives."

In RAPSODY-EX, the C (combination of knowledge) phase is supported. RAPSODY-EX also promotes the knowledge conversion to the I (internalization of knowledge) phase from the C phase and the knowledge conversion to the C phase from the E (externalization of knowledge) phase. The information of learning entity contains the expressive knowledge of the learner. This expressive knowledge is a result of expressing tacit knowledge of the learner using the language. This knowledge is converted from the learner's tacit knowledge.

In this situation, what we have to consider is as follows:
- Who are the subjects of our knowledge management work?
  Learners and the persons who support the learners are our subjects. Learners' task is to acquire the ability/skill for the problem solving. On the other hand, supporters' tasks are to support for acquisition of ability/skill of the learner, and to support of the problem solving by the learner. Supporter means a facilitator/tutor/coach/organizer, etc.
- What are the knowledge resources in the learning group?
  For learners, the knowledge for the effective and efficient problem solving is their knowledge resource. On the other hand, for the supporters, the knowledge on problem setting and activity assessment is their knowledge source.
- What is the gain for the learning group?
  The gains for learners are to acquire the ability in which to effectively and efficiently solve the problem, and to acquire the meta-cognition ability. For supporters, the acquisition of the ability of supporting the ability acquisition of the learner is their gain.
- How are the knowledge resources controlled to guarantee the maximum gain for the learning group?
  By the information processing to relate common knowledge of collaborative memory and learning context, we try to manage the knowledge in the collaborative learning. To create the collaborative portfolio between individual and group learning, extension of acquired knowledge of learners, knowledge extraction from learning history under the problem solving and making outline of problem solving process.

The examples of knowledge management in the RAPSODY-EX are shown in Figure 11. A log data of a dialog is visualized by three kinds of methods.

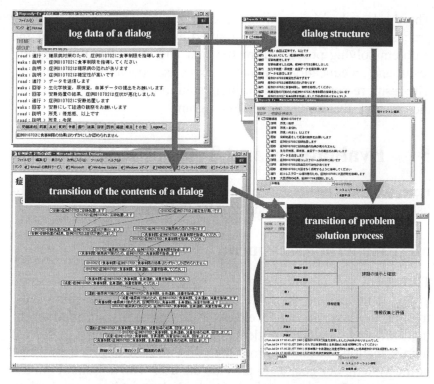

Figure 11. Examples of the Knowledge Management in RAPSODY-EX.

The first method is visualization of the dialog structure. The dialog layers are reasoned based on the dialog proceeding model (Inaba and Okamoto 1997) and the utterance intention information that were given to the dialog log. The result is shown as tree structure.

The second method is visualization of transition of the contents of a dialog. An appearance of the important term that is in a dialog is searched for using the term dictionary about the current discussion/learning domain (Chiku *et al.* 2001). This result and the timing connection of each utterance are considered to detect a transition of the contents of a dialog. The result is shown as graph structure.

The third method is visualization of transition of problem solution process. One utterance can be unified as meaningless unit for the problem solving process from the first and the second processing result and an educational mentor's expertise/educational intentions. The result re-constituted as problem solution process is shown with the structure that imitated the dendrogram.

5   Evaluations and Tests of RAPSODY

Here, we show two results of practical experiments done to establish the usefulness/effectiveness of RAPSODY.

5.1   General Assessment

To inspect the usefulness of our system, we carried out some evaluation experiments. Subjects/testees were future teaching staff, training in universities, as well as already presently enrolled teaching staff, undergraduate students, and finally, people just interested in information education. From the point of view of practical usage of the system, our goal as to provide the user with a "school" in the actual spot where the user is, be it workplace or home, and allow access via the various existing network environments. The system usage form can be classified therefore as:
- Computer connected via a relatively high-speed network, at a university or at a workplace institution,
- Computer connected via a low speed network, at the workplace or at home.

In the latter case, the system has to be proved enough practical use even for the low speed network. The evaluation of our system can be conducted from two points of view:
- Educational effect of the staff training,
- Operationality of the system and appropriateness of the functions.

We will report the evaluation experiments results concerning this point. We performed an experiment involving as testees 19 teaching staff members and 14 undergraduate students. We classified the testees according to the network speed of the used environment into as follows:

a. home (modem): 8 people,
b. home (ISDN): 5 people,
c. workplace (modem): 0 people,
d. workplace (ISDN): 4 people,
e. workplace/university (LAN): 16 people.

The testees had to use the system for a minimum of 2 hours to perform self-training. Moreover, we set up the following experimental conditions for the separate training and designing sessions.

1. The testees with specific interests about some information items could select the training program according to their interests and proceed to their training. The testees with no clear goal were assigned the "communication and networks" training program and then proceed with their training.
2. The testees had to implement also at least 3 training programs, by using the CELL construction & editing system.

Before enacting the experiment, the distance education modem database contained already 37 training programs; (information A: 8 programs; information B: 22 programs, information C: 7 programs). After more than 2 hours system usage, the testees were asked to fill in a questionnaire that contained 34 questions, organized according to points of view such as "easiness; convenience," "functions" and "computer environment." Except for questions related to the "computer environment," evaluation was performed on a linear scale of 0 to 5 points. In the following, the questionnaire result is presented and analyzed. We prepared 6 questions related to "easiness; convenience."

The global average value was high. However, the evaluation of the question "While using the system, did you loose your way?" was low (on average 2.9). When analyzing separately the self-training system and the CELL construction/editing system, we understood that the evaluation of the latter had influence on the global evaluation. As shown in Figure 12, the CELL construction/editing system allows many input items and free descriptions. It seems that it was difficult for the testees to understand the meaning of each item, and then to input the text that conformed to the respective item. Therefore, together with re-analyzing the item names (labels), it is necessary to adopt a design, where it is possible to reference both each item's description and some usage example(s). We have also prepared 12 questions about the "functions" of the self-training system, as well as 12 questions about the "functions" of the CELL construction/editing system.

Firstly, we will present the results regarding the self-training system. The average evaluation results for the questions "Did you manage to select a training program that contained novelties for yourself?," "Were the message number and contents displayed in the message window and the indication methods appropriate?" was 3.7 (so high). However, the evaluation results of the questions "Was the number of training programs (candidates) for the next step training activity in the training program list sufficient?" were 3.2 (so relatively low). Moreover, the response variance of 0.17 was, compared to the variance of other questions, 0.006 - 0.1, high. It is possible to improve this by having more candidate inputs for each training program, and implementing improved training program lists.

Next, we will present the results according to the CELL construction/editing system. The evaluation regarding the question "By using the connection/ relation editor, did you manage to design links well?" had an average of 3.5, so was highly evaluated. However, the question "Did you manage to build scenarios well by using the Guide-Script Editor?" was evaluated with a low average of 2.9. This is due to the fact that the text types defined in the Guide-Script editor were not enough.

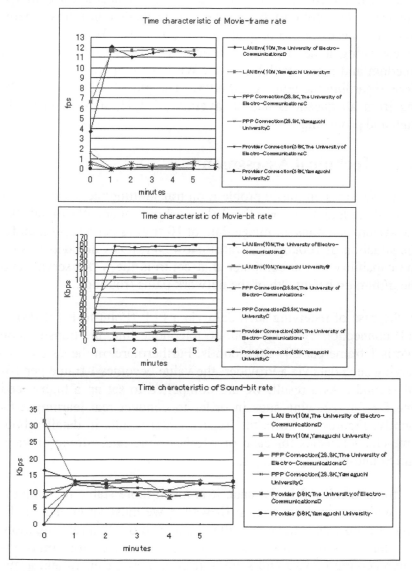

Figure 12. The time-characteristics for each of Movie-frame rate, Movie-bit rate, and Sound-bit rate.

Moreover, many testees have answered that it was difficult to construct with the editor, as the number of texts available for composing scenarios were only 6, and there were many constrains. Therefore, it is necessary to re-analyze the text types. We are currently investigating a description method that allows more degrees of freedom and more available texts. We have prepared also 4 questions regarding the item "Computer." The global evaluation resulting from all questions had an average of 3.53, so was relatively high and promising.

5.2   Technical Assessment

Here, we focus on traffic problem on transmitting/receiving data of real movie and sound via the Tele-teaching mode. We found that the system can transmit image data of 10 frames per a second under the situation of 100kbps (bit rate). However, this value depends on the capability of the computer that controls the VOD server, and the minimum bandwidth of the network paths (routing).

In the case of receiving such data via a PPP (Point-to-Point Protocol) connection by using a public telephone line, the transmission rate is 1 frame per 20 - 30 seconds. Furthermore, in the case of receiving such data via a Provider, the value becomes 1 frame per 10-20 seconds. As a result, we are compelled to set up a high-speed line for far receiving sites in order to conduct real learning efficiently. Figure 12 shows the experimental results in details about time-characteristics for each of Movie-frame rate, Movie-bit rate, and Sound-bit rate.

As for transmitting sound data, it is much more stable in comparison with transmitting movies. However, we must set up the condition of echo canceling, noise filtering and so on. In a real situation, we have used two personal computers, one for transmitting/receiving movies and sounds from a digital camera and a microphone, and another for looking at Web-materials such as Power-

Point manuscripts. From far sites, users can ask the lecturer some questions via a convenient dialogue window developed by us. In this environment, a lecturer can give collaborative calls to each of the participants and adjust/facilitate the teaching/learning process interactively.

6   Conclusions

The interactive learning environment, RAPSODY with RAPSODY-EX, can provide a modality of externalized knowledge-acquisition and knowledge-sharing via communication processes, and support learning methods such as "Learning by asking," "Learning by showing," "Learning by Observing," "Learning by Exploring" and "Learning by Teaching/Explaining." Expected learning effects are meta-cognition, distributed cognition, reflective thinking, self-monitoring and so on. Consequently, a new learning ecology scheme will emerge from our learning environment.

This paper proposed the Distance Ecological Model for building the integrated distance learning environment. This model stands for the networked virtual leaning environment based on a 3 aspects-representation, which has on the axes: (1) learning goals (on the study of the subject–matter, teaching knowledge/skills, and evaluation methods), (2) subject-contents in the designated subject-matter, and (3) learning media (forms). This represents a new framework for e-Learning environments in the coming networked age. We have mentioned the rationale of our system and explained the architecture of the training system via the Distance Ecological Model. Furthermore, we have described a Guide-Script language. The aim of our system is to support learners' self-learning, provided as in-service training. At the same time, we need to build rich databases by accumulating various kinds of teaching expertise. In such a way, the concept of " knowledge-sharing" and "knowledge-reusing" will be implemented. As a result, we believe that a new learning ecology scheme will emerge from our environment.

RAPSODY is a platform that provides various kind of learning places based on the Distance Ecological Model according to the learner's need in consideration of the relationship among Learning Objects. In this system, the function of a Tele-conference with real video/sound and the shared window of chatting/application software are provided. So, if a learner wants to change the mode of the learning media from the individual (self) one to the collaborative (group) for some reason after he/she has finished with a certain Learning Object, then the system asks a group manager for permission to attend this discussion group to satisfy lecturer's request according to the Distance Ecological Model. As another example, the system may recommend a selection of the collaborative mode for encouraging deeper recognition/understanding for that learner, if such a navigation message is described in the Guide-Script. In this way, RAPSODY provides the integrated/free environment for distance learning that can adaptively change between self/collaborative mode according to a user's needs based on the Guide-Script in the Distance Ecological Model. In this sense, the Guide-Script contains the core information about the stream developed between Learning Objects by reflecting both the learner's needs and curriculum relationships.

RAPSODY-EX is a general-purpose collaborative learning environment, which extends the functions of RAPSODY. This system aims at implementing four important features which are: (1) shared workplace (collaborative workplace), (2) API with the function of "plug in," (3) common log-collection method of learning activities and (4) knowledge managing function such as a text mining. We have already examined reliability/validity of those functions under some trials. At present, the architecture of this system is not enough to satisfy the conditions of general purpose. Hereafter, we need to reconstruct/standardize this architecture as the common platform by distinguish the domain independent parts from the domain dependent parts.

With these systems, we can construct various kinds of learning forms and design interactive and collaborative activities among learners. Such an interactive learning environment can provide a modality of externalized knowledge-acquisition and knowledge-sharing, via the communication process, and support learning methods such as "Learning by asking," "Learning by showing," "Learning by Observing, "Learning by Exploring" and "Learning by Teaching/Explaining." Among the learning effects expected from this system, we also aim at meta-cognition and distributed cognition, such as reflective thinking, self-monitoring, and so on. Therefore, we expect to build a new learning ecology, as mentioned above, through this system. Finally, we will apply this system to the real world and try to evaluate its effectiveness and usability from experimental and practical point of view.

References

Abou-Jaoude, S. and Frasson, C. (1998), "An agent for selecting a learning strategy," *Proceedings of the Conference Internationale sur les Nouvelles Technologies de la Communication et de la Formation (NTICF'98)*, pp. 353-358.

Acharya, S., Smith, B., and Parnes, P. (2000), "Characterizing user access to videos on the World Wide Web," *Multimedia Computing and Networking (MMCN)*, 3969-11.

Aoki, Y. and Nakajima, A. (1999), "User-side Web page customization," *Proceedings of 8th International Conference on Human and Computer Interaction (HCI99)*, vol. 1, pp. 580-584.

Brna, P. (1997), "Collaboration in a virtual world: support for conceptual learning?" *Proceedings of IFIP WG 3.3 Working Conference "Human Computer Interaction and Educational Tools" (HCI-ET97)*, http://www.cbl.leeds.ac.uk/~paul/papers/hci-et97paper /hci-et.html .

Chan, T., Collins, A., and Lin, J. (1997), *Global Education ON the Net*, Springer-Verlag.

Chiku, M., Yu, S., Kobayashi, Y., Inoue, H., and Okamoto, T. (2001), "A dialog visualization tool: Gijiroku," *Proceedings of the 62th Annual Conference of the Information Processing Sciety of Japan*, pp. 241-244.

Colazzo, L. and Molinari, A. (1996), "Using Hypertext projection to increase teaching effectiveness," *International Journal of Educational Multimedia and Hypermedia*, vol. 5, no. 1, pp. 23-48, AACE.

Collis, B. (1999), "Design, development and implementation of a WWW-based course-support system," *Proceedings of the 7th International Conference on Computer in Education (ICCE99)*, pp. 11-18.

Cumming, G., Okamoto, T., and Gomes, L. (1998), *Advanced Research in Computers in Education*, IOS press.

Davenport, T. (1997), *Working Knowledge*, Harvard Business School Press.

Dillenbourg, P. (1999), *Collaborative Learning, Cognitive and Computational Approaches*, Pergamon Press.

Elisabeth, A., Thomas, R., and Jochen, M. (1997), "WebPersona: a life-like presentation agent for educational applications on the World-Wide Web," *Proceedings of the workshop "Intelligent Educational Systems on the World Wide Web" at the 8th World Conference of the AIED Society*, IV-3.

Elliott, J. (1993), "What have we learned from action research in school-based evaluation," *Educational Action Research*, vol. 1, no. 1, pp. 175-186.

Fischer, G. (1999), "Lifelong learning: changing mindsets," *Proceedings of the 7th International Conference on Computer in Education (ICCE 99)*, pp. 21-30.

Frasson, C. and Aimeur, E. (1996), "A comparison of three learning strategies in intelligent tutoring systems," *Journal of Educational Computing Research*, vol.14, no 4, pp.371-383.

Hara, N. and Kling, R. (2001), "Students' distress with a Web-based distance education course, information, communication & society," http://www.slis.indiana.edu/CSI/wp00-01.html .

Hui, S. (2001), "Video-On-Demand in Education," http://www .cityu.edu.hk/~ccncom/net14/ vod2.htm .

IEEE (2000), "Draft Standard for Learning Technology -Public and Private Information (PAPI) for Learner," IEEE P1484.2/D6, http://ltsc.ieee.org/ .

IEEE-LTSC (2000), "Draft Standard for Learning Object Metadata," IEEE P1484.12/D4.0.

IMS (1998), "Learning Resourcde Metadata: Information Model, Best Practice and Implementation Guide," IMS Ver1.0, http://www.imsproject.org/ .

Inaba, A. and Okamoto, T. (1997), "Negotiation process model for intelligent discussion coordinating system on CSCL environment," *Proceedings of the AIED 97*, pp. 175-182.

Inoue, H. and Okamoto, T. (1999), "Case base reasoning system for information technology education," *Proceedings of the 7th International Conference on Computer in Education (ICCE 99)*, pp. 1083-1086.

Johnson, W.L. and Shaw, E. (1997), "Using agents to overcome deficiencies in Web-based courseware," *Proceedings of the Workshop "Intelligent Educational Systems on the World Wide Web" at the 8th World Conference of the AIED Society*, IV-2.

Kaplan, H. (1998), "Building your own Web course: the case for off-the-shelf component software," *CAUSE/EFFECT Journal*, vol. 21, no. 4, http://www.educause.edu/ir/library/html/cem9849 .html .

Kayama, K., Okamoto, T., and Cristea, A. (2000), "Exploratory activity support based on a semantic feature map," *Proceedings of the Adaptive Hypermedia Conference (AH 2000)*, pp. 347-350.

Kaye, A.R. (1994), "Computer supported collaborative learning in a multi-media distance education environment," in O'Malley, C. (ed.), *Computer Supported Collaborative Learning*, Springer-Verlag, pp. 125-143.

Kobayashi, M., Shinozaki, M., Sakairi, T., Touma, M., Daijavad, S., and Wolf, C. (1998), "Collaborative customer services using synchronous Web browser sharing," *Proceedings of the ACM Conference on Computer Supported Cooperative Work (CSCW 98)*, pp. 99-108.

Kolodner, J. and Riesbeck, C. (1993), *Case-Based Reasoning*, Morgan Kaufman Publisher.

Kuhn, T. (1962), *The Structure of Scientific Revolutions*," University of Chicago Press.

Meissner, G. (1999), "Closing in on distance learning, German institutions start to embrace wired teaching," *Educom Review*, Jan./Feb., http//www.educause.edu/ir/library/html/erm9914.html

Nishinosono, H. (1998), "A teacher education system for information education teachers at high school level in the information society," *Proceedings of the 14th National Conference of the Japanese Society of Educational Technology*, pp. 523-524.

Nkambou, R., IsaBelle, C., and Frasson, C. (1998), "Supporting some pedagogical issues in a Web-based distance learning environment," *Proceedings of the Conference Internationale sur les Nouvelles Technologies de la Communication et de la Formation (NTICF'98)*, pp. 107-116.

Nonoka, I. (1995), *The Knowledge-Creating Company*, Oxford University Press.

Okamoto, T. and Cristea, A.I. (2001), "A distance ecological model for individual and collaborative-learning support," *Journal of Educational Technology and Society*, vol. 4, no. 2, pp. 80-87.

Okamoto, T., Cristea, A.I., and Kayama, M. (2000a), "Towards intelligent media-oriented distance learning and education environments," *Proceedings of the 8th International Conference on Computer in Education (ICCE2000)*, pp.61-72.

Okamoto, T., Matsui, T., Inoue, H., and Cristea, A. (2000b), "A distance-education self-learning support system based on a VOD server," *Proceedings of the International Workshop on Advanced Learning Technologies (IWALT2000)*, pp. 71-78.

Paiva, A. (1996), "Communicating with learner modelling agents," *Workshop Proceedings of Architectures and Methods for Designing Cost-Effective and Reusable ITSs at the ITS96*, http://cbl.leeds.ac.uk/~amp/MyPapers/its96/its96-ws.html.

Peltoniemi, J. (1995), "Video-on-Demand Overview," http://www.cs.tut.fi/tlt/stuff/vod/VoDOverview/vod1.html .

Schneider, D. and Godard, R. (1996), "Virtual environments for education, research and life," *Workshop Proceedings of Virtual Environments and the WWW at the WWW5*, http://tecfa.unige.ch/moo/paris96/papers/daniel.html .

Shimizu, Y. (1999), "Toward a new distance education system," *Proceedings of the 7th International Conference on Computer in Education (ICCE99)*, pp. 69-75.

Synnes, K., Parnes, P., Widen, J., and Schefstrom, D. (1999), "Student 2000: Net-based learning for the next millenium." *Proceedings of the World Conference on the WWW and Internet (WebNet99)*, vol. 2, pp. 1031-1036.

UNESCO (1998), "World Declaration on Higher Education for the Twenty-first Century Vision and Action," report, UNESCO Paris.

The United Kingdom Government (1997), "Connecting the Learning Society," The United Kingdom Government's Consultation paper.

Woods, P.J. and Warren, J. (1996), "Adapting teaching strategies in intelligent tutoring systems," *Workshop Proceedings of Architectures and Methods for Designing Cost-Effective and Re-Useable ITS's at the ITS96*, http://advlearn.lrdc.pitt.edu/its-arch/papers/index.html .

Chapter 6

An Intelligent Tutoring System for Student Guidance in Web-Based Courses

B. Özdemir and F.N. Alpaslan

In this chapter, an intelligent agent to guide students throughout the course material in the Internet is presented. The agent will help students to study and learn the concepts in the course by giving navigational support according to their knowledge level. It uses simplified prerequisite graph model as domain model and simplified overlay model for modeling student. The system adapts the links in the contents page to help students for easy navigation in the course content. In link-level adaptation hiding and annotation technologies, which effectively support gradual learning of the learning space, are used.

1   Introduction

Internet power continues to grow rapidly. This progress has made new teaching architectures applicable on the Internet. Among these new teaching architectures, simulation-based learning, learning by doing, incidental learning, learning by reflection, case-based teaching, learning by exploring, and goal-directed learning are the most attractive ones (Schank 1994). It is a fact that almost all of these teaching architectures need computer software. The obvious advantage of the Internet is that it is time and location independent. These aspects have made the Internet the most appealing media for education for the last few years. At the beginning, the courses on the Internet were not much different than an electronic multimedia textbook. Internet has a disadvantage that it looks as a mess of links where you can rapidly confused in a minute if you are not guided well. From this view, a paper or book is better than a web-based course. There is a need for more effective learning than traditional hypertext and to encourage students to understand the concepts presented (Hammond *et al.* 1995).

Several different projects with different features have been implemented at different universities. Some of these are: University of Illinois at Urbana-Champaign's SCALE, Plattsburgh's Top Classes System, SUNY, Washington State University's Virtual Campus, University of Illinois' The Mallard Learning Environment, and Heron Laboratories' SAFARI.

Most of these systems are not intelligent tutoring systems. They are actually composed of group of programs that make preparation of course material for the Internet easy. They also have facilities such as automatic grading, conferencing with students, and making announcements on bulletin board system. Although these facilities are all necessary and form the skeleton of an Internet tutoring system, they alone are not enough to achieve the goal.

In a real intelligent tutoring system reasoning about the user actions on the domain of the course and responding immediately are essential. To achieve this, a user model should be generated for each user to make assumptions about the user's state of knowledge and learning needs.

Among these systems SAFARI developed at Heron Laboratories is a real intelligent tutoring system. It has a multi-agent architecture, defined for the pedagogical component, that uses multiple learning strategies. The system has cognitive agents that can model the human behavior in learning situations (Frasson *et al.* 1996). The system is capable of:

- Tutoring workers in an enterprise (factory, hospital) through real tasks recreated on device models using the VAPS (Virtual Applications Prototyping System) software,
- Constructing models of individual users, reflecting the user's reasoning style and state of knowledge,
- Dispensing individualize tutoring based on the user model,
- Diagnosing the actions of a student when asked to perform a task on the visual model, and
- Composing an entire curriculum for teaching, taking into account the learner's expertise and style of learning.

SAFARI thus satisfies the crucial needs of an intelligent tutoring system (Gecsei and Frasson 1994).

Experiences show that creating an intelligent tutoring system still remains difficult for various reasons. There are many different components in such a system and stabilization of these components is not easy. The structure and type of knowledge to be used are of different granularity and complexity. Another problem is that the components' design and implementation require multiple expertise in different fields such as computer and cognitive science. Integration of this expertise is a challenging task (Gecsei and Frasson 1994).

Although difficulties are many, the advantages of an intelligent tutoring system having more or less intelligent features are undeniable. In this study, we attempted to construct a base for an intelligent tutoring system. The aim was to create an intelligent agent that would present concepts in a course in a coherent way such that the learner feels that the information in the domain fits together well. While doing so, the student's knowledge level of the subject being taught is monitored. Mainly, individualized tutoring is the aim.

The system in this study is based on the creation of a course curriculum by the teacher. The curriculum is composed of concepts.

Each concept is a task to be completed by the student and connected to other concepts with prerequisite relationships. The resulting form is a conceptual network. The student is presented with a
new concept if s/he completes the concepts that are the prerequisites. This is the first point where the system reasons about the user
actions.

In a web-based course, students' learning skills are usually tested
with exams, tests and case studies. In the system proposed, the students are given a "pretest" which tests the concepts s/he must know
well before taking a real test. If there are incorrect answers, the student is advised to navigate backwards and complete the tasks related to the pretest. This is the second point where the system reasons about the user actions.

In summary, each student is modeled according to the answers s/he
gives to these tests, and the tasks s/he completes. An inference
mechanism runs in order to give student the next thing he should
learn in order to advance in the course content.

This research was supported by the national research projects "Development of Web-Based Courses at METU" (AFP-97-07-04-02),
"Development of an Intelligent Authoring Tool for Web-Based
Course Preparation As a Part of BADE Project" (AFP-06-
04DPT.98K1225) and "Development of an Intelligent Agent for
Distance Learning" (AFP-99-06-04-01). The objective of BADE
project is to develop an authoring tool for web-based course generation and administration, and to offer on/of campus web-based
courses. The intelligent agent designed and implemented in this
thesis has been integrated with the BADE Project authoring tool
developed at METU Informatics Institute.

The organization of the chapter is as follows: The underlining theories of the intelligent agent designed and implemented are explained in Section 2. In this section the theories or ideas inspired by

to construct the main components, which are curriculum and pre-test, as well as the idea of user modeling and adaptive hypermedia systems will be introduced. In Section 3, design and implementation details of the overall system will be discussed in detail. Additional features that can be added to the system are listed in the conclusion section where a summary of the study and system drawbacks can be found.

2 Theoretical Background

2.1 Intelligent Agents

An overview of intelligent agents is a good point to start to examine the functionality and the identity of the agent. Answering the following questions is a structured way to satisfy the objective:

Why do we need an agent? What is an agent? What are the key characteristics of an agent? How do we define intelligence and rationality? What types of agents are present?

2.1.1 Why Do We Need an Agent?

Due to the proliferation of computing and networking, the most people wish to be interconnected, and the need to make the data accessible at any time and any place, modern information environments have become large, open and heterogeneous. They are usually composed of both distributed and autonomous components. Recent approaches introduce software agents into such environments to deal with these characteristics. These agents represent the components in interactions, where they mediate differences and provide a syntactically uniform and semantically consistent middleware. Their greatest difficulty in achieving uniformity and consistency is the dynamism that open environment introduce. At the same time, the complexity and dynamism of the information environments has led to a pressing need for user interfaces that are active and adaptive personal assistants – in other words, agents (Huhns and Singh 1998).

The "information highway" will present us with new computer-based tasks and services. The complexity of this environment will demand a new style of human-computer interaction, where the computer becomes an intelligent, active and personalized collaborator (Maes 1994). Information filtering, information retrieval, mail management, electronic commerce, meeting scheduling, workflow management, intelligent manufacturing, education and entertainment are some of the applications or computer-based tasks that an agent can assist the user. The information has to be found, filtered, processed and presented where the agents are the integral parts.

2.1.2   What Is an Agent?

Unfortunately, there is no unique definition of an agent on which the agent researchers agree. It is possible to extract the common core concepts from these definitions. Some of these definitions that are listed by Franklin and Graesser (1997) are given:

- The MuBot Agent: "The term agent is used to represent two orthogonal concepts. The first is the agent's ability for autonomous execution. The second is the agent's ability to perform domain oriented reasoning." This pointer at definitions comes from an online white paper by Sankar Virdhagriswaran of Crystaliz, Inc., defining mobile agent technology. Autonomous execution is clearly central to agency.
- The AIMA Agent: "An agent is anything that can be viewed as perceiving its environment through sensors and acting upon that environment through effectors." AIMA is an acronym for Artificial Intelligence: a Modern Approach. This is a successful AI text that was used in 200 colleges and universities in 1995. The authors were interested in software agents embodying AI techniques. Clearly, the AIMA definition depends heavily on what we take as the environment, and on what sensing and acting

mean. If we define the environment as whatever provides input and receives output, and take receiving input to be sensing and producing output to be acting, every program is an agent. Thus, if we want to arrive at a useful contrast between agent and program, we must restrict at least some of the notions of environment, sensing and acting.

- The Maes Agent: "Autonomous agents are computational systems that inhabit some complex dynamic environment, sense and act autonomously in this environment, and by doing so realize a set of goals or tasks for which they are designed." Pattie Maes, of MIT's Media Lab, is one of the pioneers of agent research. She adds a crucial element to her definition of an agent: agents must act autonomously so as to "realize a set of goals." Also environments are restricted to being complex and dynamic. It's not clear whether this rules out a payroll program without further restrictions.

- The KidSim Agent: "Let us define an agent as a persistent software entity dedicated to a specific purpose. 'Persistent' distinguishes agents from subroutines; agents have their own ideas about how to accomplish tasks, their own agendas. 'Special purpose' distinguishes them from entire multifunction applications; agents are typically much smaller." The authors are with Apple. The explicit requirement of persistence is a new and important addition here. Though many agents are special purpose we suspect this is not an essential feature of agency.

- The Hayes-Roth Agent: "Intelligent agents continuously perform three functions: perception of dynamic conditions in the environment; action to affect conditions in the environment; and reasoning to interpret perceptions, solve problems, draw inferences, and determine actions." Barbara Hayes-Roth of Stanford's Knowledge Systems Laboratory insists that agents reason during the process of action selection. If reasoning is interpreted broadly, her agent architecture does allow for reflex actions as well as planned actions.

- The IBM Agent: "Intelligent agents are software entities that carry out some set of operations on behalf of a user or another program with some degree of independence or autonomy, and in so doing, employ some knowledge or representation of the user's goals or desires." This definition, from IBM's Intelligent Agent Strategy white paper, views an intelligent agent as acting for another, with authority granted by the other. A typical example might be an information-gathering agent, though the white paper talks of eight possible applications. Would you stretch "some degree of independence" to include a payroll program? What if it called itself on a certain day of the month?
- The Wooldridge-Jennings Agent: "... a hardware or (more usually) software-based computer system that enjoys the following properties:
  - Autonomy: agents operate without direct intervention of humans or others, and have some kind of control over their actions and internal state;
  - Social ability: agents interact with other agents (and possibly humans) via some kind of agent-communication language;
  - Reactivity: agents perceive their environment, (which may be the physical world, a user via a graphical user interface, a collection of other agents, the INTERNET, or perhaps all of these combined), and respond in a timely fashion to changes that occur in it;
  - Pro-activeness: agents do not simply act in response to their environment; they are able to exhibit goal-directed behavior by taking the initiative."

The Wooldridge and Jennings definition, in addition to spelling out autonomy, sensing and acting, allows for a broad, but finite, range of environments. They further add a communications requirement. What would be the status of a payroll program with a graphical interface and a decidedly primitive communication language?

- The SodaBot Agent: "Software agents are programs that engage in dialogs and negotiate and coordinate transfer of information." SodaBot is a development environment for a software agent being constructed at the MIT AI Lab by Michael Coen. Note the apparently almost empty intersection between this definition and the preceding seven. We say "apparently" since negotiating, for example, requires both sensing and acting. And dialoging requires communication. Still the feeling of this definition is vastly different from the first few, and would seem to rule out almost all standard programs.
- The Foner Agent: Foner requires much more of an agent. His agents collaborate with their users to improve the accomplishment of the users' tasks. This requires, in addition to autonomy, that the agent dialog with the user, be trustworthy, and degrade gracefully in the face of a "communications mismatch." However, this quick paraphrase doesn't do justice to Foner's analysis.
- The Brustoloni Agent: "Autonomous agents are systems capable of autonomous, purposeful action in the real world." The Brustoloni agent, unlike the prior agents, must live and act in a real world. This definition excludes software agents and programs in general. Brustoloni also insists that his agents be "reactive that is, be able to respond to external, asynchronous stimuli in a timely fashion."

As these definitions make clear, there is no general agreement as to what constitutes an agent, or as to how agents differ from programs. The Software Agents Mailing List on the Internet provides a FAQ (frequently asked questions) that says: The FAQ Agent: "This FAQ will not attempt to provide an authoritative definition ...". It does provide a list of attributes often found in agents: Autonomous, goal-oriented, collaborative, flexible, self-starting, temporal continuity, character, communicative, adaptive, mobile.

Although, giving a simple, precise definition may not be easy, the definition of Huhns and Singh (1998) can be said to be a synthesis of the above definitions: "Agents are active, persistent (software) components that perceive, reason, act, and communicate."

There are two extreme views of agents. One long-standing tradition takes agents, as essentially conscious, cognitive entities that have feelings, perceptions, and emotions just like humans. Under this view, all of the computational work on agents is inherently inadequate. An alternative view is that agents are merely automata and behave exactly as they are designed or programmed. This view admits a large variety of computations, including computational agents. A concern is that it might be too permissive. Which one of these views is correct? The truth lies somewhere inbetween (Huhns and Singh 1998).

2.1.3 What Are the Key Characteristics of an Agent?

The various definitions discussed above involve a host of properties of an agent. Having settled on a much less restrictive definition of an autonomous agent, these properties help us further classify agents in a comprehensive way. Table 1 lists several properties of the agents (Franklin and Graesser 1997).

Table 1. Properties of agents.

Property	Meaning
Reactive	Responds in a timely fashion to changes in the environment
Autonomous	Exercises control over its own actions
Goal-oriented	Does not simply act in response to the environment
Temporally continuous	Temporally continuous
Communicative	Communicates with other agents including people
Learning	Adaptively changes its behavior based on previous experience
Mobile	Able to transport itself from one machine to another
Flexible	Actions are not scripted
Character	Believable "personality" and emotional state

Autonomy is an important property of an agent. An agent's behavior can be based on both its own experience and the built-in knowledge. A system is autonomous to the extent that its behavior is determined by its own experience. A truly autonomous intelligent agent should be able to operate successfully in a wide variety of environments, given sufficient time to adopt (Russell and Norvig 1995).

2.1.4   Intelligence and Rationality

Intelligence is notoriously difficult to define precisely. However, we know intuitively when a system is behaving intelligently. One simplistic, but sometimes useful, definition of an intelligent system is one that performs a task that, if performed by a human, would earn the human the attribute "intelligent." However, many tasks that are performed routinely by humans are difficult to realize in a computational system. By contrast, some tasks that are difficult for a human, such as various forms of arithmetic, are easy for a machine (Huhns and Singh 1998).

The concept of rationality is intimately related to intelligence but can be formalized more easily. Most formalization requires that the agent has preferences about states of the world and chooses actions that maximize the preferences. Thus, rationality depends on the following attributes (Russell and Norvig 1995):
- The performance measure for success
- What the agent has perceived so far
- What the agent knows about the environment
- The actions the agent can perform

An ideal rational agent is defined as follows: For each possible percept sequence, it acts to maximize its expected utility on the basis of its knowledge and the evidence from the percept sequence (Russell and Norvig 1995).

Logical rationality considers qualitative notions such as the consistency of beliefs or, intentions and desires with chosen actions. Economic rationality assumes that the agent has utility functions to guide its choice of actions (Huhns and Singh 1998). Although rationality is a compelling notion for several purposes, it imposes certain artificial constraints on how we understand the world and the agents that inhabit it. Agents – artificial and human – are limited in their computational powers and in their knowledge of their environment and may not be quite as rational as they might seem (Huhns and Singh 1998).

2.1.5 Types of Agents

Agent types can be characterized by the applications for agents. There are numerous applications for agents. Many involve varieties of personal assistants, and others are specialized for information-rich environments. Still others involve topics such as art, drama, and design-well beyond the traditional applications of computing, but increasingly important (Huhns and Singh 1998).

The main interest in this study is personal assistants, a kind of software agent (FIPA 1997), and will be explained in detail in the following section.

Taxonomy of autonomous agents is depicted as in Figure 1 (Franklin and Graesser 1997).

2.1.6 Personal Assistants

One central class of intelligent agents is that of a personal assistant (PA). A personal assistant is a software agent that acts semi autonomously for and on behalf of a user, modeling the interest of the user and providing services to the user or other people/PAs as and when required (FIPA 1997).

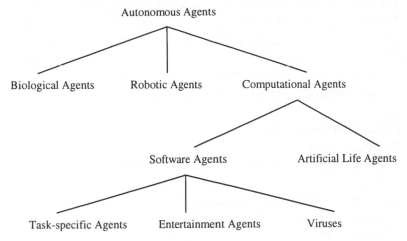

Figure 1. Taxonomy of autonomous agents.

User interfaces are now widely recognized as one of the booming areas of computing. Whereas traditional user interfaces were rigid and not helpful, the decreasing cost of computers and physical interface devices, coupled with the spread of computing to the lay population, has supported an increasing trend toward intelligent, cooperative interfaces. Also whereas traditional user interfaces were for applications such as database access, modern applications involve the control of software and hardware tools in general (Huhns and Singh 1998).

The notion of a personal assistant is very open-ended. There are many internal and external functions and services that can and will be used to provide and extend a Personal Assistant's basic functionalities. In fact, such openness to new services is a critical requirement where interoperability of PA's functions/services is desirable. The use of agent technology to support the Personal Assistant helps in achieving this requirement.

Examples of such functions/services include (Huhns and Singh 1998, FIPA 1997):

- Managing a user's diaries (e.g., meeting scheduling)
- Filtering and sorting mails (e.g., electronic mails)
- Managing a user's desktop environment (e.g., file system)
- Managing a user's activities, plans and tasks (e.g., workflow)
- Locating and delivering (multimedia) information
- Recommending entertainment (e.g., movies, restaurants, theatres)
- Purchasing desired items
- Planning travel
- Finding people with similar interests carrying out statistical reasoning
- Designing artificial environments
- Animating entities in virtual worlds
- Educating, etc.

Traditional Artificial Intelligent (AI) tries to develop automated tools that automate the reasoning process fully for solving problems. The current trend is to develop tools that assist humans in carrying out the reasoning. There are a number of good motivations for this trend (Huhns and Singh 1998):

- Many interesting problems are too complex to have tractable solutions that are fully automated.
- In many settings, for issues of ethics and responsibility, computers cannot be trusted to perform critical actions unilaterally. In such settings, it 's crucial to keep a human in the decision loop.
- Some applications inherently require the active participation of a human because the problem cannot be specified in a form that will admit to automatic solution. An important case is information retrieval, where users typically do not have a precise query that can be processed automatically. Instead, users need to ask some leading queries to understand the information space they are searching and to formulate a precise query only gradually. Another example is education: it would be inappropriate with

current technology to eliminate the human user from an educational system!

As a consequence of the above trend, modern user interfaces are playing an increasing role in complex systems. The trend has shifted from passive interfaces to active interfaces, those that have a life of their own – that is agents! Such interfaces are dialogue based, to some extent – not because they must carry out spoken or textual dialogues, but because they are aware of users and interact with them dynamically (Huhns and Singh 1998).

Personal assistants can be characterized as follows (Huhns and Singh 1998):
- Multimode: support interactions in different input and output modalities, such as voice or typing
- Dialogue based; carry out a conversation, not necessarily spoken, with the user
- Mixed-initiative: if dialogue based, let the user control the dialogue dynamically or make unexpected requests
- Anthropoid; endowed with a personality; typically emotional
- Cooperative: assist the user in defining the user's real needs – this typically requires some ability to model the user and the task the user is engaged in
- Adaptive: learn from past interactions with the user

The environment of a personal assistant has two main components: the human user and the back-end information system. These have different properties, which place interesting requirements on the designs of the assistants. Table 2 lists the key properties of users and back-end systems. It is assumed that an assistant can find all that is relevant about the user and system. It can partially predict the user's behavior, which motivates having adaptive user modeling. Because the user is historical and teleological, a dialogue functionally is required along with some task modeling. Since the assistant cannot control the user and user can change his/her mind in real time, it must allow interrupts, that is, be mixed-initiative (Huhns and Singh 1998).

Table 2. A personal assistant's environment.

Property	User	Backend System
Knowable	Yes	Yes
Predictable	Partially	No
Controllable	No	Partially
Partially	Yes	No
Teleological	Yes	Maybe
Real Time	Yes	Possibly

2.2   Conceptual Network and Curriculum

The model that will be explained in this section uses the idea similar to the components of "prerequisite graph model" explained by Nykänen (1997). The prerequisite graph model is composed of four components:

- conveniently partitioned hyperspace,
- a prerequisite graph,
- a comprehension measure, and
- an interaction formula.

Conveniently partitioned hyperspace and a prerequisite graph are the two components that are primary concerns of the model explained in this section. The main features of the prerequisite graph model are to help students studying university courses to navigate in course content hyperspace; to follow preprogrammed learning strategies and support student's goal-oriented efforts.

A course can be defined by its content. A course content is composed of several concepts to be learned (theory), examples to support the theory, and the tests to measure the student's knowledge level. The course content then can be said to be the domain of our system. The first thing we have to do is to define a way to model this domain. The study begins by dividing the course content into logical and physical sub-units.

The basic model is very simple. Course content can be divided into hierarchical sub-units. The division is shown in the Table 3: In this division entities "course" and "chapter" are logical subunits. They are composed of physical sub-units named "concept". Concept is a physical entity because each concept is associated with an .html file in the hyperspace. A concept can be one of the five different types: it can be a theorem, a definition, a lemma, or a test.

Table 3. Hierarchical division of a course content.

Unit	Composed of
Course	Chapter
Chapter	Concept
Concept	Theorem | lemma | definition | test

The relationship between concepts is represented in a network expressing the prerequisite relation. The resulting semantic network is called "conceptual network." In this network, a node is either a non-terminal node or a terminal node. A terminal node has no successors. A non-terminal node is either an AND node or an OR node. Each node in the graph is connected to one or more nodes with a direction. A node is said to be solved if all the AND nodes it is connected to are solved (Chakrabarti 1994). For example, consider the graph in Figure 2.

In the figure, the shaded nodes are AND nodes, the others are OR nodes. The node n3 is said to be solved if the nodes n5 and n6 are solved. The node n1 is said to be solved only if n3 is solved, because n3 is the only AND node, the other nodes n2 and n4 where n1 has a path to are OR nodes and need not to be solved. In other words, n5 and n6 are the prerequisites of node n3, and n3 is the only prerequisite of node n1.

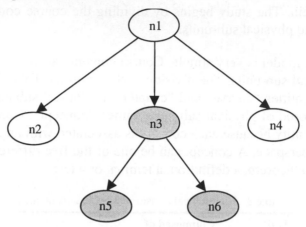

Figure 2. A sample conceptual network.

In the hyperspace terminology .html page n3 can be visited or opened if .html pages n5 and n6 were visited. Similarly .html page n1 is opened if n3 was visited beforehand. It should be noted that each concept is associated with an .html file. Thus, a conceptual network shows what concepts should be known before studying further.

Defining the course content with this model makes the student learn concepts in a step-by-step fashion upgrading their knowledge level gradually. The logical coherence is established, and a student feels comfortable, because s/he knows everything necessary to learn a concept right before to starting to study a new concept. This model also makes the study simple by giving the right guidance according to each student's individual knowledge level.

The curriculum is a simple list of concepts. If a concept is a sub-topic in a curriculum, its level is higher than the containing topic. There is a part of the curriculum for the web-based Artificial Intelligence course given in Figure 3.

```
ARTIFICIAL INTELLIGENCE
CHAPTER 1
Introduction-definition of AI
Why Study AI?
The Turing Test
Mental and Physical Machines
A Quick Survey
.
.
.
```

Figure 3. A sample curriculum.

2.3   Pretests

The knowledge level of the student may be obtained by means of a test on the concepts tutored. With this evidence, we can think that computers can guide students to increase their knowledge level gradually by considering the students' answers. However, one should keep in mind that deciding the skill level of the student according to the answers given to a test or an example is not an easy task. Computer-aided instruction or tutoring systems exist that provide individualized coaching.

A pretest is a test applied to the student prior to a real test. A pretest is composed of two types of questions: multiple choice or true/false. The questions in a pretest are on the basic concepts that the student should know before he starts studying a new chapter in the course material. Depending on the answers s/he gives to the pretests, the student will be advised to restudy the concept(s) s/he lacks. The pretest gives a student a mirror that s/he can see his knowledge level, a chance to know which concepts s/he misunderstood or forgot and to revise. This is a simplification of the idea presented as explicit evidence in overlay modeling in the paper by Carr and Goldstein (1997). The information about how the overlay model is applied to an application can be found in Weber and Specht's paper (1997).

During the attempt to solve an example the student may be supplied with a list of help topics. Help topics are the nodes in the conceptual network.

2.4   Adaptive Hypermedia and User Modeling

For years, World Wide Web (WWW) has been used to disseminate information to the Internet users. Education has become one of the areas that use WWW heavily. Initially, the systems on WWW developed for the education purpose were just electronic copies of regular textbooks. They were still hypermedia systems because they contained many hypermedia pages having different formats of information such as text, picture, sound and different links for navigation. But these systems were non-adaptive, and were unaware of student's knowledge level, goals, or preferences.

A system is said to be an Adaptive Hypermedia (AH system) if it adapts the information and links being presented to the particular user by using the user model derived from the user's knowledge level, goals or preferences. An AH system can also assist the user in navigation through the hyperspace. The working definition of an AH system (Brusilovsky 1996) is: "by adaptive hypermedia systems we mean all hypertext and hypermedia systems which reflect some features of the user in the user model and apply this model to adapt various visible of the system to the user."

There exists some adaptation techniques and methods that an AH system can apply to satisfy the main objectives. Adaptation techniques refer to methods of providing adaptation in existing AH systems where adaptation methods are defined as generalizations of existing adaptation techniques. The classification of adaptive hypermedia methods and techniques can be found in Brusilovsky's paper (1996).

There exist six kinds of hypermedia systems that are used at present for the research projects on adaptive hypermedia. These are educational hypermedia, on-line information systems, on-line help systems, information retrieval hypermedia systems, institutional information systems, and systems for managing personalized views. The list of existing AH systems classified according to their application areas can be found in Brusilovsky's paper (1996). An AH system can be shown schematically as in Figure 4 (Brusilovsky 1996).

Among these systems, educational hypermedia system is the most popular and is the system developed in this study. An educational hypermedia system has a relatively small hyperspace, which is composed of course material. The main goal of the user is to learn this material. In such a system the knowledge level of the user is the most important user feature. The course material should be presented according to the knowledge level of the student. The system should also supply navigational help for the user.

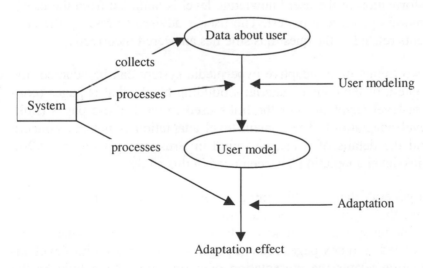

Figure 4. Classic loop "user modeling-adaptation" in adaptive systems.

The knowledge level of the user is not the only feature. The user's goal, background, hyperspace experience and preferences are other features. In this study, however, only user's knowledge level is taken into consideration. As stated earlier, the user's knowledge level is represented with simplified version of the overlay model. The overlay model is usually based on a domain model, which is a structural representation of the subject domain. Overlay models were originally developed in the area of intelligent tutoring systems and student modeling (Brusilovsky 1996).

The overlay model is the representation of the user's knowledge of the subject as an overlay of the domain model. In this model, for every concept presented in the domain, there is a value for the user knowledge level of that concept. This value can be a binary value (known-not known), a qualitative measure (good-average-poor), or a quantitative measure, such as the probability that the user knows the concept (Brusilovsky 1996). In this study a binary value is used as the value for the user knowledge level of a specific concept. The information of the user knowledge level is obtained from the user's answers given to a pretest. The user is advised to restudy the concepts related to the questions s/he has answered incorrectly.

Two things in an adaptive hypermedia system can be adapted: the content of the course material's building blocks that is pages (content-level adaptation) or the links used to reach those pages (link-level adaptation). The content-level adaptation is not our concern and the details of it can be found in Brusilovsky's paper (1996). Link-level adaptation has been used in this study.

In general, there are two information objects in a hypermedia system: the .html pages and the links which connects them. In a hypermedia system, the links can be placed in a separate page, which is called an index page, content page, or global map. Link-level adaptation adapts the presentation or permission of the links in the system. The link-level adaptation is also named as "adaptive navigation support" in Brusilovsky's paper (1996). As the name implies, it provides help for users to find their way in the hyperspace. There are five technologies for adapting link presentation: direct guidance, sorting, hiding, annotation, and map adaptation (Brusilovsky 1996).

In this study, the links are in a content page and the techniques used for adapting link presentation are based on hiding and annotation. The idea of hiding is concealing the links, which are not relevant to the user's goal. This idea is adapted in the thesis by not allowing the user to open a page if the user does not have sufficient background. This means that the prerequisites of the page have not been learned yet. Hiding can effectively support gradual learning throughout the learning space. The adaptive annotation technology mentioned by Brusilovsky (1996), Weber and Specht (1997), and Brusilovsky *et al.* (1996) suggests the augmentation of the links with some form of comments, so that user can see the current state of the link. This idea is implemented in this study by putting a "plus" sign next to a link whose associated html page is visited.

In this study, the hyperspace is formed as a conceptual network. In this network each concept is associated with an .html page. The concepts are connected with each other according to the prerequisite relationship among them. This relationship is the basis of the link-level adaptation. The concepts whose prerequisites have not been learned are hidden from the user. Putting a plus sign next to the link associated with a concept that is learned is inspired by the adaptive annotation technology. An overlay model is used to model the student.

3   Design and Implementation

3.1   System Objectives and Requirements

In this study, the main objective is to develop software that will
help the student to study a web-based course. The course content is
stored in .html pages. The agent helps students to study and learn
the concepts in the course by giving navigational support according
to their knowledge level. There are some elements in the software
to measure a student's knowledge level and these elements are created with user-friendly interfaces. Each student in the system is
modeled according to his or her knowledge level so that individual
navigational support is accomplished.

3.2   System Architecture

The modular solution to the problem stated in the previous section
comes from the ideas presented earlier. The main problem is how
the system will give navigational support to an individual student.
In order to give individual navigational support, the system should
know the student. This is accomplished by modeling each student.
As stated earlier, the particular knowledge level of a student is a
valuable feature used to model the student.

The knowledge level is a value indicating the student's knowledge
of the subject. In the system, the subject is a concept in the course.
The value representing the knowledge level can be just a binary
value, which means the student knows the concept or does not
know the concept. The elements used to measure the student
knowledge level are curriculum and the pretest. In a conceptual
network, a concept is connected to one or more concepts with prerequisite relation. In other words, to study a concept in a course the
student should study the prerequisite concepts. This property lets
the system measure the knowledge level of the student by using the

curriculum. When a student attempts to study a concept in the curriculum, the system checks if the prerequisites have been studied. If the prerequisites have not been studied, the system can guide the student to study them.

The pretest is another element used to measure the student's knowledge level. A question in a pretest is associated with a concept in the course. If there are incorrect answers given by the student in a pretest, then the student is advised to study the concepts related to the questions.

The curriculum elements and pretests can be created and maintained with some user-friendly interfaces. The data regarding to the curriculum and pretests are stored in a database. Some user interfaces are necessary to present the curriculum and the pretests to the students. There is a reasoning mechanism in the system to reason about the students' actions. The appropriate navigational support and messages will be given to the student according to the student action and the student's knowledge level. For each student, the knowledge level of each concept in the form of known/not known is stored in the database.

The user modeling is needed for navigational support. Navigational support means that the student will be helped to reach the necessary information or an .html page without getting lost in the hyperspace. The navigational support is individual in other words "adaptive". The other name for adaptive navigational support is "link-level adaptation." It is stated before that each concept in the course is associated with an .html page and a concept name in the curriculum is actually a link to the .html page containing concept information. There are different technologies for adapting link presentation. In this system, link-level adaptation effect is obtained by using hiding and annotation technologies. Hiding is implemented by not showing the .html page whose prerequisites have not been studied and the annotation is implemented by putting a plus sign next to the link associated with a concept that is studied.

According to the explanations in the above paragraphs, the list of major tasks associated with the system is as follows:
    Task 1: curriculum generation and maintenance
    Task 2: pretest generation and maintenance
    Task 3: presentation of curriculum to the student
    Task 4: presentation of pretest to the student
    Task 5: reasoning about student actions on the curriculum
    Task 6: reasoning about student actions on the pretest
    Task 7: giving the results of reasoning to the student
    Task 8: database operations
    Task 9: user interface tasks

There are two types of user in the system: the teacher and the student. The curriculum and pretests are created and maintained by the teacher. The curriculum and pretests will be presented to the student. The reasoning mechanism considers the student actions. The results of this reasoning are presented to the student in a user-friendly way. All the explanations at the above paragraphs can be figured in the system architecture as follows.

As illustrated in Figure 5, the system is composed of two modules. These modules will be explained in detail in the following sections. The database ingredients and the functions of the reasoning mechanism will also be explained in detail in the following sections.

The operation of the system is as follows:
1. The teacher creates the curriculum with a user interface in the curriculum generation module.
2. The teacher creates the pretests with a user interface in the curriculum generation module.
3. The teacher can do operations on the existing curriculum and pretests.

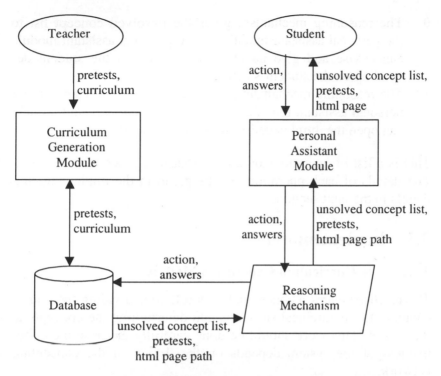

Figure 5. Agent architecture. Ovals indicate the users in the system while rectangles indicate the modules in the system. Arrows show the direction of the data flow and the labels on the arrows specify the data. The cylinder indicates the database where the data resides. The trapezoid represents reasoning mechanism working on the user actions and the database.

4. All the data regarding to curriculum and the pretests are stored in the database.
5. The curriculum and the pretests are presented to the student by means of a user interface in the personal assistant module.
6. The student can study the curriculum and pretests by using the interface in the personal assistant module.
7. The student actions are evaluated by the reasoning mechanism.
8. The reasoning mechanism updates the database according to the student's action.

9. The reasoning mechanism gives the unsolved concept list to the personal assistant module so that personal assistant module can advise and give navigational support to the student depending on the student's action.
10. The reasoning mechanism gives the .html file pathname to the personal assistant module so that the personal assistant module can open the .html page for the student to study.

This is a list of operations or actions that take place in the system. The details of each operation will be given in the implementation details in the next section.

3.3   Implementation

3.3.1   The Curriculum Generation Module

The teacher creates a conceptual network after dividing the course content into hierarchical sub-units and determining the concepts in the course. This work should be done carefully, because the effectiveness of the system depends on the design of the conceptual network.

The second step of curriculum generation is related to the conceptual network with the corresponding .html files in the database. After the curriculum is prepared and .html file pathnames is stored in the database, the teacher can input the course curriculum data into the system. The user interface shown in Figure 6 allows the teacher to create a new curriculum or modify an existing one.

Each node in the curriculum corresponds to a concept (theorem, lemma, definition, or pretest), or a collection of concepts. A node is stored as an .html file physically. The .html file pathnames should be stored in prior to creating the curriculum. The concept is a node in the conceptual network of the curriculum, so the term node will be used instead of concept from now on.

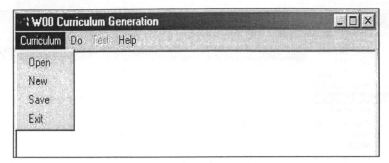

Figure 6. Curriculum Generation menu.

After the curriculum is prepared and .html file pathnames is stored in the database, instructor can input course curriculum data into the system using the Curriculum Generation Menu shown in Figure 6. This menu is used to create a new curriculum or modify an existing one.

The node operations are performed through this menu as shown in Figure 7.

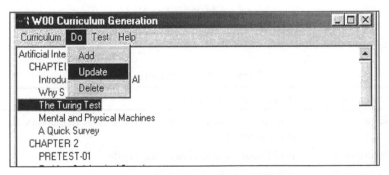

Figure 7. Node operations.

Adding a new node to the curriculum along with the node attributes and modifying the existing nodes are the main node operations as shown in Figure 8.

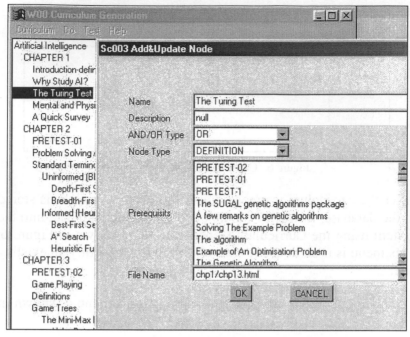

Figure 8. Add & Update Nodes.

The node attributes are shown in Table 4.

Table 4. Node attributes.

Attribute Name	Attribute Description
Name	A node is identified by its name and node name appears in curriculum.
Description	Additional information about a node.
AND/OR Type	Whether a node is an AND type or OR type in the conceptual network representation of the course concepts.
Node Type	Type of the node (Theorem, Lemma, Pretest, Definition).
Prerequisites	Prerequisite node(s) of the node. The prerequisites can be selected from the multiple-selection list box.
File Name	Indicates the html file name associated with the node.

Pretest operations are also performed through the Curriculum Generation Menu. New pretests can be generated or existing ones can be modified as shown in Figure 9. When generating pretest questions, the answers are also stored for automated grading of the tests. Each question is connected to the related concept via this menu. This is necessary for advising the students in case they have incorrect answers.

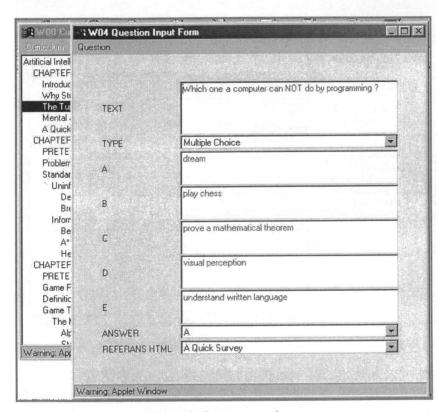

Figure 9. Pretest operations.

3.3.2   The Personal Assistant Module

A student follows the course in the Internet using the student interface in this module. Each student has a user-id and a password in order to use the personal assistant module interfaces. The interface is shown in Figure 10. The nodes in the curriculum have a plus (+) sign next to the node name if the user has already studied successfully the concept represented by that node.

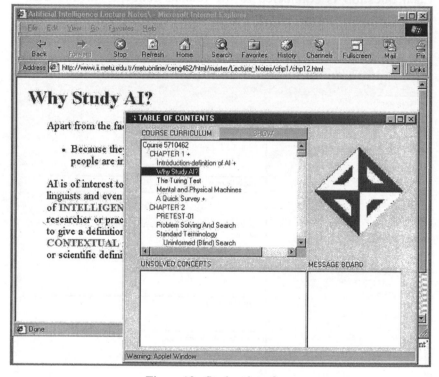

Figure 10. Student interface.

Students take pretests when a pretest node in the curriculum is selected as shown in Figure 11. Pretests are graded automatically. In case of incorrect answers, students are provided with explanation and advice (Figure 12).

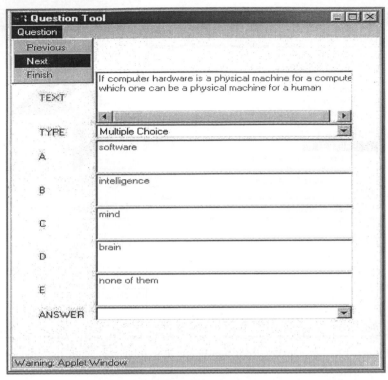

Figure 11. Question form that appears when a pretest node is selected.

The system was implemented as a standalone application with Microsoft J++ 6.0 with the features of Microsoft Developer Studio 6.0. Some of the WFC (Windows Foundation Classes for Java) developed by Microsoft were used in the system. The program was then converted to Java Applets. The database management system is Mini SQL. MsqlJava package (A Java Class Library for mSQL) is used for database operations such as executing SQL query statements, connecting to the database and closing the database.

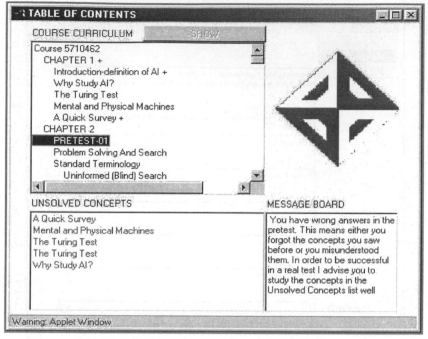

Figure 12. A snapshot from intelligent user interface when the student has wrong answers in a pretest.

3.4   System Description

According to the discussions in the previous sections, the system can be defined as an adaptive hypermedia system. The system is designed as a "personal assistant" to help teachers to generate their course curriculum and to help students to navigate through the course material. It has an intelligent user interface, which is cooperative, does adaptive user modeling, and has two main components: the human user and back-end information system. It is cooperative because it assists the user satisfying the user's needs, with the ability to model user and to adapt links. The human-user is the student and the back-end information system is in the hyperspace. The information provided by the user is historical, because system reacts to the user actions by remembering the user's knowledge level, previous actions, and the .html pages visited by the user before. Each student has an id number in the system and the system identifies each user individually by this number.

The teacher generates curriculum through a user interface. The curriculum is represented by a conceptual network and will be kept in a database table. The concepts in a course are presented to the student via an intelligent user interface having the curriculum generated. The curriculum is a simple list of concepts containing the level of information. If a concept is a subtopic in a curriculum, its level is higher than its container concept. The student can study a concept in the curriculum if s/he has already studied the prerequisite concept(s) of the current concept. The system keeps the student's knowledge level in a database table. Using this information, the intelligent user interface reasons about the individual student whether the student can study the concept s/he attempts to or not. In other words the system constructs models of individual users, reflecting the user's state of knowledge.

The system also has pretests at the end of each chapter. Pretest is a test given to the student prior to a real test. A pretest is composed of two types of questions: multiple choice or true/false. The questions in a pretest are on the basic concepts that the student should necessarily know before s/he takes a real test. Analyzing the answers s/he gives to the pretest, the student may be advised to restudy the concept(s) s/he misunderstood or forgot. In other words, the pretest reflects the user's knowledge level. The system works in the information-rich environment of the Internet.

In summary, the system is composed of a set of user interfaces working on Internet in order to:
1. Create course curriculum for teachers
2. Follow the course curriculum for students

4   Empirical Study

An educational adaptive hypermedia system with a personal assistant is best evaluated and tested by the students, because this kind of software aims to help students to learn the web-based course concepts better. The system implemented here satisfies its main objective with the adaptive link presentation. As stated before, the system accomplishes this and provides the navigational support managed by the curriculum and provides pretests. The students were asked to evaluate the system for successfulness and effectiveness of navigational support and pretests. The students also evaluated the time consideration as well as the design and the user-friendliness of the user interfaces. 22 students of the CENG 462-Artificial Intelligence course evaluated the personal assistant module. Table 5 shows the evaluation results. The numbers in the table indicates the number of students.

The results obtained show that:
1. Most of the students claim that the time needed to display the curriculum is very long.
2. Most students thought that the time needed to load a page is quite fast when a link in the curriculum is clicked.
3. The same opinion applied for the time needed to load questions.
4. Most of the students found the design of the user interface good. Few students have complaints on the design. These complaints are mainly focused on the following items:
   • The fonts are too small.
   • The question form is not designed well.
   • The .html pages should appear in the same browser window instead of opening a new window each time a link is clicked.
5. The same opinions applied to the user-friendliness of the user interface. It seems that question form should be redesigned. Fonts should be enlarged and .html pages can be opened in the same browser. However, there are students who found the original design useful since it gives the impression that browser is

only a window that shows the content of a concept and the guiding is done by the program.

6. Most students found the navigational support effective and necessary.
7. Most students found the pretests effective and necessary.

The results show that the system satisfies its objective to help the students to learn the course concepts efficiently with the adaptive navigational support. The user interface should be better designed, and the curriculum load time should be decreased. The number of students assessing this section was limited to 22.

Table 5. Evaluation results.

	Evaluation Criteria	Good	Moderate	Bad	Time
	Curriculum Load		18	4	2 min.
Time	Page Load	21		1	2 sec.
	Question Form Load	20		2	2 sec.
User	Design	12	7	3	
Interface	User Friendliness	14	3	5	
	Navigational Support	18	2	2	
	Effectiveness of Pretests	18	2	2	

5   Conclusion and Future Work

The system described in this study is an attempt to develop a base for an adaptive hypermedia system. It integrates some of the features of techniques and methods used in an adaptive hypermedia system as well as integrating some features of intelligent tutoring systems and personal assistants. It uses a simplified prerequisite graph model as domain model that is well suited for user modeling and adaptive navigation support. The simplified overlay model is used for student modeling. The overlay model takes into consideration the user's knowledge level, which can be taken from the answers of the pretests when providing adaptation. The system adapts the links in the contents page to provide easy navigation of the course content. In link-level adaptation hiding and annotation technologies are used. These effectively support gradual learning of the learning space.

There are two main drawbacks observed in the system. The first is related to the preparation of the domain model. The domain model should be prepared carefully to get maximum efficiency. The teacher should partition the system in a logical and coherent way so that all prerequisite relations among the concepts are stated correctly and completely. An incomplete or incorrect domain model would give rise to disadvantages rather than advantages for the students.

The second drawback is the insertion of the .html file path names to the database table. This process was not automated. The teacher must insert the .html file path names into the database manually before generating the curriculum.

Although the system satisfies its main objective, which is forming a base for an adaptive hypermedia system, there are some improvements which when added to the system will make it more complete. As stated earlier, building an intelligent tutoring system is not an easy task for various reasons. The previous experiences and this research show that there are many different components in such a system. The components' design and implementation requires multiple expertise from different fields of computer and cognitive science.

Two types of questions are used in pretests: multiple-choice and true/false questions. More sophisticated questions that can be solved in a number of episodes can be prepared. The solutions to these questions can then be analyzed to get more information about the student knowledge level. This is the real adaptation of the overlay model and used in ELM-ART II (Weber and Specht 1997) as episodic learner model.

The value used for the user knowledge level is binary in this study. The user either knows the subject or does not know the subject. With the addition of more sophisticated questions, this value can be a quantitative, which, then, can be used, in content-level adaptation. In the content-level adaptation, which is a lacking in our research, students with high level of knowledge can be provided with pages having more detailed and deep information while the novice students can access pages having some additional explanatory information.

User preferences and background can be taken into consideration when to hide the irrelevant information in the hyperspace. The user can inform the system directly about the preferences which are the links or .html pages preferred over others. The user background information can contain the user's profession and experience of work in related areas. The user background can be used for adaptive navigation support.

The above paragraphs describe the improvements that can be implemented in short term. In long term, some of the information retrieval techniques can be adapted to the system for letting students to ask questions of the system. The question asked by the student can be similar to the question asked in the classroom. The system will parse the question and provide information by sorting most relevant information first and least relevant information last.

There are some other components in a web-based course such as homework, forum, chat, grade-book, on-line exams, frequently-asked-questions and so on. The system can be redesigned so that student can use these facilities using the same interface. The advantage of this is that the student can access all the course material from one user interface. The same interface can be used by the instructors to prepare the instructor materials as well.

References

Brusilovsky, P. (1996), "Methods and techniques of adaptive hypermedia," *User Modeling and User-Adapted Interaction*, Special issue on: Adaptive Hypertext and Hypermedia, vol. 6, pp. 87-129.

Brusilovsky, P., Schwarz, E., and Weber, G. (1996), "A tool for developing adaptive electronic textbooks on WWW," *Proceedings of the WebNet '96 World Conf. of the Web Society, Part Six, HCI: Education and Training*, AACE, pp. 64-69.

Carr, B.P. and Goldstein, I.P. (1997), "Overlays: a theory of modelling for computer aided instruction," *AI Memo*, vol. 406, pp. 1-23.

Chakrabarti, P.P. (1994), "Algorithms for searching explicit AND/OR graphs and their applications to problem reduction search," *Artificial Intelligence*, vol. 65, pp. 329-345.

FIPA: Foundation for Intelligent Physical Agents (1997), "Personal Assistant," *FIPA'97 Specification*, Part 5.

Franklin, S. and Graesser, A. (1997), "Is it an agent or just a program?: A taxonomy for autonomous agent," *Third International Workshop on Agent Theories, Architectures, and Languages*, Springer Verlag, pp. 21-35.

Frasson, C., Mengelle, T., Aïmeur, E., and Gouardères, G. (1996), "An actor-based architecture for intelligent tutoring systems," *ITS'96 Conference*, Lecture Notes in Computer Science, vol. 1086, Springer Verlag, Berlin Heidelberg New York, pp. 57-65.

Gecsei, J. and Frasson, C. (1994), "SAFARI: an environment for creating tutoring systems in industrial training. EdMedia, World

Conference on Educational Multimedia and Hypermedia, Vancouver, (1994) 25-30.

Hammond, N., McKendree, J., Reader, W., Trapp, A., and Scott, P.J. (1995), "The Psycle Project: educational multimedia for conceptual understanding," *Multimedia-95*, San Fransisco.

Huhns, M. and Singh, M. (1998), "Agents and multiagent systems: themes, approaches, and challenges," *Readings in Agents*, pp. 1-23.

Maes, P. (1994), "Agents that reduce work and information overload," *Communications of the ACM*, vol. 37, pp. 31-40.

Nykänen, O. (1997), "Work in progress: user modeling in WWW with prerequisite graph model," *Proceedings of the Workshop on Adaptive Systems and User Modeling on the World Wide Web, Sixth International Conference on User Modeling*, Chia Laguna, Sardinia, pp. 2-5.

Russell, S. and Norvig, P. (1995), *Artificial Intelligence: a Modern Approach*, Prentice Hall, Inc., pp. 31-50.

Schank, R.C. (1994), "Active learning through multimedia," *IEEE Multimedia*, vol. 1, pp. 69-78.

Weber, G. and Specht, M. (1997), "User modeling and adaptive navigation support in WWW-based tutoring systems," *Proceedings of User Modeling'97*, pp. 289-300.

Chapter 7

Automatic Generation of Problems in Web-Based Tutors

M.V. Belmonte, E. Guzmán, L. Mandow, E. Millán
and J.L. Pérez de la Cruz[1]

Problem generation and posing are ubiquitous in education or teaching processes. However, early AI-based works on problem generation have not been followed by an abundance of generative systems in Intelligent Tutoring Systems. This chapter analyzes the above-mentioned situation and makes the case for problem generating systems. A clarification of relevant issues and options available in such systems is presented, and some selected real systems are described at length. Such systems are then classified according to a general framework which provides a better understanding of past, present, and future research in the field.

1   Introduction

Problem generation and posing are ubiquitous in education or teaching processes. It does not matter whether you adhere to an objectivist approach or a constructivist one, whether you advocate coaching or prefer tight tutoring, whether you use the Web or just pencil and paper: in every situation the need arises for a method to select or generate exercises and problems for the student. Let us say something about the role of computers in the process of problem posing.

---

[1] Authors listed in alphabetical order.

Generative or adaptive systems have a long history in Computer Aided Instruction (CAI) (Suppes 1967, Uhr 1969, Wexler 1970, Woods and Hartley 1971); in fact, they appeared in the late sixties, prior to the application of Artificial Intelligence (AI) to instructional processes. Essentially, they presented a sequence of problems to the student, received the answers, and finally assessed her/his global performance. Some systems – usually termed "adaptive drill and practice" – altered the order of presentation in response to different answers from the student.

The need for more powerful tools to generate and adapt the exercises was quickly perceived. AI techniques were the obvious choice. Koffman's early work on problem generation (Koffman and Blount 1975, Koffman and Perry 1976) shows some of the features usually found in later systems, such as the selection of a formal domain, the use of formal grammars, or the need for additional mechanisms in order to control the statements generated by the grammar. In this sense, it is a fundamental precedent and papers presenting it deserve the huge amount of citations they have obtained. However, it must be said that this encouraging start has not been followed by an abundance of generative systems in CAI or Intelligent Tutoring Systems (ITS).

Practitioners in the field have noted the relative lack of problem generating systems. Some of them have inferred that the reason is that problem generation is too complex for most tutoring domains, so it is better to resort to a fixed set of problems. This opinion is clearly stated by Maurer *et al.* (1991). They describe two systems: the first one generates functions for exercises in the symbolic differentiation domain, the other generates sets of linear equations. They found that "with present methods, the use of such procedures is neither cost-effective nor desirable. Better results with less effort seem to come from a (possibly large) database of such problems."

However, this point of view in our opinion is:

i) too pessimistic with respect to technical possibilities, and;
ii) too optimistic with respect to possibilities of a fixed database of
   problems or questions.

Concerning (i), it is indisputable that an independent, random choice of numerical values inside a template often leads to inappropriate or, even worse, nonsensical statements. However, this is not the only tool available in the practitioner's tool-case. Context-free grammars, attribute grammars, inverse generation or post-generation constraining can avoid such undesirable cases.

Concerning (ii), the "possibly large database" is a difficult thing to achieve in many domains. As every instructor knows, students are very good at learning by heart the correct answer to a posed question, without any real understanding of underlying processes or principles. In order to avoid such a "memorizing" effect, the database should be very, very large; and hence the burden of generating the database is comparable to the efforts needed for tuning a good generating device.

In the rest of this chapter, we will make the case for problem generating systems. In Section 2, a clarification of relevant issues and options available in such systems is presented. In Section 3, some selected real systems will be described at length, which prove empirically the feasibility of the methods. Finally, in Section 4, some conclusions are presented.

2 A General Framework for Problem Generation

2.1 Types and Methods

Problem statement generation is a fundamental element in many tutoring systems. Particularly, the ability to pose new problems – depending on the interactions with the student – provides an important degree of flexibility over systems with predefined sets of canned problems.

While the variety of tutoring systems described in the literature is large, the kinds of problems used to tutor different subject matters also seem to present a similar richness. This section discusses a general framework where different kinds of problems can be classified and compared. Before engaging in the subject of problem generation, it is a wise step to make a distinction between the concepts of task, problem, and exercise:

- The term *task* refers to a kind of job that needs to be done. According to Chandrasekaran *et al.* (1998), a task is a *goal type*, where goals are defined as "attitudes on world descriptions." For example, the diagnostic goal "Explain abnormal observations of a system" is made up of an attitude term (explain), and a world description (abnormal observations). Examples of other attitude types are "make true that", "prevent", "determine whether", "identify", and "assign likelihood to".
- The term *problem* refers to a statement or proposition that aims to find a course of action that, given some data, should produce certain results. A problem is a particular instance of a task.
- The term *exercise* will be used here to refer to a kind of problem restricted to practicing the application of particular formulae, concepts, or mathematical theorems. The term *drill* evokes the image of a repetitive kind of exercise.

The proposed framework rests both on the notion of task, and on the kinds of problem-solving procedures that can be used to achieve them.

Problem-solving in general, and knowledge-intensive tasks in particular, have been the subject of study of Artificial Intelligence over the last decades. In the early years of AI, an important distinction was drawn between *well-structured tasks* (WST)[2] that were amenable (at least in theory) to computer solution using algorithmic or search procedures, and the so-called *ill-structured tasks* (IST). Theorem proving and chess playing were usually regarded as well structured, while architectural design and general real-world interaction were considered ill structured. Simon (1973) argued that "the boundary between well structured and ill-structured problems is vague, fluid and not susceptible to formalization" and that ISTs are a "residual concept" in the sense that "a problem is a [IST] if it is not a [WST]." The aim of his work was to provide a positive characterization of ISTs. In short, Simon's argument was that the boundary between WSTs and ISTs "derives from our insistence that notions of computability in principle be replaced by notions of practicable computability in the definition of [WSTs]," and that given a knowledge base of sufficient size, natural language understanding, and perceptual and pattern recognition capabilities, no new concepts or mechanisms are needed to automate all kinds of problem solving. Nevertheless, a practical boundary exists between the tasks that, at any given time, can be successfully formalized and, at least in theory, solved in a computer (the WSTs), and the rest (the ISTs).

Within the class of WSTs another basic distinction can be made between tasks that can be solved using existing special-purpose algorithms, and those that involve at least some kind of trial and error search. The latter is often referred to as the class of knowledge-intensive reasoning tasks. These have been extensively studied in the field of Knowledge Engineering, where efforts to define an ontology of problem-solving knowledge are currently under way (Chandrasekaran *et al.* 1998).

Meanwhile, several definitions and classifications of knowledge-intensive reasoning tasks have been proposed or adapted from cog-

---

[2] Given the previous definitions it is probably more accurate in current Knowledge Engineering terms to use the terms well-structured and ill-structured *tasks*, instead of the original terminology of well-structured and ill-structured *problems*.

nitive psychology. For example, in a paper by Schreiber *et al.* 2000), knowledge-intensive tasks are classified as *analytic* and *synthetic*. Analytic tasks take as input the description of a system, object, or artifact, and produce some characterization of it as output. Some examples of analytic tasks are classification, diagnosis, prediction, assessment, and monitoring. Synthetic tasks, on the other hand, aim at producing the description of a new system, object, or artifact, and take as input sets of requirements it should satisfy. Some examples are configuration, planning, assignment, and scheduling. This division can be extended to ill-structured and algorithmic tasks as well.

All the above distinctions provide a basic framework for task classification, which is summarized in Figure 1. Rather than sharply defined classes, a continuum exists between the difficult ill-structured tasks and the simplest algorithmic exercises. Note also that often a complex non-algorithmic task can be decomposed into subtasks, some of which may be algorithmic in nature. In addition, ill-structured tasks, such as design tasks, have often been decomposed into subtasks, some of which are well structured. Therefore, the capability to solve most of the mentioned tasks often implies mastering several kinds of algorithms in addition to other abilities.

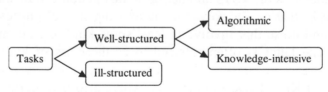

Figure 1. A general framework for tasks and problem-solving.

In some tutoring contexts, such as coached instruction, it is important for the tutor to pose problems and to be able to solve them. This imposes important constraints on the kind of problems that can be posed, given the current problem-solving capability of computers. However, other kinds of tutoring contexts, such as discovery learning, do not have this limitation.

2.2   Generation Context

The context in which the generation of a problem takes place is represented in Figure 2 and can be described as follows:

1. The ITS, by means of the corresponding module (e.g., instructional planner) determines that the next best instructional action is to pose a problem to be solved by the student.
2. The type of problem needed is determined by the system, according to the current learning strategy and the information contained in the student model. This information can be of many different kinds:
   - *experience* (with computers, with the domain, and so on),
   - *knowledge* (essentially, parts of the curriculum that are mastered/non-mastered by the student),
   - *goals* (e.g., get deep/shallow knowledge),
   - *preferences* (student's favorite learning style, and so on).

   In other words, the generated problem can be customized for the particular student at many different levels. Of course, a high level of customization increases the difficulty of the problem generation process. Therefore, most existing systems only take into account the student's current state of knowledge.
3. Once the type of problem has been determined, the problem generator is asked to generate a problem of this type. The result is a problem statement, which is passed back to the ITS engine. According to the established visualization techniques (which can include text, video, graphics, sounds, applets, among others) the problem is presented to the student for solution.

2.3   Generating Devices

This section discusses several generating mechanisms that are used in different ways in the systems described in Section 3.

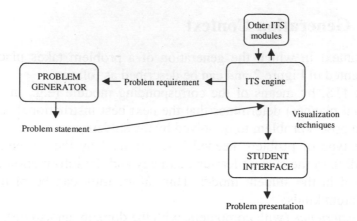

Figure 2. Generation context.

2.3.1 Simple Mechanisms

Almost every programming language or environment provides a (pseudo-)random number generator (Knuth 1997). This generator typically returns an integer value in a given interval with uniform probability, and suitable transformations are available to generate other entities, such as enumerated objects or character strings. This simple device is the basis for more complex generators and it is sometimes enough to achieve the functionality required by a *problem schema*. In this context, a problem schema is a *template* for generating an indeterminate number of problems by filling some holes with suitable values.

For example, let us consider XAIDA (Hsieh *et al.* 1999), a system for the development of computer-based maintenance training. A semantic network is used for the representation of the physical characteristics of a device to be taught. To generate a question about the domain, first a part-attribute pair or an attribute-value pair is randomly chosen and then an exercise schema is randomly chosen from among those that fit the selected pair. For example, the selected pair could be (*attribute* = "function", *value* = "store hydraulic fluid for the system"). By then applying the schema "Select the part(s) with a(n) *attribute* of *value*", we obtain the exercise "Select the part(s) with a(n) function of store hydraulic fluid for the system" (taken from Hsieh *et al.* (1999)). In highly structured conceptual domains, suitable for such representations, this procedure (random elements + problem schema) can produce very good results.

Regrettably, independent choices are usually not enough when posing exercises. For example, let us consider the following schema: "Two x are moving along the same way at the same speed of v km/h. If they start at time t_1 and meet at time t_2, how far was one from the other at the beginning?" Some constraints for x, v, t_1, and t_2 are obvious: t_1 must be less than t_2; if x="cars," v cannot be greater than, say, 150 km/h; and so on. Generally speaking, certain values constrain the others and hence additional mechanisms are needed to ensure coherence.

Besides this mechanism based on the use of templates, *taxonomies* can also be used for exercise generation in hierarchically structured domains. Examples that illustrate this approach are discussed in Sections 3.4 and 3.7.

2.3.2 Grammars

A further step in exercise generation is provided by *context-free grammars*. Context-free grammars (CFG) were introduced by Chomsky (1959) to describe natural languages; however, they have found their main application in the definition of formal devices. CFG's are standard in computer science and the interested reader can check any introductory book on the subject. Several examples of CFG-based generative systems are presented in Section 3. However, some modifications must be done to a standard CFG in order to generate exercises. First, the terminals of the grammar are often generated by the system by means of simple devices such as the ones mentioned in the preceding section. Moreover, productions in the grammar may be weighted, yielding a probabilistic grammar where different problems (i.e., kinds of sentences in the grammar) have different probabilities of occurrence.

CFGs have many potential advantages over template-filling mechanisms. For example, they allow fairly complex statements to be generated from a small, simple set of productions. One feature, perhaps even more useful, is the capability to express a *top-down* process of generation. For example, let us suppose that we need an exercise in the domain of symbolic differentiation. A CFG for generating elementary functions can mimic the human process of selecting operators: "we want a fraction whose numerator is a polynomial and whose denominator is a logarithmic function." This *inverse generation* is usually needed in order to fulfill the requirements of the rest of the tutorial system.

However, the same domain of symbolic differentiation shows the drawbacks or, at least, the limitations of CFGs. For example, it is very cumbersome to set a limit in the depth of the derivation in a pure CFG. Sometimes it is even impossible to express very natural constraints.

Attribute grammars (Waite and Goos 1985) – another standard tool in computer science – are handier than CFGs. An attribute grammar is based upon a CFG and associates a set of attributes with each symbol (non-terminal or terminal.) Attributes represent properties of the symbol and are context-sensitive. Attributes are either synthesized or inherited. Synthesized attributes of a symbol A are computed from values of the symbols originating from A; inherited ones are computed from the environment of A. In this way, a suitable selection of attributes and attribution rules can express in a concise and natural way a lot of information about the problem statements to be generated. For example, if the only productions are

$$1.\ S \Rightarrow (S)$$
$$2.\ S \Rightarrow a$$

and we want to compute the level of nesting, we add the attribute
S.depth and the attribution rules

$$1.\ S \Rightarrow (S_1), \quad S.depth = S_1.depth + 1$$
$$2.\ S \Rightarrow a, \quad\quad S.depth = 0$$

2.3.3   Ad Hoc Techniques

Sometimes it is necessary to use "tricky" knowledge that would be
difficult to express even in an attribute grammar. The last choice is
then to filter the output of the grammar by means of an ad hoc procedure that imposes *post-generation constraining*. If the output
does not pass the filter, a new statement is generated – in the hope
of better luck – or a heuristic modification of the statement can be
done in order to satisfy the constraints.

3   Systems and Issues

This section reviews the more relevant web-based educational systems that use some kind of problem generation. Koffman's early
work, described in Section 3.1 is not concerned with web-based
systems. However, it has also been included, since it set the basis
for problem generation in tutoring systems.

3.1   Early Problem Generation Systems

The systems described in (Koffman and Blount 1975, Koffman and
Perry 1976) share a common architecture, but present generating
devices for two different kinds of problems. The systems provide
tutoring for a set of concepts organized in a *concept tree* using prerequisite or subconcept relations. Each concept has specific problem generation and coaching (problem solving) routines. The student's knowledge is modeled using different levels of proficiency
in each concept, together with statistical information regarding usage of the system. Both problem generation and coaching are controlled with these proficiency levels. Details on how concepts are

selected for tutoring are described in (Koffman and Perry 1976), the structure and maintenance of the student model is described in (Koffman 1972), and all three papers (Koffman 1972, Koffman and Blount 1975, Koffman and Perry 1976) describe different features on the operation of the coaching routines.

The systems operate in the following way. Once a concept has been selected for instruction a related problem is generated. Then the coaching procedure monitors and/or guides the student's problem solving actions. The difficulty of the problem as well as the degree of guidance depend on the student's level of proficiency. Each time the student gives right or wrong responses the level is updated accordingly.

The kinds of schematic problem statements described by the authors call for the student to apply specific algorithmic procedures to certain data. Some examples are "form the logical 'and' of numbers X and Y given in binary|octal|hexadecimal base," or "form the truth table associated with logical expression L." The algorithms to "form the logical 'and' of two numbers" or "form the truth table of an expression" are clearly defined and available to the student in textbooks. The coaching procedures ask the student to follow these algorithms step by step. The granularity of the steps depends on the student's level. An example follows where level 0 denotes a proficient student (maximum granularity) and level 3 a non-proficient student (minimum granularity):

- Calculate the logical 'and' of two numbers in binary|octal|hexadecimal base (asked for at levels 0-1).
- Calculate the binary equivalent of a number depending on its base (octal or hexadecimal) (asked for at levels 0-1).
- Add leading or/trailing zeroes to both numbers if needed until both have the same number of digits (decimal and non-decimal) (asked for at levels 1-2).
- Calculate the logical and of two binary digits (asked for at levels 2-3).

Koffman and Perry (1976) propose a context-free probabilistic grammar as a viable model for problem data generation. Let (S, N, T, P) be the usual components defining a formal grammar, where S is the initial symbol, N the set of non-terminal symbols, T the set of terminal symbols, and P the set of productions or rules. For example, the following grammar generates simple logical expressions that can be used to fill the data in one of the schematic problem statements already described – see (Koffman and Perry 1976) for an extended example –:

```
N = {S, A, *}
T = {p, q, r, not, and, or, xor}
P = {S → A,    A → (A * A),   A → (not A),
     A → p,    A → q,         A → r,
     * → and,  * → or,        * → xor}
```

The generation of expressions is controlled with two additional elements. The first one is a set of probabilities associated to each rule in the grammar. All rewrite rules sharing the same non-terminal symbol in their left-hand side should have nonzero probabilities that sum up one. A different set of probabilities is devised for each of three different difficulty levels. The student's previous level of performance determines the set of probabilities chosen to generate new problems. The second is a difficulty function and a set of difficulty thresholds associated to each rule. Rules are considered for rewriting only when their threshold is higher that the value returned by the difficulty function applied to the partially generated expression. The function may take into account different factors, such as the length of the generated expression and the student's level. According to Koffman and Perry, "this makes the probabilities context sensitive and keeps the problems from getting out of hand" (Koffman and Perry 1976).

Koffman and Blount (1975) describe an additional problem generation mechanism for MALT (MAchine Language Tutor), a system that teaches machine-language programming. All programming problems consists of the following sub-problems: input of information; processing of core-resident information; and program output. A set of alternatives is provided for each sub-problem, and all of them are decomposed into a sequence of logical tasks. These may be accomplished in one or more ways by primitive tasks, or consist of a sequence of other tasks. All programs are constructed using a set of twenty-six primitive tasks that the system knows how to solve (e.g., reading or printing an ASCII character, or transferring data into and out of memory). Therefore "the logic sequence which the system will use to code the problem is pretty well determined by its implied structure. The only freedom that exists is in the selection of the code to implement each primitive task." This context presents formidable requirements for a coaching procedure. Taking the partially designed problem of a student and determining whether it accomplishes what is intended is an example of ill-structured task. For this reason, MALT incorporated only a canned set of flowcharts for each primitive task, and showed them to the student upon request.

Problem generation can be viewed as the selection of a path through a tree of depth three. The problem generator has seven alternatives for input, thirteen for processing, and ten for output. Each problem is generated selecting an input sub-problem (depth 1), a compatible-processing sub-problem (depth 2), and a compatible output sub-problem (depth 3). The probability of a particular sub-problem being selected depends on the student model. Therefore, this generating device can easily be assimilated to a probabilistic grammar. This time, parameterized problem statements are generated. The parameters in the statement (e.g., specific memory registers to be used) are generated randomly. A sample input problem statement generated by MALT is "Your problem is to write a program that will: Read in *10* (octal), *four*-digit numbers and store their value starting in register *205*." Randomly generated parameters are in italics.

Probabilistic grammars continue to be an important alternative in problem generation, and some of the more recent systems described below use similar mechanisms. However, Koffman and Perry (1976) highlighted some of the limitations they encountered with this approach, namely, that too much information needed to be specified in the grammar itself in order to generate broad but meaningful classes of problems.

3.2   ILESA

ILESA (http://alcor.lcc.uma.es/~jmlopez) is a web-based intelligent learning environment, where learners of Linear Programming can practice their problem solving skills while being coached by the system. From a pedagogical point of view, ILESA is based in the theory of coached problem solving, described by VanLehn (1996) and Collins *et al.* (1989).

The goal of Linear Programming problems is to find the optimum of a linear function subject to a set of linear constraints, i.e.:

Optimize $c_1x_1 + ... + c_nx_n$,
Subject to $a_{11}x_1 + ... + a_{1n}x_n \sim b_1$,

$$\vdots$$

$a_{m1}x_1 + ... + a_{mn}x_n \sim b_m$,

where $\sim$ denotes either $\geq$, $\leq$ or $=$.

The most commonly used method to solve these problems is the Simplex algorithm. It is an iterative procedure that finds the solution in a finite number of steps. Using ILESA, students can solve linear programming problems with the Simplex algorithm. In fact, ILESA can be used in two different ways: a) as a problem solver; and b) to solve a problem while being coached by the system. In the latter case students can choose between solving a problem entered by themselves or a problem posed by the system. When the second option is selected, the system automatically generates a problem at the right level of difficulty, based on the current estimation of the student's knowledge level. Figure 3 shows a snapshot of ILESA's interface, captured while a student was solving a problem.

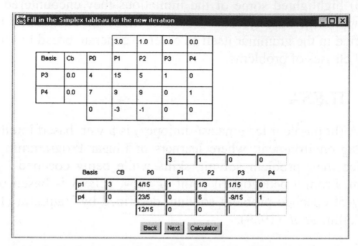

Figure 3. Window for an iteration (partially filled-in by the student).

Problems are generated according to the information contained in the student model. A detailed description of this model can be found in a paper by López *et al.* (1998). The generation of problems in this domain may seem easy at first sight. A simple scheme is the generation of random coefficients for the objective function and the linear constraints. However, the real difficulty lies in generating problems *at the right level of difficulty*. Moreover, it is not of pedagogical value to pose problems that involve excessive computations. Both requirements are taken into account in ILESA's generation mechanism.

First of all, problems have been grouped into seven levels of increasing difficulty:

- *Level 1.* In this level the system poses problems to the student with the following characteristics:

$$\text{Optimize} \quad c_1x_1 + c_2x_2 + \ldots + c_nx_n \,,$$
$$\text{Subject to} \quad a_{11}x_1 + a_{12}x_2 + \ldots + a_{1n}x_n \leq b_1 \,,$$
$$\vdots$$
$$a_{m1}x_1 + a_{m2}x_2 + \ldots + a_{mn}x_n \leq b_m \,,$$
$$x_1, x_2, \ldots, x_n \geq 0,$$

where all b_i are non-negative, which is the simplest structure of a linear programming problem. We will call these types of problems LP_0 problems, and the general problem will be called an LP problem. In this first stage we will pose only maximization LP_0 problems.

- *Level 2.* In this step the student is posed LP_0 problems that have alternative opti*mal solutions.*
- *Level 3. Unbounded* LP_0 problems are added.
- *Level 4.* In this step *minimization* LP_0 problems can also be posed.
- *Level 5. Unfeasible* problems (non-negativity of b_i's is no longer required) are added.
- *Level 6.* Any problem with non-negativity constraints for all the variables can be posed.
- *Level 7.* In this level any LP problem can be posed.

This decomposition of the domain constitutes a *learning strategy*, and was proposed by one of the authors of this paper who lectures on Operations Research. However, other strategies could be used: levels 2 and 3 could be interchanged between them or posed before level 4, as proposed by Winston (1994).

In order to solve these problems, a student needs certain skills. The relationships between skills and problems is described in Figure 4, where round nodes represent abilities and square nodes represent abilities that can be identified with the seven levels of problems.

The number of variables and constraints in the problem are limited to 3 each (i.e., 3×3 is the maximum problem size) in order to avoid problems which are too long and involve too many calculations. However, even in these restricted size problems, the behavior of a set of constraints is not trivial. Specially devised heuristics are used to control both the problem's solution and the difficulty of the computations involved. These heuristics ensure that the problem generator is *correct* but not *complete*, i.e., all the problems generated have the desired type of solution, but not only those problems adapt to the requirements.

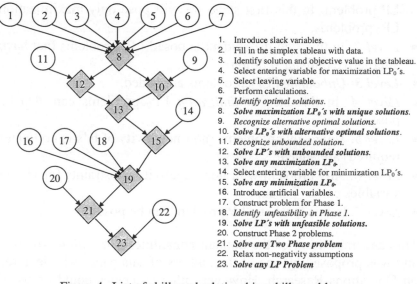

1. Introduce slack variables.
2. Fill in the simplex tableau with data.
3. Identify solution and objective value in the tableau.
4. Select entering variable for maximization LP_0's.
5. Select leaving variable.
6. Perform calculations.
7. *Identify optimal solutions.*
8. *Solve maximization LP_0's with unique solutions.*
9. *Recognize alternative optimal solutions.*
10. *Solve LP_0's with alternative optimal solutions.*
11. *Recognize unbounded solution.*
12. *Solve LP's with unbounded solutions.*
13. *Solve any maximization LP_0.*
14. Select entering variable for minimization LP_0's.
15. *Solve any minimization LP_0.*
16. Introduce artificial variables.
17. Construct problem for Phase 1.
18. *Identify unfeasibility in Phase 1.*
19. *Solve LP's with unfeasible solutions.*
20. Construct Phase 2 problems.
21. *Solve any Two Phase problem*
22. Relax non-negativity assumptions
23. *Solve any LP Problem*

Figure 4. List of skills and relationships skills-problems.

In Figure 4, we can see that the difficulty of the problem is strongly correlated to the type of solution. The system must be able to generate problems which have: (a) a unique solution; (b) alternative optimal solutions; (c) an unbounded solution; and (d) no solution (i.e. non-feasible problems). For illustration purposes, we will refer to size 2×2 problems (2 variables and 2 constraints). Similar techniques have been used for other problem sizes.

- *Generation of problems with unique solution.* The goal is to generate a problem with two variables and two constraints that has a unique solution. This type of problem is illustrated in Figure 5.

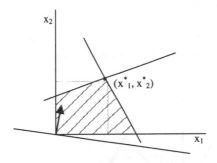

Figure 5. Problem with a unique solution.

Apparently, it is enough to generate values for the coefficients of the constraints such that there is an intersection point with non-negative components between them, and an objective function which is not parallel to any of the constraints. However, in order to guarantee simplicity in the calculations, the following algorithm is used:

Algorithm for generating $2{\times}2$ LP_0 problems

---

1. *Generate four values y_1, y_2, a and b, which are positive rational numbers (with denominators 2,3, or 4) or positive integer numbers. The solution of the problem will be (y_1, y_2), and a and b will be the intersection points with OX and OY, respectively.*
2. *Compute the equation of the straight lines between $(a, 0)$ and (y_1, y_2) and (y_1, y_2) and $(0, b)$. Let these equations be $a_{11}x_1+a_{12}x_2=b_1$ and $a_{21}x_1+a_{22}x_2=b_2$, respectively. Then the constraints for the problems are $\{a_{11}x_1+a_{12}x_2 \le b_1$ and $a_{21}x_1+a_{22}x_2 \le b_2\}$, together with the non-negativity constraints $x_1,x_2 \ge 0$.*
3. *Generate a vector (c_1, c_2) of positive integer values that is not proportional to any of the vectors (a_{11}, a_{12}) and (a_{21}, a_{22}). The goal function for the problem is $f(x_1,x_2) = c_1x_1+c_2x_2$.*

This procedure ensures that the coordinates of the vertexes of the feasible region are either rational numbers with denominators 2,3,4 or integer numbers. Since the Simplex algorithm searches for the optimal solution exploring these vertexes, we can expect that the computations involved are not too difficult.

- *Generation of problems with alternative optimal solutions.* The goal now is to generate a problem of the type represented in Figure 6.

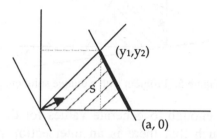

Figure 6. Problem with alternative optimal solutions (segment).

The procedure to generate these types of problems is identical to the procedure described for generation of LP_0 problems, except for step 3. Now the goal is to have an objective function that is parallel to one of the constraints. Step 3 is now as follows:

3. *Generate a vector (c_1, c_2) that is proportional either to the vectors (a_{11}, a_{12}) or to the vector (a_{21}, a_{22}). The goal function for the problem is $f(x_1,x_2) = c_1x_1+c_2x_2$.*

- *Generation of problems with unbounded solution.* Now the goal is to generate problems in which the optimum of the goal function cannot be reached, as shown in Figure 7.

The resulting procedure is as follows:

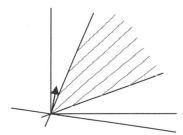

Figure 7. Problem with an unbounded solution.

Algorithm for generating 2×2 unbounded problems
1. *Generate four values a, b, c and d, which are positive integers and satisfy c<a and b<d.*
2. *Compute the equation of the straight lines between (a, b) and (0,0) and (c,d) and (0, 0). Let these equations be $a_{11}x_1+a_{12}x_2=0$ and $a_{21}x_1+a_{22}x_2=0$, respectively. Then the constraints for the problems are $\{a_{11}x_1+a_{12}x_2 \geq 0$ and $a_{21}x_1+a_{22}x_2 \leq 0\}$, together with the non-negativity constraints $x_1,x_2 \geq 0$.*
3. *Generate a vector of positive integer values (c_1, c_2). The goal function for the problem is $f(x_1,x_2) = c_1x_1+c_2x_2$.*

- *Generation of non-feasible problems.* In this case, the feasible region of the problem should be empty. The simplest way for size 2×2 problems is to generate a constraint $a_{11}x_1+a_{12}x_2 \leq b_1$ and a number k, and then add the constraint $k(a_{11}x_1+a_{12}x_2) \geq kb_1$. In these problems the goal function is not important. Therefore, random values can be assigned to the costs.

As already pointed out, the size limit (2×2) has been used only for illustration purposes, but combining the different problem sizes and types, ILESA is able to generate around 40 different problems with similar techniques.

3.3   ICDC

ICDC (http://www.geocities.com/Athens/Agora/6948/derivadas/index .html) is a web-based intelligent learning environment where students can practice their problem-solving abilities in the domain of differential calculus. In Figure 8 we can see part of a possible learning strategy:

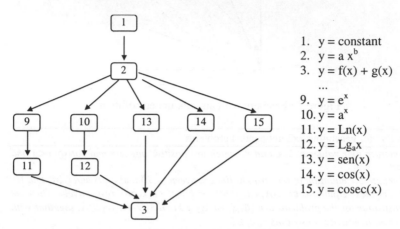

1. $y = $ constant
2. $y = a\,x^b$
3. $y = f(x) + g(x)$
   ...
9. $y = e^x$
10. $y = a^x$
11. $y = Ln(x)$
12. $y = Lg_a x$
13. $y = sen(x)$
14. $y = cos(x)$
15. $y = cosec(x)$

Figure 8. Section of a graph describing a possible learning strategy.

ICDC was designed for students taking their first course of differentiation. In order to improve student motivation, the system proposes a trip through the solar system, beginning at the Sun. Each time the estimation of the student's knowledge changes, the student will be taken to a new planet. Problems are posed as multiple choice items, with one correct solution and several incorrect ones that are also automatically generated by the system. In Figure 9 we can see a snapshot of the student's interface.

When the student selects the wrong answer, a feedback message explains to him/her which rules he/she needs to apply in order to get the correct solution.

The problem generation procedure in ICDC is quite simple. The system has a library of basic functions (polynomial, trigonometric, logarithmic, exponential, and so on) and a library of basic operators (sum, difference, multiplication, division, and composition). Functions are chosen randomly from the library of basic functions and combined by using operators randomly chosen from the corresponding library. In order to avoid excessive complexity, a maximum size limit has been set to problems involving four functions and four operators. Mechanisms that avoid the generation of trivial problems such as $[\cos^2(x) + \sin^2(x)]\text{Ln}(x)$ have also been included.

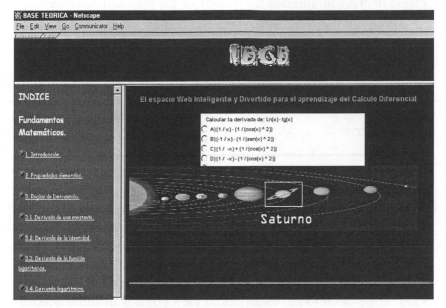

Figure 9. Snapshot of ICDC interface.

The different options for each item are also automatically generated. The procedure is very simple. One of the options is the correct solution, which is computed internally. To generate the incorrect options, we use a library of common misconceptions that was proposed by a mathematics teacher. As an example, Table 1 shows the correct solution and common misconceptions for the functions involved in the problem presented in Figure 9.

Incorrect answers are generated combining common misconceptions with the appropriate operator. Sample options generated in this fashion are presented in Figure 9. This wrong-answer generation procedure is based on VanLehn's repair theory (Brown and VanLehn 1980). It is important to stress that this work is in a preliminary stage. An initial prototype has been implemented and both the prototype and the problem generator are currently being evaluated. The preliminary results are encouraging, but further work is needed in order to improve the quality of the problem generator.

Table 1. Sample entries in the library of misconceptions.

Function	Correct solution	Common misconceptions
$Ln(x)$	$1/x$	$\dfrac{-1/x}{Ln(x)}$
$tg(x)$	$1/\cos^2(x)$	$-1/\cos^2(x)$ $-1/\sin^2(x)$ $1/\sin^2(x)$

3.4   Multibook

Multibook (Fisher and Steinmetz 2000) is an adaptive hypermedia system in the technical domain of multimedia systems. The content of Multibook is a printed book called: "Multimedia: Computing, Communications and Applications" (Steinmetz and Nahrstedt 1999). The goal is to have individual views of this material according to the needs and preferences of the users. These views are created using the sequencing approach (Seeberg *et al.* 1999), which is based on a knowledge base. The knowledge base uses two spaces: the ConceptSpace and the MediaBrickSpace.

The ConceptSpace contains an ontology of keywords (concepts) that allows the outline of a lesson or its table of contents to be produced. This space uses a set of semantic relations of types such as superconcept, application, or instance. Each particular navigation on the ConceptSpace generates a sequencing of the lessons according to a specific learning strategy. The MediaBrickSpace has the necessary elements (contents) for filling the outline once the table has been created. This space uses a second set of relations – e.g., "illustrates", "is-an-example-of", "is-the-opposite-of", or "is-analogous-to" – taken from the natural language processing area and called rhetorical-didactic relations.

In order to address the automatic creation of exercises, Multibook automatically derives multi-choice-style exercises from the ontology ConceptSpace. These exercises are very simple and only *Part-of* and *Application-of* questions can be generated. For example: "Which are the parts of <concept>. Please select the correct answer," or "What are the applications of <concept>. Please select the correct answer." Multibook uses the following algorithm to create the exercises:

1. Generate the text of the question.
2. Construct a list of correct answers using the proper ontology relation (*Part-of* questions use the "uses" relation and *Application-of* questions use the "application" relation).
3. Construct a list of wrong answers.
4. Merge both lists in a random way.
5. Check the student answer, and if it is wrong the system recommends the student to repeat the lesson being learned.

The construction of a proper list of wrong answers is an important issue. In order to avoid random and nonsense answers it is important to generate wrong answers that are in close relationship with the correct answers. In order to achieve this, it is necessary to reduce the ontology to a taxonomy where concepts, which are semantically close to the correct answer, are located.

3.5   WEAR

WEAR (**WE**b-based authoring tool for **A**lgebra **R**elated domains) (Virvou and Moundridou 2000a, 2000b) is a web-based authoring tool for intelligent tutoring systems. Its main objective is to be useful to instructors and students in different domains that use algebraic equations (e.g., economic, physics, or chemistry). WEAR provides assistance in the construction of exercises and mechanisms for student error diagnosis that monitors them, and provides appropriate feedback. In this sense WEAR is a generative and adaptive web-based system; generative, since it provides the ability of problem construction, and adaptive (Brusilovsky and Cooper 1999), since the tool performs an intelligent analysis of student solutions and offers an interactive support to problem solving. In addition, the tool allows the instructor to control the sequence in which problems are introduced to the students by means of a "level of difficulty" that they can associate to each problem.

On the other hand, the instructors can also take advantage from other problems that have been previously constructed with WEAR. These problems are stored in the system problem database, and the instructors can retrieve them for their usage. However, this approach has some disadvantages, as these problems may: (i) be related to several domains; (ii) be assigned to different levels of difficulty; and (iii) be repeated in different domains. WEAR solves these problems providing an instructor modeling component (Virvou and Moundridou 2001) which allows the system to adapt itself to the preferences and needs of each individual instructor.

The initial input to the tool is a description of a particular algebra-related domain given by the instructor. This domain description is made in terms of formulae, variables, and units of measure and their relationships. In Table 2 we show an example of an instructor's input from the economic domain. The instructor does not need to give all the information (variable, formulae, and so on) in a single interaction, since the tool saves the information related to the domain every time that the instructor interacts with the system.

Figure 10 shows the system's architecture. The "Domain and Problem Generator or Selector" allows the instructor to develop new problems and to retrieve others previously stored in the "Domain

Description and Problems." This component stores the problems and the domain knowledge, and, in addition, provides exercises to the "Problem Selector" and communicates their level of difficulty to "The Instructor Model."

Table 2. Example of instructor output.

Variables	Formulae
Income (Y)	Y=C+I
Consumption (C)	C=a+b*Y
Investment (I)	I=i-c*r
Autonomous consumption (a)	
Marginal propensity to consume (b)	
Autonomous investment expenditure (i)	
Interest rate (r)	
Sensitivity of investment in interest rates (c)	

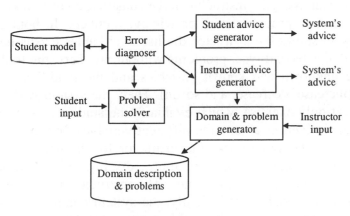

Figure 10. WEAR Architecture.

The system components related to the student are the following: (1) "The Problem Solver", that is a module that interacts with the student while he/she is solving an exercise; (2) "The Error Diagnoser", that performs an individualized error diagnosis of the student; and (3) "The Student Model", that generates, according to the above information, progress reports and allows the instructor to modify the difficulty levels of the problems. The system's implementation uses a client-server architecture. The tool is on a WWW server, and the students and instructors may use it by means of any WWW browser.

The system provides a procedure that guides the instructor step by step in problem construction. First, the instructor must select the domain parameters that are going to be used in the construction of the new problem. After that, he/she has to specify which of these parameters are given and which are asked. Then, the tool generates the problem statement and checks its correctness and consistency avoiding data redundancies. Finally, the system displays the full text of the problem and its solution, asking the instructor for an adequate level of difficulty.

The tool can assist the instructor in the construction of two kinds of problems, i.e., problems with or without numbers. In both cases, the system shows the instructor the list of variables he/she has entered. In the second type, problems without numbers, the tool asks for the unknown and known variables and the modifications on these (increase, decrease, and so on). Then, the system will generate a text-only exercise, which evaluates the student's skill to discover the influences among the different variables. In the first kind of problem, the system asks the instructor for the unknown variables and, according to the equations, displays all the variables "depending" on the unknown ones. The instructor must enter values for these variables and, finally, the system communicates any inconsistencies producing the problem statement. Of course, the instructor may always change the statement in order to make it better.

3.6   LispGen

Intelligent tutors for Lisp programming are among the best known achievements in the field (Anderson *et al.* 1993, Brusilovsky *et al.* 1996). LispGen (formerly LispTutor2) is a less ambitious system

whose aim is to guide the student in the first steps in learning Lisp
(Fernández *et al.* 2000). Currently, exercises concerning the
evaluation of Lisp expressions are present in the system; in later
stages we hope to implement a more complete set of exercises. This
can be found at http://alcor.lcc.uma.es/lisptutor2/. A screen dump
of LispGen is shown in Figure 11.

Figure 11. A screen dump in LispGen.

The general procedure used in LispGen is as follows:

1. A suitable problem schema is selected according to the learning
   strategy and the student model.
2. A problem of this type is generated and presented to the student.
3. The student solves the problem.
4. The solution is compared to the one given by the system. According to the result, the student's model is modified and the
   next type of problem is selected, that is, we return to step 1.

Let us describe how the system works (from the student's point of view). When the student starts the session, the system asks for her/his personal data (name, surname, and identification number). In this way, the system can create and afterwards handle the student model. Then, the system poses a problem (whose type is determined according to the information contained in the student model). The student can solve it, ask for a clue or give up. Every time he/she asks for a clue the system shows one evaluation rule that has to be used in the resolution of the problem. When all the available clues have been presented, the student is informed that there are no more clues available. After asking for each clue the student has the opportunity to solve the problem or to give up. When the student gives up a problem (either after asking for a clue or not) the tutorial shows the solution and proposes a new problem. Students are not penalized when they ask for a clue or fail to solve a question. Problems will be posed till the pupil wants to finish the session or completes the course.

Next, we will describe the problem generator. When generating a Lisp expression E for tutorial purposes, several issues must be taken into account:

- the evaluation of E will require the application of the evaluation rule which is the current instructional focus.
- the evaluation of E will not require the application of evaluation rules which have not been taught.
- the level of complexity (nesting) of E will be bounded by some "suitable" value.
- some non-evaluable expressions must be generated, since negative examples are at least as useful as positive ones.

On the other hand, the system must be flexible enough to allow modifications and customizations from different instructors or for different classes.

To fulfill these requirements, a generator of Lisp expressions has been implemented based upon the concept of *attribute constrained probabilistic context-free grammar* (see Section 2.3). The main attribute is the type of a grammar symbol. Three types have been considered: (Lisp) *symbol*, *number*, and *list*. In fact, the list type is the union of infinite disjoint types given by the length and the type of the elements. These features can be described in our generator. For example, the constraint $(L > 3 ((1\ S)))$ expresses that the (grammar) symbol must finally become a list (L) of four or more elements (> 3) whose first element is a (Lisp) symbol $(((1\ S)))$.

For example, let us consider the derivation of the CDR form (CDR (CDR '(KK))) (Table 3). In the column **string** we show the (non)terminal string that the grammar is generating, beginning from the initial symbol expr. In the column **production#**, the number of the applied production is given. Notice that a special procedure is needed in the last step in order to generate the terminal KK. At each step, several productions have been considered, with probabilities proportional to their weights. For instance, expr-cdr could yield with equal probability either expr-cdr-list (constraint $(L > 0)$) or expr-cdr-sym (constraint $(L = 0)$). In this case, the former derivation has been followed.

Table 3. A derivation in LispGen.

String	Constraints	Production #
expr $\Rightarrow$		
expr-cdr $\Rightarrow$	(L)	86
(CDR expr-cdr-lista) $\Rightarrow$	(L > 0)	88
(CDR (CDR expr)) $\Rightarrow$	(L > 0)	90
(CDR (CDR expr-quote)) $\Rightarrow$	(L)	8
(CDR (CDR (QUOTE expr-in-quote))) $\Rightarrow$	(L)	9
(CDR (CDR (QUOTE (atom-q)))) $\Rightarrow$	(S)	10
(CDR (CDR (QUOTE (atom)))) $\Rightarrow$	(S)	13
(CDR (CDR (QUOTE (symbol)))) $\Rightarrow$	(S)	21
(CDR (CDR (QUOTE (KK))))		terminal generation

In the column constraints, we show the type constraints imposed on non-terminal symbols occurring in the string. Additional constraints (such as nesting level and others) are not shown in Table 3.

Currently 323 productions have been coded to implement the generation of 35 items, ranging from numbers to DO forms. Elementary list functions, conditional and iterative constructs such as COND, IF, MAPCAR or DOTIMES, and functional constructs such as FUNCALL or lambda expressions are covered by the courseware.

3.7   SIETTE

SIETTE (Ríos *et al.* 1999) is a web-based tool for adaptive evaluation based on tests. SIETTE is aimed at two different types of users: teachers (test developers) and students (evaluation subjects). To this end, SIETTE has two different online interfaces: *test editor*, where teachers (with no programming knowledge) can define their customized tests, and *virtual classroom*, where students can take the tests previously defined. Tests in SIETTE are hierarchically structured as shown in Figure 12.

In SIETTE, items are selected automatically by the system according to the current estimation of the student's knowledge. In this way, each student that takes a SIETTE test is presented with a different set of items, i.e., SIETTE tests are *adaptive*. The underlying psychometric theories in the SIETTE systems are Computer Adaptive Testing (Wainer 1990) and Item Response Theory (Rudner 1998, Van der Linden and Hambleton 1997).

Many different types of items can be included in a SIETTE test. Some of them can be automatically generated. Next, we will review all the different type of items, and then we will describe how automatic generation is achieved in some types.

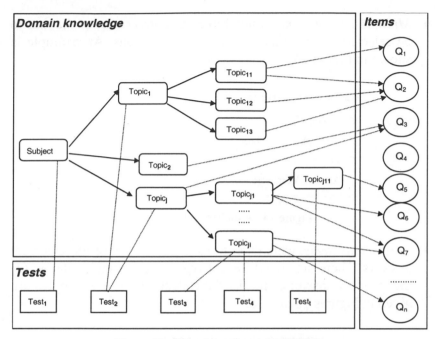

Figure 12. Structure of tests in SIETTE.

SIETTE items can be classified into two different groups: (a) *items that are predefined* in the system (some of them are controlled by Java applets) and therefore no programming knowledge is needed to include them; and (b) *items that are controlled by Java applets* implemented by the test developer. The items in the first group are:

- *Dichotomous items* (true/false questions). An example is shown in Figure 13.

Chistopher Columbus discovered America in 1492

○ True

○ False

Figure 13. A dichotomous item.

- *Multiple-choice items*, which have one correct answer that has to be selected by the student from several options. An example is shown in Figure 14.

> Who discovered America in 1492?
>
> ○ Abraham Lincoln
> ○ Chistopher Columbus
> ○ James Cook
> ○ Americo Vespuccio

Figure 14. A multiple-choice item.

- *Polytomous items*, which are items that have two or more correct answers. There are two different types of polytomous items: (a) independent answers; and (b) dependent answers. Examples are given in Figures 15 and 16.

> Which are members of the European Comunity?
>
> ☐ France   ☐ Italy   ☐ Germany
> ☐ Japan   ☐ Russia   ☐ Switzerland
> ☐ Poland   ☐ Norway   ☐ Belgium
> ☐ Holland   ☐ Finland   ☐ Spain

Figure 15. A multiple-choice item with independent answer.

> Which is the combination of the chemical components of water?
>
> ☐ Carbon   ☐ Oxygen
> ☐ Potassium   ☐ Sodium
> ☐ Lithium   ☐ Calcium
> ☐ Hydrogen   ☐ Fluoride

Figure 16. A multiple-choice item with a dependent answer.

- *Fill-blanks items*, in which the student needs to fill some blanks in a text. The correctness of the answer is checked by means of regular expressions (in the case that the blank needs to be filled with text) or formulas (in the case that the answer is a number). Examples are shown in Figures 17 and 18.

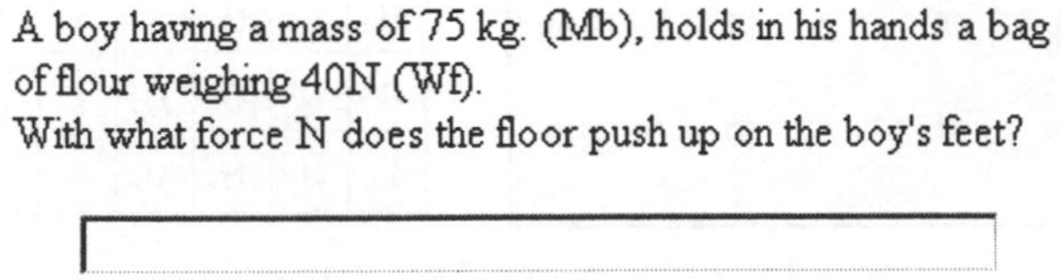

A boy having a mass of 75 kg. (Mb), holds in his hands a bag of flour weighing 40N (Wf).
With what force N does the floor push up on the boy's feet?

Figure 17. A fill-blank item (numeric).

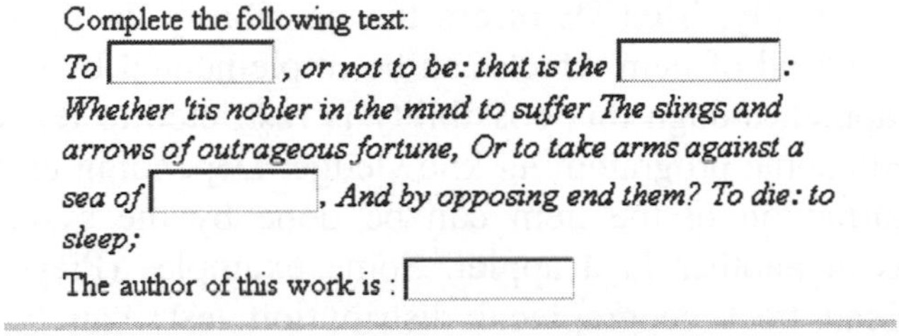

Complete the following text:
To [   ] , *or not to be: that is the* [   ]:
Whether 'tis nobler in the mind to suffer The slings and arrows of outrageous fortune, Or to take arms against a sea of [   ], *And by opposing end them? To die: to sleep;*
The author of this work is : [   ]

Figure 18. A fill-blank item (text).

- *Pastime-like items*. In order to improve the presentation of items, SIETTE offers some other options, in the style of pastimes. These items include (among others): *connection items* in which the student must form pairs by connecting elements in two different columns, *word search items*, which consist of locating the missing word in a matrix of letters. Examples are shown in Figure 19.

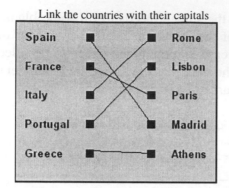

Figure 19. Examples of pastime-like items.

- *Items controlled by Java applets implemented by the test designer.* Finally, SIETTE offers the possibility to include virtually any kind of item which can be implemented by means of a Java applet, though this possibility is restricted to test developers with some programming knowledge. Depending on the case, the correction of the item can be done by the system or by means of another Java applet. Some examples (Piagetian test, European trees geographical distribution test) can be seen at http://www.lcc.uma.es/siette.

Under certain particular conditions that vary according to item type, most of the items we have just described can automatically be generated by the system. To this end, there are several possibilities:

- *Procedures based on random mechanisms.* For multiple choice, polytomous, and connection, item generation is as easy as selecting the correct combination of answers and merging it with a randomly selected set of wrong answers. In this way, item repetition and all its disadvantages can be avoided.
- *Use of item templates*, which are instantiated in real time generating a new item. These templates can be implemented by using HTML or extensions, such as PERL, PHP, JSP, and so on. An example of a template in PHP is shown in Figure 20.

Which is the value of x at the end of this program?


```
<?
  srand(date("U"));
  $randMax=getRandMax();
  $rand=Rand();
  $x =intval(doubleval($rand)*doubleval(10)/doubleval($randMax));
  echo "<CODE><PRE>";
  echo "  x=$x;<BR>";
  echo "  x++;";
  echo "</PRE></CODE>";
>
```

``` $sol = $x+$x; echo $sol; >```	``` $sol = $x+1; echo $sol; >```	``` $sol = $x-1; echo $sol; >```	``` $sol = $x; echo $sol; >```

Figure 20. An example of an item template in PHP.

This template is then preprocessed by the system and generates the item shown in Figure 21.

Which is the value of x at the end of this program?

```
x = 6;
x++;
```

☐ 12   ☐ 7   ☐ 5   ☐ 6

Figure 21. Item generated by the template in Figure 20.

- *Generation of items according to domain hierarchy.* In hierarchically structured domains, the ontology/taxonomy can be taken into account when generating test items. Let us consider the following example: Forestry European trees can be classified according to the taxonomy shown in Figure 22.

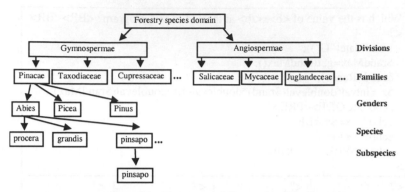

Figure 22. Taxonomy for tree classification.

Items that are commonly used in tests about tree recognition include: (a) identifying which is the tree shown in a photograph; and (b) identifying which of the photographs shown corresponds to a given tree. The first type is very easy to generate as generation in this case is reduced to randomly selecting a photograph from the database. For generating an item of the second type, the correct photograph should be merged with some others, in such a way that the resulting item is challenging for the students. To this end, the taxonomy can be taken into account as follows: depending on the desired difficulty, the incorrect photographs can be randomly chosen within the same species, genders, families or divisions. Another possibility is that if, for example, the correct photograph corresponds to the tree leaf, the incorrect photographs should be chosen within trees that have the same type of leaf. Examples of questions generated according to these schemas are shown in Figure 23.

However, not all of the options described are fully implemented in the current version of the SIETTE system. The next version of SIETTE is expected to be available at the beginning of year 2002.

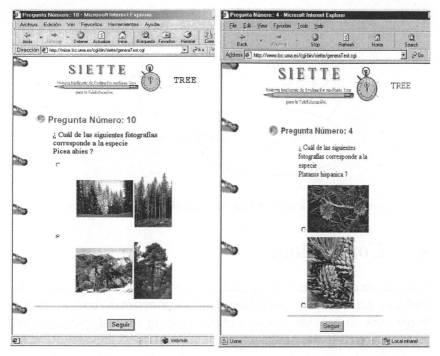

Figure 23. Example of items in a SIETTE test for tree recognition.

3.8   Summary

In this section several systems that implement different problem generating mechanisms have been presented. Such systems can be classified according to the general framework described in Section 2.3, in which problem generation mechanisms were divided into three different groups: simple, those based on grammars, and ad hoc techniques. In Figure 24 we can see that some of the systems described use a combination of two mechanisms: ILESA uses random generation of the coefficients combined with ad hoc techniques to control problem solution and difficulty, and the simple generating mechanism in ICDC could also be described by a grammar.

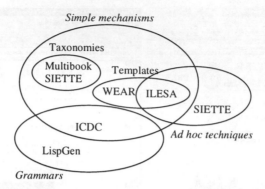

Figure 24. Classification of systems according to generating devices.

4   Conclusions

This chapter presents both a global view of the state of the art in problem generation in Web-based tutoring systems, and a general framework to provide a better understanding of past, present, and future research in the field.

First of all, Artificial Intelligence is an empirical science (Simon 1995). In the previous sections a representative set of tutoring systems with problem generation capabilities have been described in detail. The credibility and validity of the techniques described come to a great extent from the success of the systems implementing them. The availability of these systems on the Web should facilitate their dissemination and empirical testing by independent researchers. In short, these systems display the availability of current techniques and their practical applicability in different domains.

On the other hand, the need for a general framework on which to base future research in the area is clear to the authors. Early CAI researchers turned to the AI techniques of the day to build the first generative systems. The time has come to turn to current developments in Artificial Intelligence and Knowledge Engineering to build the next generation of tutors and learning environments. Our discussion began with statements about the different kinds of problems and problem statements, and the different kinds of generating devices. General problem generation based on real-world interactions between tutor and student is clearly an ill-structured task. However, the generation of meaningful instances of particular classes of problems, and at the right level of difficulty, can be formalized as a well-structured knowledge-intensive synthetic task.

However, this venture has obviously some difficulties. In particular, the use of formal grammars presents well-known problems. Generating useful problem statements involves both syntax and semantics. While defining a grammar may be a difficult task in itself, the controlled generation of particular sentences using the grammar becomes harder with the size of the grammar. Designing a good grammar-based problem generator is simply a knowledge engineering task, not an impossible one. Results are promising, but there is still a long way to go.

References

Anderson, J.R., Conrad, F.G., and Corbett, A.T. (1993), "The Lisp tutor and skill acquisition," in Anderson, J.R. (ed.), *Rules of the Mind*, Hillsdale, N: Lawrence Erlbaum Associates, pp. 143-164.

Brown, J.S. and VanLehn K. (1980), "Repair theory: a generative theory of bugs in procedural skills," *Cognitive Science*, vol. 4, pp. 379-426.

Brusilovsky, P. and Cooper, D.W. (1999), "ADAPTS: adaptive hypermedia for a Web-based performance support system," *Proceedings of the 2th Workshop on Adaptive Systems and User Modeling on the World Wide Web*," edited as Eindhoven University of Technology Computing Science Report TUE 99-07, pp. 41-47.

Brusilovsky, P., Schwarz, E., and Weber, G. (1996), "ELM-ART: an intelligent tutoring system on the World Wide Web," *Vol. LNCS 1086. Intelligent Tutoring Systems*, Springer Verlag.

Chandrasekaran, B., Josephson, J.R., and Benjamins, R. (1998), "The ontology of tasks and methods," *Proceedings of the 11th Knowledge Acquisition Modeling and Management Workshop KAW'98*.

Chomsky, N. (1959), "On certain formal properties of grammars," *Information and Control*, pp. 137-167.

Collins, A., Brown, J.S., and Newman, S.E. (1989), "Cognitive apprenticeship: teaching the crafts of reading, writing, and mathematics," in Resnick, L.B. (ed.), *Knowing, Learning, and Instruction: Essays in Honor of Robert Glaser*, Hillsdale, NJ: Lawrence Erlbaum Associates, pp. 453-494.

Fernández, I., Millán, E., and Pérez-de-la-Cruz, J.L. (2000), "Adaptation and generation in a Web-based Lisp tutor," *Vol. LNCS 1892. Adaptive Hypermedia and Adaptive Web-Based Systems*, Berlin: Springer Verlag, pp. 297-300.

Fisher, S. and Steinmetz, R. (2000), "Automatic creation of exercises in adaptive hypermedia learning systems," *Proceedings of Eleventh ACM Conference on Hypertext and Hypermedia (Hypertext 2000)*, ACM Press, pp. 49-55.

Hsieh, P.Y., Halff, H.M., and Redfield, C.L. (1999), "Four easy pieces: development systems for knowledge-based generative instruction," *International Journal of Artificial Intelligence in Education*, vol. 10, pp. 1-45.

Knuth, D.E. (1997), *The Art of Computer Programming*, Reading, Massachusetts: Addison-Wesley.

Koffman, E.B. (1972), "Individualizing instruction in a generative CAI tutor," *Communications of the ACM*, vol. 15, no. 6, pp. 472-473.

Koffman, E.B. and Blount, S.E. (1975), "Artificial intelligence and automatic programming in CAI," *Artificial Intelligence*, vol. 6, pp. 215-234.

Koffman, E.B. and Perry, J.M. (1976), "A model for generative CAI and concept selection," *International Journal of Man-Machine Studies*, vol. 8, pp. 397-410.

López, J.M., Millán, E., Pérez J.L., and Triguero F. (1998), "ILESA: a web-based intelligent learning environment for the simplex algorithm," *Proceedings of the 3rd International Conference on Computer Aided Learning and Instruction in Science and Engineering CALISCE'98*.

Maurer, H., Stone, M.G., Gillard, P., and Stubenrauch, R. (1991), "Question/answer specification in CAL tutorials (Automatic problem generation does not work)," in Dörfler, W. *et al.* (eds.),, *Schriftenreihe Didaktik der Mathematik*, Hölder-Pichler-Tempsky - B.G. Teubner, vol. 21, pp. 191-197.

Ríos, A., Millán, E., Trella, M., Pérez-de-la-Cruz, J.L., and Conejo, R. (1999), "Internet based evaluation system," *Open Learning Environments: New Computational Technologies to Support Learning, Exploration and Collaboration. Proceedings of the 9th World Conference of Artificial Intelligence and Education AIED'99*, Amsterdam: IOS Press, pp. 387-394.

Rudner, L. (1998), *An On-line, Interactive, Computer Adaptive Testing Mini-Tutorial*, http://ericae.net/scripts/cat/catdemo .

Schreiber, G., Akkermans, H., Anjewierden, A., de Hoog, R., Shadbolt, N.R., and Wielinga, B. (2000), *Knowledge Engineering and Management*, MIT Press.

Seeberg, C., Steinacker, A., Reichenberger, K., Fisher, S., and Steinmetz, R. (1999), "Individual tables of contents in Web-based learning systems," *Proceedings of the 10th ACM Conference on Hypertext and Hypermedia.*

Simon, H.A. (1973), "The structure of ill-structured problems," *Artificial Intelligence*, vol. 4, pp. 181-201.

Simon, H.A. (1995), "Artificial intelligence: an empirical science," *Artificial Intelligence*, vol. 77, no. 1, pp. 95-127.

Steinmetz, R. and Nahrstedt, K. (1999), *Multimedia: Computing, Communications and Applications*, Prentice-Hall.

Suppes, P. (1967), "Some theoretical models for mathematics learning," *Journal of Research and Development in Education*, vol. 1, pp. 5-22.

Uhr, L. (1969), "Teaching machine programs that generate problems as a function of interaction with students," *Proceedings of the 24th National Conference*, pp. 125-134.

Van der Linden, W. and Hambleton, R. (eds.) (1997), *Handbook of Modern Item Response Theory*, New York: Springer Verlag.

VanLehn, K. (1996), "Conceptual and meta-learning during coached problem solving," *Lecture Notes in Computer Science: Vol. 1086. Proceedings of 3rd International Conference ITS'96*, Berlin Heidelberg: Springer Verlag, pp. 29-47.

Virvou, M. and Moundridou, M. (2000a), "Modelling the instructor in a Web-based authoring tool for algebra-related ITSs," *Lecture*

Notes in Computer Science 1839. Proceedings of 3rd International Conference on Intelligent Tutoring Systems ITS2000, Berlin Heidelberg: Springer Verlag, pp. 633-644.

Virvou, M. and Moundridou, M. (2000b), "A Web-based authoring tool for algebra-related intelligent tutoring systems," *Educational Technology and Society*, vol. 3, no. 2, pp. 61-70.

Virvou, M. and Moundridou, M. (2001), "Student and instructor models: two kinds of user model and their interaction in an ITS authoring tool," *8ᵗʰ International Conference UM 2001*, LNAI vol. 2109, pp. 158-167.

Wainer, H. (ed.) (1990), *Computerized Adaptive Testing: a Primer*, Hillsdale, NJ: Lawrence Erlbaum Associates.

Waite, W.M. and Goos, G. (1985), *Compiler Construction*, Berlin: Springer Verlag.

Wexler, J.D. (1970), "Information networks in generative computer-assisted instruction," *Transactions on Man-Machine Systems*, vol. 11, pp. 181-190.

Winston, W. (1994), *Operations Research: Applications and Algorithms*Duxbury Press.

Woods, P. and Hartley, J.R. (1971), "Some learning models for arithmetic tasks and their use in computer-based learning," *British Journal of Educational Psychology*, vol. 41, pp. 35-48.

Chapter 8

The Design of Internet-Based Interactive Learning Models Using Agents and Their Applications

T. Ichimura, M. Nakamura, K.J. Mackin,
K. Yoshida, S. Otsuki and T. Yamashita

In this chapter, we describe a web based training system, where sequencing learning tasks is automatically determined. For a simple problem, the problem solution is defined in the system development stage. However, for an intricate and complex problem, the problem cannot be settled uniquely. In the case of creating an examination, teachers must select problems uniformly from areas covered. For a solution to such problems, we propose a sequencing method by Fuzzy Structural Modeling and Fuzzy Petri Net.

Further, we describe a group learning environment where learners in different locations can have a discussion on a problem solving process. Learners can not only express their individual opinions privately and arrange them, but they can also share structures of each other's individual opinions among them. If one learner does not actively participate, he/she hardly acquires new knowledge. So, the pertinent software agent generates questions in order to prompt him/her to join in the discussion and acquire new knowledge.

1   Introduction

Various research, development, and practice in e-learning have already been performed in institutions of higher education, companies, and other organizations. E-learning has clearly shown the validity and effectiveness with the educational model and the business model. In Japan, the government determined the "e-Japan strategy" and "the e-Japan master plan." Such governmental policy has helped boost the explosive spread and development of e-learning in Japan.

Recently, partially as an effect of the rapid development of Internet technology, the range of research on e-learning has expanded. Some example areas of e-learning research include distributed cooperative study environments, synchronous or asynchronous study environments, the study contents corresponding to its environment, the history management in cooperative study, and knowledge management of students.

In this chapter, we describe a web based training system we have developed, where sequencing learning tasks is automatically determined. For a simple problem, the problem solution is defined in the system development stage. However, for an intricate and complex problem such as a comprehensive examination, the problem cannot be settled uniquely. In the case of creating an examination, teachers must select problems uniformly from areas covered. For a solution to such problems, we propose a sequencing method by FSM (Fuzzy Structural Modeling) and FPN (Fuzzy Petri Net). Furthermore, we developed a web-based training system for the National Examination for Medical Practitioners.

Further, in this chapter we describe a group learning environment where students can have a discussion on a common problem solving process among participants in different locations. Not only can participants express one's opinions privately and rearrange these opinions, but can also share structures of each participant's individual opinions among the group. If a student does not actively take part in the learning process, it is difficult for the student to acquire new knowledge. So, the pertinent software agent generates questions in order to prompt the user to join in the discussion in order to acquire new knowledge.

Section 2 describes an algorithm for the design of courses using Fuzzy Petri Net and describes an e-learning system for the National Examination for Medical Practitioners that we developed. Section 3 describes the method of collaborative learning support using multi-agents, and an Internet-based visual interface for group learning.

2   The Design of Courseware by Fuzzy Petri Net

The process of designing a class can be referred to as a system with a cycle of planning, practice, and evaluation as shown in Figure 1. This figure shows the structuring, the sequencing, and the instructional analysis in its process. We consider that some of the most important phases in the development of CAI (Computer Assisted Instruction) courseware are structuring learning tasks and defining a model of the instructional system. The learning tasks have a complex structure and it is often desirable and sometimes essential to synthesize its hierarchies. The process of arranging elements in a hierarchy is usually dealt with intuitively. In order to deal with such a system systematically, ISM (interpretive structural modeling) (Warfield 1976) is a useful method and the design of courseware by ISM has been proposed by Sato (1989). This method enables us to depict a graphic structure theory from a subordination matrix representing a binary relation among elements based on graph. However, the subordination matrix represented in a fuzzy binary relation rather than a binary relation includes various kinds of information, because it will not be always reasonable to use the binary relation among elements. The FSM (fuzzy structural model-ing) method (Tazaki and Amagasa 1979) proposed by Tazaki is an effective method for structuring hierarchy to depict graphic struc-ture from a subordination matrix representing a fuzzy relation among elements (Yamashita *et al.* 1998, Ichimura *et al.* 1999).

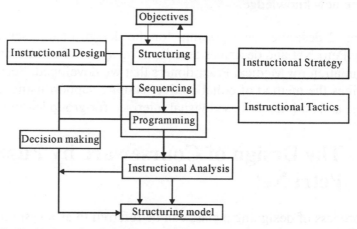

Figure 1. A cycle of planning, practice, and evaluation for instruction.

After we obtain the structural model by the subjects, the next prob-lem is how to implement a sequence of learning tasks for teaching strategies. For a solution of such a problem, Akahori (1991) has proposed a method of Sequencing Learning Tasks. This model pre-sents combinations of concept such as task applicability, funda-mental necessity, and fundamental relativity. The method requires a subordination of tasks and their fundamental elements. By such a specified relation of the tasks, this method makes it possible to de-velop sequences of learning task automatically and simulate opti-mum teaching strategies quantitatively. However, the obtained se-quences have many variation and we cannot determine the optimum one to implement the teaching strategies. When an "OR" relation exists in the original subordination, the method does not represent its relation.

In order to provide a solution for such a problem, we develop an interactive tool for implementing a sequence of learning tasks by Fuzzy Petri Nets (Chen *et al.* 1991, Shiizuka 1992, Paul *et al.* 1996). After obtaining a structural model by FSM, the system shows a graphical model. Then, we add IF-THEN rules as knowledge to the arc representing relations among learning tasks. The system draws the sequence of learning tasks based on the fuzzy structural model and IF-THEN rules. In implementing the teaching strategy by Fuzzy Petri Nets, the process of reasoning is drawn automatically on the graph according to tasks' achievement of students.

2.1   FSM (Fuzzy Structural Modeling) Method

When we study complex systems, develop plans, treat various kinds of human actions, it is often desirable and sometimes essential to synthesize hierarchies. The process of arranging elements in a hierarchy is usually dealt with intuitively. In order to deal with such a system systematically, ISM, DEMATEL, and so forth have been proposed. ISM (Warfield *et al.* 1972) and DEMATEL (Gabus and Fontela 1973) are developed on the basis of graph theory. Especially, ISM is effective for achieving the consenting structure of a problem. In this method, a matrix representing a subordination relation among the elements of system is called a subordination matrix and the elements contain a binary relation. However, it will not always be reasonable to use the binary relation among elements.

Fuzzy Structural Modeling (FSM) (Tazaki and Amagasa 1979), which is a method for structuring hierarchy for complex problems, is an effective method on the basis of fuzzy theory. An important requirement for the structural modeling of complex systems is that the necessary data is acquired and organized into a form, from which a structural model can be developed. A fuzzy reachability matrix is one such form. The main purpose of this method is to describe and illustrate a formal procedure for constructing the graphic representation of the hierarchical arrangement, given the necessary information concerning the relationship of each element to each other element. The procedure permits the automatic development of the graphic structure that portrays the hierarchy. The entries in the matrix take values on the interval [0,1] by virtue of fuzzy relation. According to the matrix, a fuzzy digraph describes a contextual relation among the elements of the system and can be transformed into an interpretive structural model of the system with respect to the relationship.

A significant step in the development of the proposed fuzzy structural modeling consists of the relation of transivity, irreflexivity and asymmetry with respect to the construction of subordination matrix. The relaxation extends the flexibility and applicability for the structural modeling of systems.

2.1.1   Preliminaries of FSM [3]

FSM defines several properties with respect to fuzzy subsets, $S = \{s_1, s_2, ..., s_n\}$, and fuzzy relations between s_i and s_j, with $i, j = 1, 2, ..., n$. A fuzzy binary relation and its complement in a direct product space S and S, S×S are respectively characterized by f_r and $f_{\bar{r}}$ as follows:

$$f_r : S \times S \rightarrow [0,1]$$
$$f_{\bar{r}} : S \times S \rightarrow [0,1] \tag{1}$$

where the relation of f_r and $f_{\bar{r}}$ is given by

$$f_{\bar{r}}(s_i, s_i) = (1 - f_r(s_i, s_i))/(1 + \lambda f_r(s_i, s_i)).$$

Let p be a real number given on the semi-open interval (0,1) and a parameter λ be a real number in $-1 < \lambda < \infty$. According to such a p, some definitions with respect to the fuzzy relations are given as follows.

Definition 1 (fuzzy irreflexive law).

When $f_r(s_i, s_i) < p$ for $\forall(s_i, s_i) \in S \times S$, the relation is called fuzzy irreflexive.

Definition 2 (fuzzy asymmetric law).

When either $f_r(s_i, s_j)$ or $f_r(s_j, s_i)$ for $\forall s_i, s_j \in S(i, j)$ is less than p, the relation is called fuzzy asymmetric.

Definition 3 (fuzzy semi-transitive law).

Let $M = (f_r(s_i, s_j) \; f_r(s_j, s_k)) \geq p$ for $\forall(s_i, s_j), (s_j, s_k) \in S \times S$ $(i \neq j \neq k)$.

When $f_r(s_i, s_k) \geq M$ for $\forall(s_i, s_k)$, the relation is called fuzzy semi-transitive.

Under these definitions, FSM method uses p as a threshold and λ as a fuzzy structuring parameter. In FSM, we should determine an appropriate p and λ.

Next, we construct a fuzzy subordination matrix A, which represents a fuzzy subordination relation among the elements of S on the basis of a certain contextual relation:

$$A = [a_{ij}], \quad i, j = 1, 2, \cdots, n, \tag{2}$$

where A is a square $n \times n$ matrix and the element a_{ij} of A is given by the fuzzy binary relation f_r as follows:

$$a_{ij} = f_r(s_i, s_j), 0 \leq a_{ij} \leq 1, \quad i,j=1,2,\cdots,n.$$

This shows the grade of which s_i is subordinate to s_j.

When a fuzzy subordination matrix A satisfies Definitions 1 to 3, such a matrix may represent several hierarchies. To obtain a structural model on the basis of several hierarchies, the concept of level set is defined as follows.

Definition 4.

A top level set $L_t(s)$, an intermediate level set $L_i(s)$, a bottom level set $L_b(s)$ and an isolation level set $L_{is}(s)$ are, respectively defined as follows:

$$L_t(s) = \left\{ s_i \middle| \bigvee_{j=1}^{n} a_{ij} < p \le \bigvee_{j=1}^{n} a_{ji} \right\}, \tag{3}$$

$$L_i(s) = \left\{ s_j \middle| \bigvee_{k=1}^{n} a_{kj} \ge p, \bigvee_{k=1}^{n} a_{jk} \ge p \right\}, \tag{4}$$

$$L_b(s) = \left\{ s_i \middle| \bigvee_{j=1}^{n} a_{ji} < p \le \bigvee_{j=1}^{n} a_{ij} \right\}, \tag{5}$$

$$L_{is}(s) = \left\{ s_i \middle| \bigvee_{k=1}^{n} a_{kj} < p, \bigvee_{k=1}^{n} a_{jk} < p \right\} \tag{6}$$

Each element of the top level set is not subordinate to any other element. Each element of the intermediate level set is subordinate to some other and has some other subordinated to itself. Each element of the bottom level set has nothing subordinate to itself. Each element of the isolation level set is not subordinate to an other, and has nothing subordinated to itself.

2.1.2 The Procedure of Structural Modeling

The procedure of structural modeling algorithm is given by the flowchart as shown in Figure 2.

2.1.3 Experiment Result

We explain the calculation using literal expressions in mathematics in junior high school. Now, let us consider a fuzzy subordination matrix in 8 different learning tasks as given in Equation (7).

These elements are 1) Multiplication and division of polynomial and monomial, 2) Multiplication and division with parenthesis, 3) Multiplication and division of monomial, 4) Multiplication and division, 5) Degree, 6) Monomial, 7) Polynomial, and 8) Calculation containing four operations. Figure 3 depicts a structural model by FSM. Figure 4 is constructed on the basis of Figure 3 and it gives an example of literal expressions.

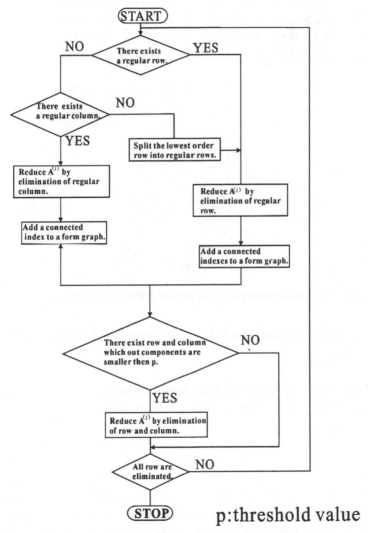

Figure 2. The procedure of fuzzy structural modeling.

$$\begin{array}{cccccccc}
0.00 & 0.65 & 0.20 & 0.50 & 0.40 & 0.40 & 0.20 & 0.80 \\
0.45 & 0.00 & 0.50 & 0.15 & 0.50 & 0.40 & 0.40 & 0.80 \\
0.85 & 0.50 & 0.00 & 0.60 & 0.25 & 0.25 & 0.50 & 0.70 \\
0.50 & 0.90 & 0.50 & 0.00 & 0.50 & 0.25 & 0.25 & 0.70 \\
0.65 & 0.50 & 0.80 & 0.50 & 0.00 & 0.50 & 0.50 & 0.60 \\
0.65 & 0.65 & 0.80 & 0.80 & 0.50 & 0.00 & 0.50 & 0.60 \\
0.85 & 0.65 & 0.50 & 0.80 & 0.50 & 0.50 & 0.00 & 0.60 \\
0.25 & 0.25 & 0.35 & 0.35 & 0.45 & 0.45 & 0.45 & 0.00
\end{array} \tag{7}$$

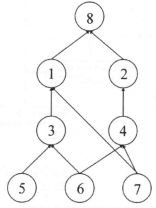

Figure 3. A structural model in a calculation using literal expressions by FSM.

2.2 Sequencing and Reasoning by Fuzzy Petri Net

FSM can depict a graph of structural model of objects in learning tasks and its graph gives a visual understanding. However, FSM draws only a condition where such objects are divided into some level sets. Especially, the sequencing of objects requires knowledge of them. When we consider IF-THEN rule as knowledge representations and a designer reflects the teacher's concept on such IF-THEN rules, it is difficult to draw this knowledge from the teacher. Because teachers consider each relation between objects and they do not have a clear relationship for all combinations, this requires effort on our part to construct sequencing from such relationship systematically.

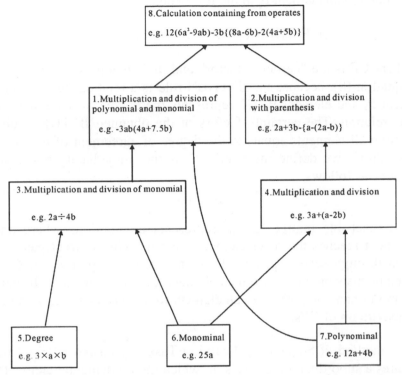

Figure 4. A structural model included objects in the calculation using literal expressions.

We propose a method of sequencing by Fuzzy Petri Nets (Ichimura *et al.* 2001). This method adds each IF-THEN rule which represents relations among objects to the arc of each element in the obtained structural model. Especially, the outstanding technique in this method can represent not only "AND" but also "OR" relation in the antecedent or conclusion part of IF-THEN rules.

First, we use the IF-THEN rule format, which represents the arc from a place P_i corresponded to an element E_i to a place P_j corresponded to an element E_j in the following:

$$\text{IF } P_i \text{ THEN } P_j, \text{ CF} = \mu_{ij} \ (1 \leq i.j \leq n), \tag{8}$$

where CF is the "certainty factor" and μ_{ij} is given by a teacher. In Equation (8), because the IF-THEN rule is a relation between element P_i and element P_j, CF represents the degree of agreement of the relation. The certainty factors of the obtained IF-THEN rules among all elements equals to the degree of agreement of relations. Therefore, we define the matrix D as the immediately reachable matrix as follows:

$$D = (d_{ij}) = (\mu_{ij}). \tag{9}$$

The reachable matrix $X(=x_{ij})$ represents all relations where one element reaches the other element not only with a direct path but also through several paths. The matrix X is the product of CFs, which exists on the arc from an element to another element. If there is more than one path from an element to another element, x_{ij} takes a maximum of CFs.

The method of Sequencing Learning Tasks by Akahori (1991) requires a subordination of tasks, in which the fundamental elements, their relativity and characterized vector is defined as their measurement. In this section, we define a fuzzy characterized vector on the basis of fuzzy theory.

As a subordination of tasks, the fundamental elements, L and S, are defined in the following:

$$L_j = \sum_{i=1}^{n} g(i, j), \ S_i = \sum_{j=1}^{n} g(i, j), \tag{10}$$

where $g(i, j)$ is defined as follows:

$$g(i, j) = \begin{cases} 1 & (x_{ij} \geq \theta) \\ 0 & (otherwise) \end{cases}.$$ (11)

On the other hand, because the tasks' relativity among reachable elements is the reachable matrix X by architecture of FPN, we define a matrix representing its degree $\Phi(=\phi_{ij})$ in the following,

$$\phi_{ij} = \begin{cases} x_{ij} & (reachable\,from\,i\,to\,j) \\ 1 & (i = j) \\ 1 - x_{ji}/1 + \lambda x_{ji} & (x_{ji} \geq \theta,\,reachable\,from\,j\,to\,i) \end{cases}$$ (12)

When an element E_j is reachable from an element E_i and its relatively is given x_{ij}, if an element E_i is reachable from an element E_j, the relativity is complement of ϕ_{ij}. If and only if an element ϕ_{ij} is not reachable and the inverse of ϕ_{ji} is reachable, we consider that ϕ_{ji} is influenced to ϕ_{ij}. Then ϕ_{ji} is complement of ϕ_{ij} appropriately. Φ in Equation (12) is confirmed by the teacher and if the matrix should be modified, then the teacher gives a new appropriate ϕ_{ij}.

Furthermore, to define a fuzzy characterized vector, we define a summarized index of a subordination of tasks and their fundamental elements as follows;

$$Z = (z_1, \cdots, z_h, \cdots, z_n) \quad (1 \leq h \leq n),$$

$$z_h = \max\left(A \frac{\min_r (L_r)}{L_h}, B \frac{S_h}{\max_s (S_s)} \right) \quad (1 \leq r, s \leq n),$$ (13)

where A and B represent parameters of subordination of tasks and their fundamental elements respectively. We give a fuzzy characterized vector as an index of Z and the tasks' relatively in the following.

$$Z' = C\Phi Z$$ (14)

where C represents a parameter of the tasks' relativity.

Figure 5 shows a FPN representation in Equation (8). FPN has places, transitions, and tokens. In Figure 5, the place P_i shows the element E_i and the transition t_i shows the value of CF_i. If the place Pi has some token value z_i, a result of reasoning by FPN, y_j is calculated in Equation (15) and the token value Z_j is set as y_j. Equation (15) is the agreement value of results of reasoning and a fuzzy characterized value.

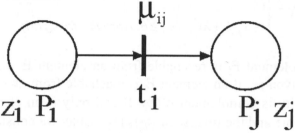

Figure 5. Fuzzy Petri Net in Equation (8).

$$y_j = \min(y_i \cdot \mu_{ij}, z_j) \tag{15}$$

Furthermore, the following 4 types of IF-THEN rules by extending Equation (8) are defined in Equation (16). Figure 6 shows the FPN model of Equation (16). However, Type4 cannot derivate clear implication, so we do not consider this model in this paper. The token values are calculated by Equations (17), (18), and (19), respectively.

TYPE1: IF P_{j1}, AND P_{j2} AND $\cdots$ AND P_{jn} THEN P_k,
$$CF = \{\mu_{j1k}, \mu_{j2k}, \cdots, \mu_{jnk}\}$$
TYPE2: IF P_j THEN P_{k1} AND P_{k2} AND $\cdots$ AND P_{kn},
$$CF = \{(\mu_{jk1}, \mu_{jk2}, \cdots, \mu_{jkn}\}$$
TYPE3: IF P_{j1}, OR P_{j2} OR $\cdots$ OR P_{jn} THEN P_k,   (16)
$$CF = \{\mu_{j1k}, \mu_{j2k}, \cdots, \mu_{jnk}\}$$
TYPE2: IF P_j THEN P_{k1} OR P_{k2} OR $\cdots$ OR P_{kn},
$$CF = \{\mu_{jk1}, \mu_{jk2}, \cdots, \mu_{jkn}\}$$

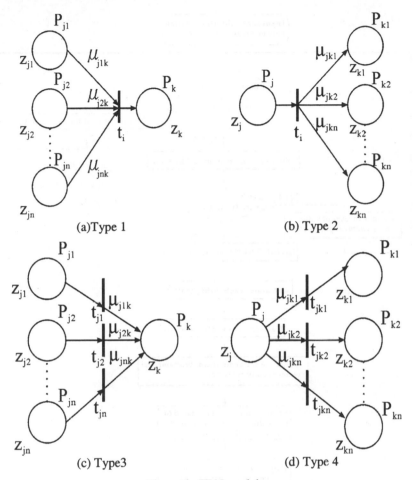

(a)Type 1   (b) Type 2

(c) Type3   (d) Type 4

Figure 6. FPN models.

$$y_k = \min(\min_n(y_{j1} \cdot \mu_{j1k}, y_{j2} \cdot \mu_{j2k}, \cdots, y_{jn} \cdot \mu_{jnk}), z_k) \qquad (17)$$

$$y_{kl} = \min(y_j \cdot \mu_{jkl}, z_{kl}) \qquad (1 \le l \le n) \qquad (18)$$

$$y_k = \min(\max_n(y_{j1} \cdot \mu_{j1k}, y_{j2} \cdot \mu_{j2k}, \cdots, y_{jn} \cdot \mu_{jnk}), z_k) \qquad (19)$$

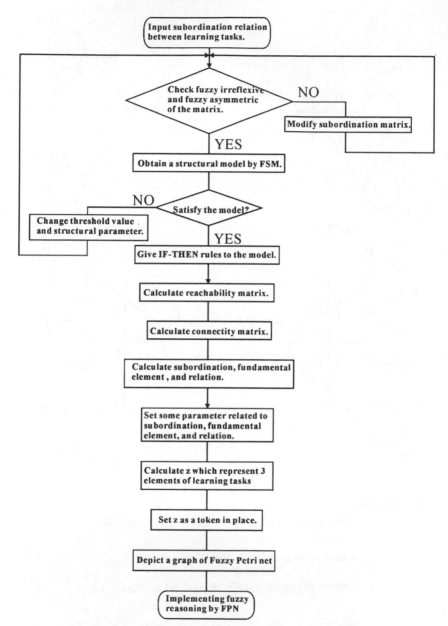

Figure 7. Flowchart of structuring, sequencing and implementing.

Figure 7 shows a flowchart of structuring, sequencing and implementing by FPN. First, a subordination relation among learning tasks is required, and then the system asks the relationship among each task in fuzzy numerical value between [0,1]. After the system determines a structure model, we add IF-THEN rules and calculate a fuzzy characterized vector from Equation (8) to Equation (14). After an FPN model is constructed, the system implemented the practice process of tasks for students.

2.3 Experimental Result

Let us consider an example of the FSM model in Figure 3 and the following additional IF-THEN rules.

$$\text{IF } P_5 \text{ AND } P_6 \text{ THEN } P_3., \text{ CF}=\{\mu_{53}=0.800, \mu_{63}=0.900\} \quad (20)$$
$$\text{IF } P_6 \text{ AND } P_7 \text{ THEN } P_4., \text{ CF}=\{\mu_{64}=0.900, \mu_{74}=0.800\} \quad (21)$$
$$\text{IF } P_3 \text{ AND } P_7 \text{ THEN } P_1., \text{ CF}=\{\mu_{31}=0.850, \mu_{71}=0.600\} \quad (22)$$
$$\text{IF } P_4 \qquad \text{THEN } P_2., \text{ CF}=\{\mu_{42}=0.800\} \quad (23)$$
$$\text{IF } P_1 \text{ AND } P_2 \text{ THEN } P_8., \text{ CF}=\{\mu_{18}=0.800, \mu_{28}=0.900\} \quad (24)$$

For such IF-THEN rules and CF values in Equations (20)-(24), an immediately reachable matrix D is obtained as follows:

$$
\begin{array}{llllllll}
0.000 & 0.000 & 0.000 & 0.000 & 0.000 & 0.000 & 0.000 & 0.800 \\
0.000 & 0.000 & 0.000 & 0.000 & 0.000 & 0.000 & 0.000 & 0.900 \\
0.850 & 0.000 & 0.000 & 0.000 & 0.000 & 0.000 & 0.000 & 0.680 \\
0.000 & 0.800 & 0.000 & 0.000 & 0.000 & 0.000 & 0.000 & 0.720 \\
0.680 & 0.000 & 0.800 & 0.000 & 0.000 & 0.000 & 0.000 & 0.544 \\
0.765 & 0.720 & 0.900 & 0.900 & 0.000 & 0.000 & 0.000 & 0.648 \\
0.600 & 0.640 & 0.000 & 0.800 & 0.000 & 0.000 & 0.000 & 0.576 \\
0.000 & 0.000 & 0.000 & 0.000 & 0.000 & 0.000 & 0.000 & 0.000 \\
\end{array}
$$

In the case of $\lambda=1.5$, ϕ calculated in Equation (12) is modified in elements having a 0.0 value in the above matrix. In this experiment, we give appropriate values less than the threshold value of FSM parameters. The modified ϕ is as follows.

$$
\begin{array}{cccccccc}
1.0000 & 0.1674 & 0.0624 & 0.0450 & 0.3099 & 0.2103 & 0.3821 & 0.8000 \\
0.2067 & 1.0000 & 0.2771 & 0.0204 & 0.3994 & 0.2485 & 0.2338 & 0.9000 \\
0.8500 & 0.1703 & 1.0000 & 0.2529 & 0.0682 & 0.1023 & 0.1883 & 0.6800 \\
0.1555 & 0.8000 & 0.0768 & 1.0000 & 0.3044 & 0.3824 & 0.0837 & 0.7200 \\
0.6800 & 0.2716 & 0.8000 & 0.0483 & 1.0000 & 0.0504 & 0.1264 & 0.5440 \\
0.7650 & 0.7200 & 0.9000 & 0.9000 & 0.2187 & 1.0000 & 0.0561 & 0.6480 \\
0.6000 & 0.6400 & 0.2834 & 0.8000 & 0.3209 & 0.3528 & 1.0000 & 0.5760 \\
0.0507 & 0.3834 & 0.3979 & 0.3607 & 0.1937 & 0.3799 & 0.1674 & 1.0000
\end{array}
$$

A fuzzy characterized vector Z' is calculated in Equations (10), (11), and (13).

$Z'=(0.5323, 0.5698, 0.5179, 0.6291, 0.7232, 1.0000, 0.9809, 0.5154)$

Based on the flow of Figure 10, the fuzzy characterized vector creates the following sequences.

seqence1:(6,7,5,4,3,2,1,8)
seqence2:(6,7,4,2,5,3,1,8)
seqence3:(6,7,4,5,3,2,1,8)

Finally, we can obtain an FPN model. Figure 8 shows the FPN model of sequence 3.

2.4   E-Learning System for the National Examination for Medical Practitioners

We developed an e-learning system for the national examination for medical practitioners. Because the system is constructed on web based database technology, teachers and students can use it through the Internet. At first, a user registers the user's identification information. The identification information becomes a key, and he/she can confirm his/her historical record after studying with this system.

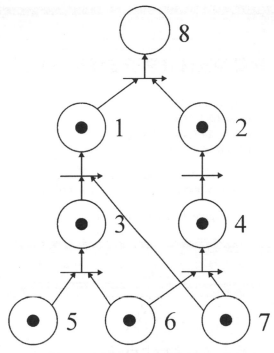

Figure 8. A FPN model from Equation (20) to Equation (24).

In this system, a student selects a category in one of the fields covered by the national examination. However, the examination has many categories in each department of medicine. Furthermore, the categories have 4 levels of classification; "term," "large," "medium," "small." Not only students but also teachers are at a loss as to determine which category to start.

Figure 9 shows the selection window of categories. The student selects some categories with this window. After selection of categories, the FSM method determines a structure model, some sequences are considered, and then FPN implements reasoning for a selected sequence of tasks. Figure 10 shows the selected FPN model for 20 categories.

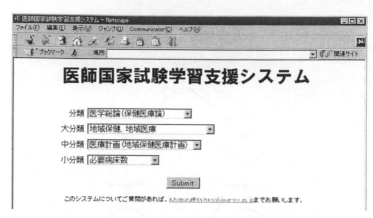

Figure 9. Selection of categories.

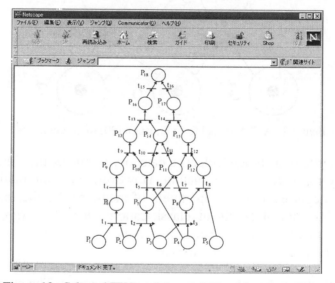

Figure 10. Selected FPN model on web based learning system.

The student answers 10 questions for each category as shown in Figure 11. The answers are stored in the historical database, and the achievement status for each person is recorded. The privilege to view such records is given in 3 levels; administrator, teacher, and student. The student can see his/her own record and the teacher can view data related to the problems that he/she had created and inserted into database. The administrator has all rights to maintain this system, and can take statistics of the students' learning results as shown in Figure 12. All requirements to this system for learning, teaching, and statistics are executed on his/her web browser. A new question to the database is added through the Internet.

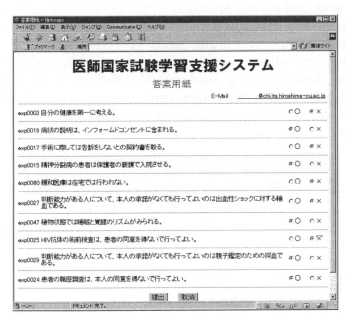

Figure 11. Answer-sheet.

The system has been developed in cooperation with St. Marianna University in Japan and is currently in operation at Hiroshima City University, Japan.

2.5 Discussion

We described structuring by applying the FSM method and the sequencing of learning tasks for teaching strategies by extending Akahori's (1991) method of Sequencing Learning Tasks. The sequencing of objects required knowledge of the directed domain. To introduce IF-THEN rules as knowledge representations in which a designer reflects the teacher's concepts on such IF-THEN rules, we proposed a method of sequencing by Fuzzy Petri Nets (Ichimura *et al.* 2001). This method adds each IF-THEN rule, which represents relationship among objects as the arc of each element in the obtained structural model. Specifically, the outstanding technique in this method can represent not only "AND" but also "OR" relation in the antecedent or conclusion part of IF-THEN rules. This model presents combinations of concepts such as task applicability, fundamental necessity, and fundamental relativity. Our proposed method helps reduce the complexities in sequencing of learning tasks by drawing a graph structure of the relationship among task's elements.

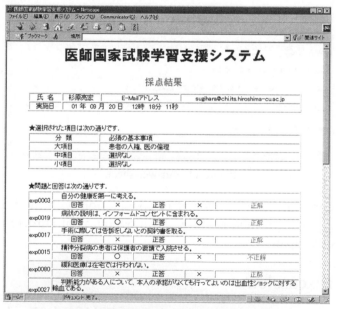

Figure 12. Confirmation sheet for corrected answers.

This method is applied into an e-learning system for the national examination for medical practitioners. Medical experts are required to study from a complex structure in different departments of medicine. It is difficult to define a studying program to study systematically. We hope that the system assists medical students master his major field in medicine.

3 Assisting a Good Grasp of Opinions and Learning Support in Group Learning

Learners can communicate with each other easily in different places by Internet-based communication tools (e.g., chat, e-mail, and NetNews). However, they can not necessarily always make out the target domain well because these communication tools do not assist them to arrange their opinions fully. This section describes a group learning environment where learners in different places can have a discussion on the basis of problem solving process (Nakamura and Otsuki 2001). There is a memo tool where a learner can express his/her opinions privately and arrange them. There is a communication tool where learners can share structures of each learner's individual opinions among them. The memo tool and the communication tool are integrated seamlessly. The learner can grasp differences between two learners' opinions easily by highlighting the opinions with different colors. Then he/she can notice differences among their opinions, contradictions in their opinions, and various thinking ways, and make his/her position clear. Furthermore, after the discussion, the learners can also replay the discussion in chronological order to ruminate over and examine the contents of the discussion. If a learner speaks nothing, he/she can hardly acquire a new knowledge. So, the pertinent agent generates questions in order to prompt him/her to join in the discussion and acquire a new knowledge (Nakamura *et al.* 1999). The design, a result of basic evaluation, and the group learning support are described in Sections 3.1, 3.2, and 3.3, respectively.

3.1   Design of Group Learning Environment

Figure 13 shows a snapshot of our group learning environment. All learners join in the discussion via each individual client computer. A synchronous discussion is announced on the web page when a teacher or a learner registers a theme and starting time. The learners log on the session by the starting time and join in the discussion. On the other hand, an asynchronous discussion starts whenever a teacher or a learner registers a theme. Each learner logs on the session at his/her convenience and joins in the discussion.

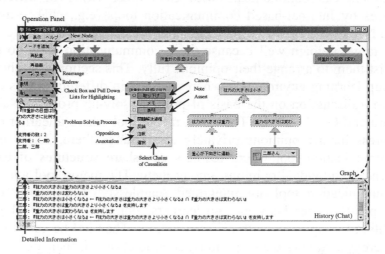

Figure 13. Snapshot of group learning environment.

A learner adds a node on the graph by using a button "new node" on the operation panel to express his/her opinion. He/she adds an arc in order to set up a relation between plural opinions (Section 3.1.1). Nodes and arcs are arranged automatically according to the problem solving processes (Section 3.1.1). He/she not only can express his/her opinions and arrange them but also can share the structure with other learners (Section 3.1.2). He/she can look at detailed information (e.g., the names and the number of the learners who agree to a designated node or arc) if necessary. He/she can also grasp the opinions easily by highlighting them with different colors (Section 3.1.3) and confirm the history of the discussion by using the history (chat) (Section 3.1.4).

3.1.1 Primitive Objects

Nodes and arcs are introduced as primitive objects in order for learners to express their opinions, ask about an opinion, and reply to a question. A node is a primitive object which means an opinion. If its contents are not written, it means a question. At the same time, a learner can express whom he/she asks about. On the other hand, an arc is a primitive object which means a relation (i.e., a problem solving process or an opposition) between plural opinions. The shape of a problem solving process is an arrow and the shape of an opposition is a bi-directional arrow. The following six relations are expressed. Figure 14 shows an example of a structure of opinions.

1. opinion α $\leftarrow$ opinion β: An arrow is drawn from an opinion β (i.e., cause, reason, and so on) to an opinion α (i.e., result, conclusion, and so on) when a learner expresses the problem solving process.

2. opinion α $\leftarrow$ opinion β (question): An arrow is drawn from a question node to an opinion α (i.e., result, conclusion, and so on) when he/she asks about an opinion β (i.e., cause, reason, and so on) which the opinion α originates from.

3. opinion α (question) $\leftarrow$ opinion β: An arrow is drawn from an opinion β (i.e., cause, reason, and so on) to a question node when he/she asks about an opinion α (i.e., result, conclusion, and so on) which the opinion β produces.

4. opinion α $\leftarrow$ (question) $\leftarrow$ opinion β: A question node is inserted between an opinion β (i.e., cause, reason, and so on) and an opinion α (i.e., result, conclusion, and so on) when he/she

asks about a question why the opinion α originates from the opinion β.

5. opinion α ↔ opinion β: A bi-directional arrow is drawn between opposed nodes.

6. no-relation: This is an isolated node that has no relation to any other nodes yet.

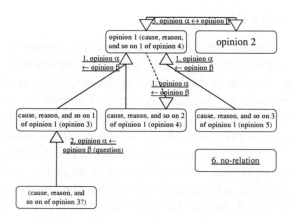

Figure 14. Example of structure of opinion.

A relation between plural nodes which share the end of an arc is "and" and a relation between plural nodes which share the same destination node (i.e., result, conclusion, and so on) but do not share the end of an arc is "or." A source node (i.e., cause, reason, and so on) is arranged automatically under the destination node (i.e., result, conclusion, and so on). If there is a conflict in relations between two nodes, the arc is drawn with a broken line.

3.1.2   Memo Tool and Communication Tool

Functions of both a memo tool and a communication tool are defined. A learner can express his/her opinions privately by using the memo tool. The learners can share structures of each learner's individual opinions among them by using the communication tool.

An opinion (i.e., a node or an arc) has three attributes: cancel, note, or assert. A learner selects one of the three attributes at a time. An asserted opinion is added on all the other learners' graphs, too. This is a way of communication among the learners and all the learners can refer to asserted opinions. A noted opinion is not added on the other learners' graphs. This is a way of private memorandum and only the owner can refer to opinions noted by him/her. A canceled opinion is deleted from all the graphs if no learner supports the opinion. But if the other learner notes the opinion privately, the opinion is not deleted only from his/her graph. In case that a learner notes an opinion he/she has asserted, the opinion is regarded as a canceled one from viewpoints of the other learners.

All the learners can refer to asserted opinions and note/assert the opinions by themselves. An opinion asserted by plural learners is piled up repeatedly. A frequency of repetition is proportional to the number of the learners who assert it. Furthermore, if a learner has noted the opinion, an extra is piled up only on his/her graph. But we think an opinion asserted by many learners may make graphs complicated and have bad influence on learner's cognition, the number of repeat times is suppressed within four times. Of course, the whole pile can be drawn always if necessary.

Opinions are drawn with the following colors and made a distinction among them. Figure 15 shows an example of a structure of discussion (if monochromatic printing is used here, a reader may hardly recognize differences of objects. Numbers in parentheses are for explanation).
- noted opinions: green
- asserted opinions: blue
- opinions asserted by other learners: light gray

The private tool (i.e., the memo tool) and the shared tool (i.e., the communication tool) are integrated seamlessly. The learners not only can share their opinions but also can express their opinions and arrange them on the basis of problem solving process. Otherwise, if these tools are prepared as two separate tools, the learners have a tiresome work of copying opinions from a tool and pasting it to the other tool. Furthermore, it is difficult for a learner to compare their own opinions with the other learners' opinions.

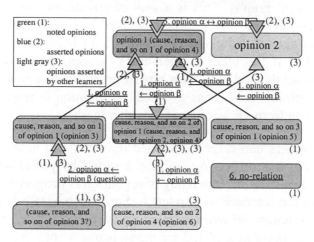

Figure 15. Example of structure of discussion.

The communication tool can be regarded as a set of transparent layers, each of which expresses a structure of opinions asserted by one learner. The memo tool can be regarded as a transparent layer, which expresses a structure of all opinions noted by a learner on the set of the transparent layers. Table 1 shows the access control rules about these layers.

Table 1. Access control rules about primitive objects.

	layer noted by learner α		layer assered by learner α	
	write in	refer to	write in	refer to
learner α	Y	Y	Y	Y
other learners	N	N	N	Y

3.1.3   Assisting a Good Grasp of Opinions

The learners not only can share their opinions but also can express their opinions and arrange them on the basis of problem solving process by using the memo tool and the communication tool. Thus, it becomes easier to grasp relations between plural opinions (e.g., what does a result originate from? what does an opinion oppose to?) and an outline of discussion (e.g., which opinions have many learners asserted?). However, it is difficult for the learners to make opposed points between different opinions clear and make their own positions clearer, because it is still difficult to grasp detailed information (e.g., which opinions has the learner α asserted? what points are the learner α's opinions different from the learner β's ones?). These difficulties may come from indistinguishability of different layers. Does it become easier to grasp detailed information if opinions are drawn with distinctive colors? No. If many learners join in discussion or many opinions are asserted, the learners may be thrown into cognitive confusion.

Here, six functions are introduced: (1) highlighting opinions asserted by a specified learner, (2) emphasizing selected opinions, (3) emphasizing chains of problem solving processes, (4) making a distinction between changed opinions and the other opinions, (5) making a distinction between new opinions and old opinions, and (6) drawing a graph on a reduced scale. These functions have no influence on the other learners' graphs. Outlines of these functions are given.

(1) Highlighting opinions asserted by a specified learner: As defined in Section 3.1.2, noted opinions are drawn with green and asserted opinions are drawn with blue. This is a default effect of highlighting opinions. A learner can change an effect of highlighting opinions:
- green: noted opinions (default) / none
- blue: asserted opinions (default) / learner α's opinions

- red: none (default) / learner β's opinions
- light gray: other opinions (default).

In other words, these four highlighting methods pick out a structure of opinions asserted by a specified learner in a structure of discussion. These methods may be of use in the following cases (Table 2 and Figure 16). If he/she does not want to make a distinction between the noted opinions and the other opinions, he/she may as well change an effect of highlighting opinions: the noted opinions are drawn with light gray.

1. In case that he/she wants to grasp a structure of his/her own opinions or compare his/her own opinions with the other learners' opinions, he/she uses the default effect of highlighting opinions (Figure 16.1).
2. In case that he/she wants to grasp a specified learner's opinions or compare the specified learner's opinions with the other learners' opinions, he/she changes an effect of highlighting opinions: the specified learner's opinions are drawn with blue and no opinion is drawn with red (default) (Figure 16.2).

Table 2. Effective usages of highlighting opinions.

	a learner wants to	effect of highlighting opinions
1	grasp a structure of his/her own opinions	default (blue: aserted opinions, red: none)
	compare his/her own opinions with other learners' opinions	
2	grasp a specified learner's opinions	blue: the specified learner's opinions, red none (default)
	compare the specified learner's opinions with other learners' opinions	
3	compare his/her own opinions with a specified learner's opinions	blue: asserted opinions (default), red: the specified learner's opinions
4	compare two specified learners' opinions	blue: the first learner's opinions, red: the second learner's opinions

3. In case that he/she wants to compare his/her own opinions with a specified learner's opinions, he/she changes an effect of highlighting opinions: the specified learner's opinions are drawn

with red and asserted opinions are drawn with blue (default) (Figure 16.3).

4. In case that he/she wants to compare two specified learners' opinions, he/she changes an effect of highlighting opinions: the first learner's opinions are drawn with blue and the second learner's opinions are drawn with red (Figure 16.4).

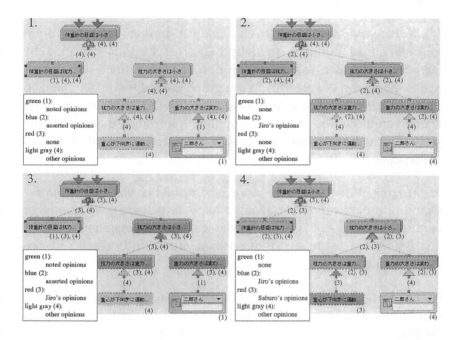

(2) Emphasizing selected opinions: If a structure of discussion is complicated, it may become difficult to trace a chain of problem solving processes. Emphasizing selected opinions makes cognition of relations in the graph easy. Bi-directional arrows also cause a difficulty of cognition of relations in the graph, because they cross over the chains of problem solving processes. Thus, only ends of a bi-directional arc are usually drawn, and the whole line is drawn

only when it is selected. Of course, the whole line can be drawn always if necessary.

(3) Emphasizing chains of problem solving processes: Emphasizing the chains of problem solving processes, which an opinion originates from or produces, makes cognition of relations in the graph easy.

(4) Making a distinction between changed opinions and other opinions: Changed opinions (i.e., opinions asserted or canceled by learners) are drawn with a broken line in a predefined duration. It makes cognition of relations in the graph easy. Of course, changed opinions can be drawn with a normal line always if necessary. If no learner supports the canceled opinion, it is deleted from all the graphs. It is drawn with dark gray in a predefined duration before the deletion.

(5) Making a distinction between new opinions and old opinions: Opinions are drawn with gradation colors which are proportional to opinions' freshness. It assists for the learners to grasp an outline of discussion (e.g., a process of discussion and recently discussed topics) at a glance.

(6) Drawing a graph on a reduced scale: The graph can be drawn in a reduced scale. It assists for the learners to view the whole of the graph at a glance and grasp an outline of discussion.

3.1.4   Other Functions

History (chat) is a tool where the learners grasp chronological information of discussion. Whenever every opinion is asserted or cancelled, the history (chat) records it. Relations between plural opinions (i.e., a problem solving process, an opposition, or an "and") are represented by symbols (i.e., ←, ↔, or ∩).

A learner can replay the contents of the discussion in chronological order in order to ruminate over and examine the contents of the discussion. According to the record of discussion (opinions asserted or canceled by the learners), nodes and arcs are added or deleted.

3.2   Basic Evaluation of Group Learning Environment

A result of a basic evaluation of the environment is described shortly. Although we expected that learners not only made out the target domain but also got meta-cognitive skills, we only measured whether cognition of opinions became easier by structures of opinions, a set of transparent layers, and highlighting opinions in this evaluation. Testees were requested to pick out common opinions between two learners' opinions from the following different views of a part of the same discussion, which three learners participated in. The part included 13 sentences (586 characters) in Japanese. It was on physics.

1. Structure of <u>discussion</u>: The view is a printed-paper structure of discussion. It is a set of transparent layers, each of which expresses a structure of opinions asserted by one learner. The layers are collected into one structure by the communication tool. The two learners' opinions are highlighted with different colors.

2. <u>Separate</u> structures of two learner's opinions: The view is two separate printed-paper structures of two learner's opinions. They are two independent layers of the structure of discussion, not collected by the communication tool. For reasons of arrangement of opinions, some opinions are not placed at the same location. The testees were not provided with the other learner's opinions, which were not related to the work.

3. <u>History</u> (Chat): The view is a printed-paper set of sentences recorded by the history (chat). However, the sentences are arranged so that topics may not be jumped from one to another.

There are the following three combinations in picking out common opinions between two learners' opinions from the three learners' opinions: (a) common opinions between the first learner's opinions and the second learner's opinions, (b) common opinions between the first learner's opinions and the third learner's opinions, and (c) common opinions between the second learner's opinions and the third learner's opinions. Thus, the three views multiplied by the three combinations produce nine works entirely. Furthermore, the learners are labeled differently in different views so that the works might have smaller influences on each other. For the same reason, the works were carried out in the order of (1a), (2b), (3c), (1b), (2c), (3a), (1c), (2a), and (3b). The order is determined not to continue the same view and the same learners' opinions.

We measured the time used by the testees and the number of faults in each work. The works were finished by testee's reports. The testees were five students belonging to a graduate school of information science (called a, b, c, d, and e). Table 3 shows averages of the time used by the testees for the works. Records of the first three works (i.e., (1a), (2b), and (3c)) are removed from the table because they are works where testees enriched their experience.

Table 3.   Averages of time (in seconds) used for picking out common opinions between two learners' opinions.

	(1) Discussion	(2) Separate	(3) History	(3) - (1)	(2) - (1)	(3) - (2)
a	19.5	46.0	142.0	122.5	26.5	96.0
b	14.5	43.5	129.5	115.0	29.0	86.0
c	31.5	53.5	142.0	110.5	22.0	88.5
d	42.0	44.0	94.5	52.5	2.0	50.5
e	22.0	66.0	82.0	60.0	44.0	16.0
average	25.9	50.6	118.0	92.1	24.7	67.4

(1) Discussion took significantly shorter time than (3) History by the Wilcoxon matched pairs signed ranks test with 5% significance level. The column of "(2) - (1)" in Table 1.3 means an effect of both a set of transparent layers and the highlighting opinions. The

column of "(3) - (2)" means an effect of the structure of opinions. The number of faults is counted as opinions (i.e., nodes and arcs): (2a) testee c: one shortage, (3a) testee b: five surpluses, testee c: six shortages, one surplus, testee e: one shortage, (3b) testee d: two shortages. The testees took long time but made a lot of mistakes when he/she picked out common opinions from a set of sentences. As a result of this evaluation, the structures of opinions, a set of transparent layers, and highlighting opinions can assist a good grasp of opinions. Especially, testee a, b, c, and d grasped opinions well by the structure of opinions and testee e grasped opinions well by a set of transparent layers and highlighting opinions.

3.3   Group Learning Support

If a learner does not assert his/her opinion, he/she can hardly acquire a new knowledge. In this case, it is expected that the environment supports group learning. A agent, called private agent, is assigned to each learner in a client site. The private agent constructs a difference model, which consists of differences between the opinions privately noted by the pertinent learner and all asserted opinions. The private agent generates questions based on the pertinent learner's difference model if he/she has asserted nothing longer than a predefined interval. However, a case that plural learners need to be assisted at the same time may occur. If each private agent speaks freely, the discussion may become confused. It is desirable that the private agents support group learning cooperatively. The private agents negotiate among them in order to dissolve the above condition and select the private agents in charge of the assistance from the instructional viewpoints. Thus, the private agents have two functions of assisting the pertinent learners. One is to activate the discussion by inviting an inactive learner into the discussion, and the other is to prompt the learners to share their opinions. The function of group learning support consists of four steps: (1) construction of models, (2) generation of candidates of questions for assistance, (3) negotiation, and (4) assistance.

3.3.1 Construction of Models

There are three kinds of models in the environment: student models, a discussion model, and difference models.

1. Privately noted opinions are recorded in the pertinent learner's student model. Unlike student models in Intelligent Tutoring Systems, the student models in the environment include no process inferred by computers but all contents directly expressed by the pertinent learner. The pertinent learner's student model is updated whenever he/she updates a noted opinion.
2. Asserted opinions are recorded in the discussion model. The discussion model includes the chronological order of opinions, the name of a learner who writes an opinion, the names of learners who agree with an opinion, and whether and when an opinion is canceled or not. The discussion model is updated whenever an asserted opinion is updated.
3. A difference model is used when the private agent generates candidates of instructional questions in order to assist the pertinent learner. The private agent assists the pertinent learner in asking about his/her noting opinion which has not been asserted. Thus, the difference model needs to record differences between the opinion noted by him/her and all asserted opinions. The difference model shows not only whether an opinion is known by the pertinent learner or not, but also whether an opinion has been spoken in the discussion or not. The pertinent learner's difference model is updated whenever his/her student model or the discussion model is updated.

3.3.2 Generation of Candidates for Assistance

A private agent generates the following questions based on the pertinent learner's difference model as candidates for assistance if he/she has not spoken longer than a predefined interval and a destination node (i.e., result, conclusion, and so on) has been asserted (Figure 17):

1. a question that asks the pertinent learner about a source node (i.e., cause, reason, and so on), which has not been asserted but has been noted privately
2. a question that asks about a source node (i.e., cause, reason, and so on), which has not been asked about but has been asked about.

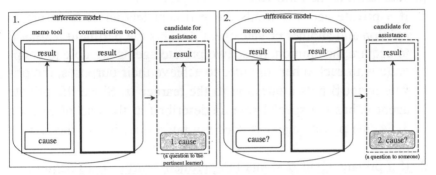

Figure 17. Examples of candidate for assistance.

When not only a destination node (i.e., result, conclusion, and so on) has been asserted but also a source node (i.e., cause, reason, and so on) has been asserted, a private agent generates candidates for assistance.

The candidates are evaluated from the following instructional viewpoints and the best-evaluated one is offered:

• The longer the pertinent learner has not spoken, the higher the private agent evaluates the candidate in order to prompt him/her to join in the discussion.
• The newer a candidate is, the higher the private agent evaluates it in order to give priority to the continuity between the topics in the discussion.

The reminders of the candidates are reserved for negotiations.

3.3.3 Negotiations

If plural private agents offer their candidates simultaneously, the private agents negotiate among them. Each offered candidate is sent from a private agent, called sender, to the other private agents, called receivers. A private agent is able to cooperate with another private agent in the following cases (Figure 18):

1. If a private agent α wants the pertinent learner α to assert an opinion and another private agent β wants the pertinent learner β to acquire the opinion, these two private agents are able to cooperate with each other. In order to achieve their purposes, the private agent β puts a question to the learner α. Since the private agent α has the special role as described at the end of Section 3.3.4, the private agent α does not put a question to the learner α.

2. If a private agent α wants the pertinent learner α to acquire an opinion and another private agent β wants the pertinent learner β to acquire the opinion, these two private agents are able to cooperate with each other. In order to achieve their purpose, either the private agent α or the private agent β puts a question.

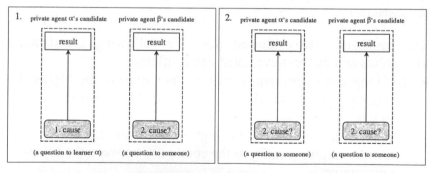

Figure 18. Example of cooperative candidate.

The receivers answer to the sender in the following ways and the private agents compare the offered candidates by the sum of evaluations and select the best-evaluated one out of all the candidates:

1. Cooperation: If a receiver is cooperative with the sender in the receiver's best-evaluated candidate, the receiver agrees with the offered candidate by telling the evaluation to the sender.
2. Compromise: If a receiver is not cooperative with the sender in the receiver's best-evaluated candidate but the receiver is cooperative with the sender in another candidate, the receiver agrees with the offered candidate by telling half of the evaluation to the sender.
3. Competition: If a receiver can not even compromise with the sender, that is, if the offered candidate has no influence on the pertinent learner, the receiver tells nothing to the sender.

3.3.4 Assistance

In general, there exist plural learners, whose private agents want each of the pertinent learners to assert an opinion. We call a set of the learners "explainer set." On the other hand, there exist plural private agents, who want each of the pertinent learners to acquire a new knowledge. We call a set of the private agents "questioner set." Except for the special case as described later, the assistance by the private agents is limited to only putting a question. The private agent in charge of the assistance is selected out of the questioner set in the following ways: one private agent of the questioner set puts a question to a learner in the explainer set who has not spoken for the longest interval. In case that the questioner set is null or the explainer set is null, a special agent is needed. The agent supplements this deficient role.

The private agents need to wait until the explainer replies to the question or a predefined amount of time has elapsed. In other words, the private agents do not negotiate among them in this interval. If no learner speaks in this interval, the explainer's private agent puts a question to another learner in the explainer set. If there is not another learner in the explainer set, the explainer's private agent replies to it instead of the explainer. Why the explainer can not reply to the question although he/she knows it? The explainer's opinion may be suppressed by the majority's opinion. Although one of the strong points of group learning is that learners are motivated by the existences of the other learners, it often falls into a tendency of superficially shared cognition because learner's opinion, which may induce disagreement, is suppressed (Levine and Moreland 1991). Especially, it is difficult for a learner to speak an opinion which no learner might agree with. If the explainer knows that there is at least one learner who agrees with his/her opinion, he/she is encouraged. It is of use that the explainer's private agent replies to it instead of him/her.

3.4   Discussion

The shared working environment of Suthers *et al.* (1995), a pioneering work in the area of the study on tools assisting group learning, was designed as a tool assisting a collaborative work rather than a cooperative work. The similarity between Suthers *et al.*'s one and ours is that learners can obtain deep comprehension by using graphical objects and sharing the objects among them. The difference is that their environment lacks the following functions: (1) a restriction on deletion of graphical objects, (2) a way to support an opinion on the diagram, and (3) a way to privately work on the diagram by trial and error.

Learners can learn something by using KJ method (Kawakita 1967), which accelerates arrangement and thinking. The learners are requested to (1) collect (brainstorming) and record (creation of cards), (2) classify (grouping of cards), and (3) conquer opinions cooperatively. This process is entirely bottom up and the participants do not express relations among plural opinions explicitly when they (1) collect and record, and (2) classify opinions.

A lot of features of group learning environments are common to ones of CSCWs. However, some features, target domain's characteristics, purposes of assisting, and so on are different. For example, gIBIS (Conklin and Begeman 1988), a pioneering work in the area of the study on tools assisting cooperative work, proposed a way of visualizing an internal structure of design decisions in order to assist users to understand it. The visualized structure by gIBIS is reflected by users' positions: support, object to, and so on.

4　Conclusion

In this chapter, we described internet-based interactive learning. Specifically, we proposed group learning for the targeted students. An interactive learning system provides an agent that assists a student. When an agent notices an opportunity to make a better influence, it negotiates with other agents.

Further, we developed our methods taking into consideration that most teachers favor methods using real world problems that give a clear response, are easy to understand, and are possible to implement in a regular classroom lesson. To verify the effectiveness of our method, we developed the e-learning system for the National Examination for Medical Practitioners.

Such methods are effective in constructing a computer assisted instruction system and will shed a new light on the future of the research of educational technology.

References

Akahori, K. (1991), "Sequencing learning tasks in junior high school mathematics," *Japan Society for Educational Technology*, vol. 15, no. 2, pp. 57-71. (In Japanese.)

Chen, S.M., Ke, J.K., and Chang, J.F. (1991), "Knowledge representation using fuzzy petri nets," *IEEE Trans. on Knowledge and Data Engg.* vol. 2, no. 3, pp. 311-319.

Conklin, J. and Begeman, M.L. (1988), "gIBIS: A Hypertext tool for exploratory policy discussion," *Proc. of CSCW*, pp. 140-152.

Gabus, A., and Fontela, E. (1973), *DEMATEL Reports*, nos. 1, 2, and 3, Battelle J. Inst.

Ichimura, T., Kuriyama, Y., and Yamashita, T. (1999), "Analyses of college students' concept by Fuzzy Structural Modeling (FSM) method with planar lattice neural network," *Proc. of Intl. Conf on IEEE SMC*, vol. III, pp. 298-303.

Ichimura, T., Sugihara, A., Takahama, T., Isomichi, Y., and Yoshida, K. (2001), "A proposal of interactive tool for implementing a sequence of learning tasks in a drill and practice by Fuzzy Petri Nets and its application to e-learning system for the National Examination for Medical Practitioners," *Proc. of The 2nd Vietnam-Japan Bilateral Symposium on Fuzzy Systems and Applications*.

Kawakita, J. (1967), "Method of thinking," *Chuokoronsha*. (In Japanese.)

Levine, J.M. and Moreland, R.L. (1991), *Culture and Socialization in Work Groups. Perspectives on Socially Shared Cognition*, Washington, D.C.: American Psychological Association.

Nakamura, M., Hanamoto, K., Tsutsumi, Y., Fukuda, M., and Otsuki, S. (1999), "Models and negotiations for group learning support," *Proc. of ICCE*, vol. 1, pp. 677-684.

Nakamura, M. and Otsuki, S. (2001), "Assisting a good grasp of opinions in group learning," *Proc. of ICCE*, vol. 2, pp. 755-762.

Paul, B., Konar, A., and Mandal, A.K. (1996), "Estimation of certainty of knowledge with fuzzy petri nets," *Proc. of the IEEE Intl. Conf. on Fuzzy System*, part 2, pp. 951-955.

Sato, T. (1989), *Educational Informatics' Engineering*, Corona Publishers. (In Japanese.)

Shiizuka, H. (1992), "Fuzzy petri nets," *Journal of Japan Society for Fuzzy Theory and Systems*, vol. 4, no. 6, pp. 1069-1085. (In Japanese.)

Suthers, D., Weiner, A., Connelly, J., and Paolucci, M. (1995), "Belvedere: engaging students in critical discussion of science and public policy issues," *Proc. of AI-ED*, pp. 266-273.

Tazaki, E. and Amagasa, M. (1979), "Structural modeling in a class of systems using fuzzy sets theory," *Fuzzy Sets and Systems*, no. 2, pp. 542-553.

Warfield, J.N. (1976), *Societal Systems Planning. Policy and Complexity*, Wiley, New York.

Warfield, J.N, *et al.* (1972), *A Unified Systems Engineering Concept*, Battelle M. Inst.

Yamashita, T, Ichimura, T., and Koshiya, T. (1998), "An application of fuzzy structural modeling to the usability of computer systems," *Journal of Japan Society for Fuzzy Theory and Systems*, vol. 10, no. 3, pp. 569-574.

Chapter 9

Supporting Personalization in Distance Education Virtual Communities

E. Gaudioso and J.G. Boticario

Web based distance learning is benefiting from the improvement in communication services and currently most web based educational systems offer forums, chats and any other available channel for students' communication. This development is changing the teaching model and nowadays lecturers and students are becoming active members of virtual educational communities. In this chapter we describe, aLF (active learning framework), an environment for web-based distance learning developed to support the requirements for collaborative work between all the different communities involved. However, we will see that although this framework is specially intended for supporting collaborative work, a significant number of students are reluctant to actively participate in aLF communication services. This is partly due to the fact that a very similar response is provided to students with changing needs and whose level of experience on the subject being taught and on the use of resources available on the web site are different. Thus it is needed some kind of personalization to adapt to the students interests and requirements, based in the data that the system has about the student. Such information is stored in the so-called user model. In this chapter we describe, a user modeling subsystem framed within aLF aimed at providing an adaptive response which can meet users' knowledge state, preferences and goals.

1   Motivation

Distance education takes place when a lecturer and student(s) are separated by physical distance. The proliferation of accesses to the Internet has made the World Wide Web (WWW) an ideal environment for lecturer-student communication with no restrictions of time and space. When a web site is designed to support certain courses it is called an *educational web site*. Educational web sites reduce student isolation by offering a number of communication channels, usually newsgroups, e-mail, mailing lists and chats. They may also provide the necessary course material that can be downloaded by the students, offer HTML pages that guide students through the course contents or provide references to other information sources, as well as many other educational possibilities.

Often the contents provided by an educational web site are fully static. The HTML page navigation sequence, the set of references, and the newsgroup messages are the same for every student on the course. This homogeneous response is to students with changing needs and whose level of experience on the subject being taught and on the use of resources available on the website are different. Furthermore, adaptation is essential in distance education because students are isolated and have a wide variety of backgrounds and interests. Therefore an environment that adapts to each individual student appears to be desirable. Examples of such adaptation could be to order or highlight newsgroups messages, page annotations and files on student interests, and to group the students with similar levels or slightly higher levels of experience.

In order to solve this problem, the web-based adaptive educational systems (Brusilovsky 1998) carry out an adaptation based on a user model, representing the user's knowledge state, preferences and goals. These are not entirely new kinds of systems as they borrow heavily from intelligent tutoring and adaptive hypermedia systems.

The objective of Intelligent Tutoring Systems (ITS) is to use the domain knowledge provided by an expert, the knowledge available on the student, and the tutor knowledge to offer flexible and personalized teaching. Because of the possibilities that the Internet offers, these systems began to be implemented on the Web, and are known as Web-based ITS (Brusilovsky 1995).

Adaptive hypermedia systems (Brusilovsky 1996) apply different forms of user models to adapt the contents and the hypermedia page links to the user. The main goal of this adaptation is to provide the user with efficient access to the site by first presenting the links that should be of interest.

To summarize, although distance learning benefits from the use of the educational web sites, it poses several challenges regarding the management of student collaboration and the adaptation of the contents to student needs. Thus some kind of personalization is required to adapt to student interests and requirements. For this reason it is necessary to have some data on the user such as personal and interaction data. In this chapter we describe how we are facing some of these problems within aLF (active learning framework). This is an environment for web-based distance learning developed to support the requirements for collaborative work between all the different communities involved.

2   Fundamental Points

On-line communities use tools that facilitate on-line contact among users who are browsing the same pages. They also encourage the creation and management of different interest groups. As we will comment later on, sites that are based on the storage of site information and user interactions have been developed to support these communities. Stored information is used to generate dynamic page information, and to extend their contents via user on-line annotation, and also to identify user types and register navigation traces.

Sites which support on-line communities offer a wide variety of services and information sources for each community which may make the user feel overwhelmed.

In Section 3 of this chapter we will describe aLF and the services it offers, and we will see that it is a good option for cooperative work on the Web. Nevertheless, owing to the increasing number of materials and users who access the web site, more and more problems are being detected in the management of these communities. There are many unresolved questions such as: How should the groups be organized on the course? How can we detect that a student has difficulties on the course?, and many others.

aLF monitors student actions on the platform and stores this data in the database. Using the database an adaptive system may infer student requirements or interests. Such information is usually called a user model and an introduction to this field will be presented in Section 4.1.

Traditional user modeling systems often make use of knowledge representation techniques. Knowledge representation formalisms offer facilities for maintaining knowledge bases (using representation formalism) and for reasoning (using the inference procedures of representation formalisms). Usually these facilities must be defined a priori by the system designer. This definition is very time-consuming and costly because there are a huge variety of data and rules to represent (Pohl *et al.* 2001).

In addition, for a system to be really adaptive, simple memorization of its interaction with the user in the user model is not enough. Ideally, adaptation results from generalizing previous experiences and applying these generalizations to new user interactions. That is from a learning process.

As a result of applying machine learning techniques, user models can be automatically modified as the users interact with the system. Yet in contrast, no explicit knowledge about the user can be obtained.

Another key feature in these systems is the acquisition of feedback from the student. Usually adaptive systems rely on dangerous assumptions about the interests of a particular user (for instance, if a user has not chosen a particular HTML page then he/she is not interested in that page at all) or make the user explicitly express his/her interests (for instance, the user must rate each page in the system as "interesting" or "not interesting"). The latter requirement may be both boring and subjective for the user.

In Section 4.3 we will present a hybrid approach combining both knowledge-based user models and machine learning components, which allows us to acquire better user models without any loss in representation.

Learning plays a key role in user model acquisition. Its design goes far beyond the simple application of a learning method. In this chapter we show that the application of a single method is not sufficient to learn some user features and we propose using an ensemble of several machine learning methods or classifiers to improve the accuracy of this task. In this chapter, we will not present the whole architecture of the system in detail since it is described elsewhere (Boticario *et al.* 2000, 2001).

2.1   Computer Support Collaborative Work

Over the past decade we have seen an explosion of network-based technologies that enable traditional and non-traditional distance learners alike to learn together. These environments enhance traditional distance-learning curricula by giving students the opportunity to interact with other students and share ideas (Jermann *et al.* 2001), and are called Computer Support Collaborative Systems (CSCL).

There is a general framework for all these systems: a private environment for each student and another public or shared environment where the students collaborate; in addition each student has a coach at his/her service. The coach is a personal assistant recommends certain actions to the student in order to improve his/her collaboration with his/her partners. These recommendations implemented based are on the student's interaction in his/her private area and in the shared workspace, and by applying certain predefined rules.

There are two important open questions. How can the user be made aware of fellow participants' actions and what is the behavior of the student personal assistant. These two aspects are related to correct user modeling, user interaction and the group model to which the user belongs.

Regarding the paper by Jermann *et al.* (2001) we can distinguish four fundamental stages:
- Data capture of the user interaction.
- Identification of the actual state of the interaction.
- The interaction can be diagnosed by comparing the current state of interaction with an ideal model of interaction. An ideal model is a set of indicators describing desirable and undesirable interaction states. For instance, we might want learners to be verbose, agree frequently, and all to participate.
- Simple remedial actions (e.g., "You have not participated enough") might result from analyzing a model containing only one indicator (e.g., word or action count), which can be directly computed from the data. More complex remedial actions might require a more sophisticated computational model.

These stages are always the same. First data is collected, then an interaction model is constructed and instantiated to represent the current state and possibly the desired state. Finally, some decisions are made about how to proceed.

Jermann *et al.* (2001) distinguish three types of supportive collaborative learning systems in the context of the collaboration management model. Systems that reflect actions, systems that monitor the state of interaction, and systems that analyze the state of the collaboration.

Systems that reflect actions, termed mirroring systems, collect raw data in log files, and display it to the collaborators. This is the most basic level since the system only discloses the actions that a particular student is doing to the rest of the group components.

Systems that monitor the state of interaction fall into two categories: those that aggregate the interaction data into a set of high-level indicators and display them to the participants, and those that internally compare the current state of interaction to a model of ideal interaction but do not reveal this information to the users. In the first case, the learners are expected to manage the interaction themselves, after having been given the appropriate information to do so. In the second case, this information is either intended for later use by a coaching agent, or analyzed by researchers in an effort to understand and explain the interaction.

Lastly, there are the systems that analyze the state of collaboration using an interaction model, and offer advice intended to increase the effectiveness of the learning process. The coach in an advising system plays a role similar to that of a lecturer in a collaborative learning classroom.

3   An Environment for Web-Based Student Collaboration

3.1   Overview

Our research is developed in a distance-learning university (UNED[1]) with over 180,000 students and a traditional distance-education model. UNED is especially for those people who want to be given a second chance to study, whose time is very limited, for whom distance is a problem, and who may even be physically handicapped. It is also for corporate workers who want to update their knowledge. This last group can also take advantage of the postgraduate courses offered. In this context we can find students of different ages and with very different backgrounds and motivations. There is therefore a set of educational requirements and needs to be fulfilled that are different for each student. Distance-education tools have been shown to be useful in such situations and, particularly, web-based adaptive educational systems seem to be one of the best solutions.

A platform called aLF (active learning framework) has been developed in order to support the requirements for collaborative work between all the different communities involved. The platform builds upon the ArsDigita Community System[2], a multiplatform and open source set of tools for constructing web-based applications. aLF is composed of a Web server connected to a relational database and a set of TCL (*Tool Command Language*) scripts allowing management of the interaction with the data model.

The first important feature of aLF is using a relational database to manage the information provided by the web server. This informa-

---

[1] www.uned.es

[2] www.arsdigita.com

tion is usually managed directly through the file system tools provided by the operating system. Although this approach can provide adequate functionality for static sites, it is neither flexible nor reliable enough when it has to manage large amounts of transactions. In a collaborative environment like aLF, there is a huge stream of information flowing between users and through the site. These sites are very dynamic since users are regularly interacting in a variety of ways, such as sending messages to the bulletin boards, organizing interactive meetings or publishing materials. Accordingly, the relational database component of aLF provides support for these requirements. This database does not only store the user personal information and the contents they send, but also serves to structure potentially everything that is happening in the site.

Another key feature of aLF is that it offers different views based on user navigation and actions through the site. All kinds of information on users can thus be gathered with TCL scripting language. The scripts can interface with the database so that this information can be easily stored and retrieved on demand. TCL scripts can also contribute to maintaining a dynamic environment, since they enable web pages to be dynamically constructed and this process can make use of the database information if required.

Users registered on aLF are grouped into *workgroups* (Figure 1). The administration of each workgroup is done by the person in charge who may not be the web site manager. The setting up of these kind of workgroups is particularly useful for distance learning since it allows different university departments, courses, study groups and research groups to be managed.

3.2   Services

aLF workgroups offer several services thus allowing a learning and collaborative environment to be easily set up:

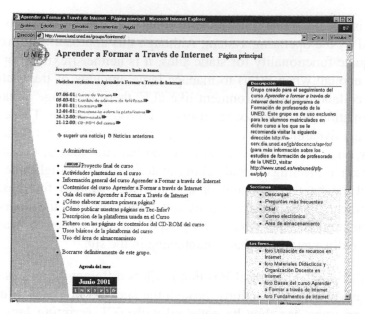

Figure 1. aLF course workgroup.

- *Newsgroups*: They can be reached via HTML pages (Figure 2), and automatically index the messages by categories defined by the manager or establish a notification system so users are automatically informed about new replies. They can be moderated or unmoderated. They are very useful in an educational community because they permit communication between students and lecturers.

- *Bulletin boards*: With this service aLF users can create news for the rest of the community members without having to use electronic mail. The author of the news item or message can control the date of publication of the news, its expiry date and even the group of people for whom it is intended. It is particularly useful since the rest of the workgroup members can comment on the news item and group interaction is thereby enhanced (Figure 3).

- *Document management*: A user can manage all his/her documents on line by having them in a central place and accessible to

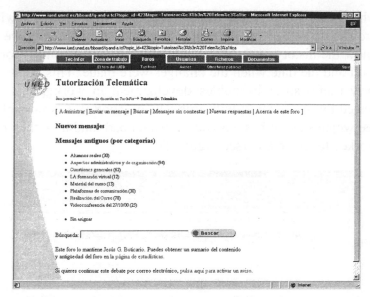

Figure 2. An example of newsgroups pages.

Intranet
_____

Noticias en www.iued.uned.es
19-09-00: Páginas de Materiales Didácticos del IUED
18-09-00: Creado un potente foro web
11-09-00: Jornadas de Teleformación y Teletrabajo para
personas con discapacidad
11-09-00: Poenalis: Derecho penal en la red
15-08-00: Dos mil cien millones de páginas web
04-08-00: Inversiones en Rediris
01-08-00: Los españoles en Internet
06-07-00: Reflexiones de Alfons Cornellá sobre la Educación

sugiere un asunto | archivos

Figure 3. An example of an aLF bulletin board.

all those users that he/she desires. The system has a permission
management service so that each document can be read, modified or managed by a particular user, by a series of users or by a

whole workgroup. These users can access from anywhere with a browser to see, update or delete their files. Furthermore, we can know the history of the document and thus see who has worked on it and the date when the changes were made. This is particularly useful since it enables development in workgroups suggested by the lecturer; with this version control it is possible to see which student has worked on which part, and how they have worked together, etc. (see Figure 4).

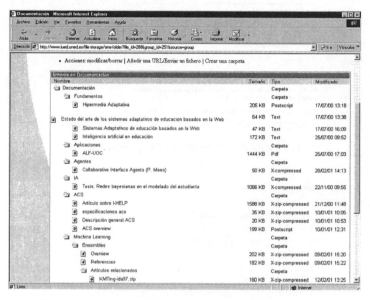

Figure 4. Document Management in an aLF workgroup.

- *Chats*: Internet group work is useful particularly from an asynchronous point of view, i.e., when the different collaborators do not work at the same time. Sometimes distance and the feeling of isolation can be counterproductive. With the chat tool small group chats can be organized, thereby avoiding the problem of overcrowded chats which make the service unintelligible. The advantage of this service in aLF, as well as gaining access via the HTML pages, is that all the conversations are recorded so that the lecturer can select relevant information from his/her conversation with the students and thus avoid repetition. Key chat issues can be transferred to the forum.

- *Calendar*: There are private calendars for each of the users, group calendars and a public calendar for all the aLF communities. The most commonly used service is the fixing of appointments within the workgroup.

- *Presentations*: They allow, by just completing forms, to prepare an instant presentation for the Web which is quickly downloaded. There is therefore no need to send files to the server. They have automatic indexes and all the necessary links for navigation support. They are really useful for teaching since they allow both lecturers and students to specify certain contents on a few screens, each screen being a HTML page. They also have a further advantage in that you do not need to know the web format to edit the screen with a pleasant and navigable visual structure.

- *Project management*: It allows certain project tasks to be created. For each task, project or tasks assignments can be created which become the responsibility of the task owner. These assignments can be different types (error, improvement or new task), have different levels of severity (critical, serious, medium or low) and states (open, need clarification, fixed waiting approval, deferred or closed). From the point of view of distance learning, the usefulness of a project management tool as presented here is obvious. We can create projects for certain student workgroups and tasks for these projects, so that students work in their corresponding area as they receive assignments, either from their lecturer or their fellow students. The group members can check their work on a list where all the group member tasks are described, as well as progress reports on each one of them. Each project can have forums, project marks and a task and assignment monitoring system, thereby creating a user-friendly project knowledge base which can be consulted and accessed from the web.

- *Tools to contact the other users*: There are a set of different tools enabling users to publish their own personal pages, to see which users are connected at the same time, to see which users are already in the community and what their participation is. This utility promotes the use of the chat tool.

It is important to point out that aLF manages all these services through the database. Information about the messages sent to a forum or a bulletin board, the task assignments (tickets) sent to the project management tool, the appointments on the calendar, the annotations to a particular news item on the board or the conversation in a chat are stored in the database, so a great amount of information on user interaction with the platform is available.

3.3   An aLF Course Experience

We will now describe an experience of a distance course being taught through aLF. The goal of this course was precisely to teach the use of the Internet in education.

We set up a group in aLF for the students on the course; this group had a bulletin board, news service, chat, file-storage area and a personal web-pages storage area where the students could publish their own web pages.

Regarding the conceptual organization of the contents, it was based on the proposal made by Roger Schank in the ASK system (Schank and Cleary 1995). The course concepts were organized as a conceptual network where each node was a course concept for the student to learn and the arcs represented certain links between concepts such as, prerequisite, consequence, example or exercise. These links were presented by several questions or options that the student could choose (see Figures 5 and 6).

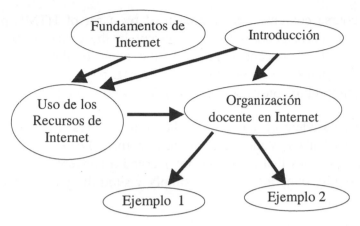

Figure 5. Partial conceptual network of the course contents (in Spanish).

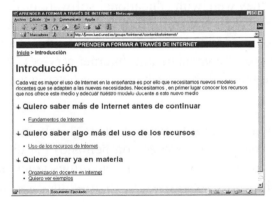

Figure 6. Course page resulting from the conceptual network of Figure 5.

As we have mentioned before, the whole goal of the course was to teach the use of the Internet in education for lecturers. It started by introducing basic concepts about the Internet and its services. It then taught a possible organization of the courses using these services. The course also had certain general subgoals that the student may attain, such as **Basis of the course, Fundamentals of the Internet, Use of the Internet** in education, and **Practices.**

The course contents were represented by a set of HTML pages, each one corresponding to one concept in the course conceptual network. This conceptual network, the goals of the course, and other elements are represented by an XML page[3] that the system may interpret to construct the student knowledge model.

For each student on the course, the system stores a model of the contents that the student has already learned. For this course the system assumes that a student has learned a concept if he/she has successfully done a test or has simply visited the pages related to the concept.

First we presented the students with a survey in order to evaluate how familiar they were with educational software or the Internet. In most cases the students were in turn lecturers interested in the use of the Internet in education, and on the whole, they had little experience in the use of computers and Internet services. As the course proceeded we realized that we had a very heterogeneous group of students.

Consequently, the course lecturers had to closely monitor the students on the course. They solved (on demand) the difficulties that arose. The lecturers proposed several activities (such as sending a message to the bulletin board) in order to guide the students more closely.

Although there was also the possibility of contacting the lecturers by phone or face-to-face, the main channels of communication were the course bulletin boards and electronic mail. The lecturer also visited the chat room established for the course to detect if the students had difficulties in the course.

---

[3] XML is a meta-language, i.e., it is a language to define languages. It is composed of certain elements that provide information about the contents of the document and not only about its physical structure or presentation as occurs in HTML pages

We have also discovered that students do not collaborate among themselves except when they use the chats and send personal e-mails. If this lack of collaboration could have been foreseen, lecturers could have suggested scenarios or tasks where students were encouraged to interact.

These problems could have been avoided if the system had detected student difficulties, such as problems in the use of the course services. Then lecturers could have been informed of these problems right from the beginning and they could have set up subgroups of students with similar characteristics, needs and interests. The system could also automatically do this.

Thus our proposal for a personalized environment is based on a cooperative tutoring scheme. In this scheme the lecturer, besides solving the doubts of the students in a personalized way, is responsible for improving collaboration between the group components.

4   Adaptive Tasks

So far we have reviewed a wide range of functionalities required for user interaction and collaboration from the point of view of web technology. However, this technology does not fully exploit all the information gathered in the database. Accordingly, the next stage is to incorporate support for *adaptive tasks*.

Generally, it is desirable that educational systems provide some kind of support to the student in the learning process. There a number of ITS techniques suitable for this task such as intelligent analysis of student solutions, interactive problem-solving support or example-based problem solving support (Brusilovsky 1998). However, in a collaborative work environment like aLF, it is also important to incorporate another type of support for the so-called *adaptive navigation* and *adaptive collaboration* tasks. In addition, on postgraduate courses, where the system is currently being applied, support for these tasks is usually needed more than for the ITS techniques.

The adaptive navigation support task aims to assist the student navigate over a web site's pages by changing the appearance of the links available, for example, highlighting those considered to be the most important. In particular, systems incorporating this feature can arrange, annotate or hide the links dynamically to make it easier to select the link that must be chosen. Adding adaptive navigation support to an educational web site can help the student find the optimal path through the course contents. Moreover, this technique simply advises, i.e. all the links on a page are available so that the student can decide the following step to take, what concept he/she wants to learn or what problem he/she wants to do. This ties in with the goal of this research of promoting significant and active learning by stimulating student participation in the use of the different resources (Boticario and Gaudioso 2000).

Adaptive collaboration support is a very recent technique that is beginning to be incorporated in ITS and it has coincided with the advance of Internet educational systems. The goal of this technique is to use the knowledge that the system has on the students stored in the user models, to constitute workgroups and put students with similar interests and levels of experience in contact with one another. Usually there can be different kinds of collaboration between students and lecturers, such as collaboration via public annotations in the exercises, collaboration via synchronous communications of the people connected at a specific moment, and collaboration via the setting up of workgroups based on student similarities. Although we can achieve all these functionalities in aLF, we try to adapt all these possibilities to the real needs and interests of the user so that the user does not feel overwhelmed by the amount of services provided here.

All these tasks are done by using models that represent certain characteristics of the user, such as personal data, requirements or personal interests. This information is used by the adaptive system to achieve the adaptive tasks described above. We will now briefly describe the fundamental points of user modeling.

4.1   User Modeling

The user model is an integral part of any intelligent user interface aiming to adapt to its user requirements. A *user model* (Ross 2000) is an explicit representation of the properties of an individual user; it can be used to reason about the needs, preferences or future behaviour of the user. Most computer systems that interact with humans contain some kind of implicit model of the user. For example, a program using the mini-max game playing strategy has an implicit model of a single canonical user; it assumes that the user will always make the best possible move. This model affects the program, but is not stored explicitly. The paper "User modeling via stereotypes" (Rich 1979) is widely regarded as marking the beginning of user modeling. Rich investigates the possibilities for allowing computers to treat their users as individuals with distinct personalities and goals.

User modeling is now a mature field, and demonstrably useful research systems exist. Yet few commercial implementations of user modeling exist, since there are some difficulties encountered when incorporating a user model into the design of existing systems. User models are sometimes quite complicated, meaning implementation requires significant development resources. This problem is exacerbated by a lack of empirical studies of user model performance benefits and effects on user training. Performance overheads should therefore be considered. These problems have motivated research into minimalist user models, which aim to provide the benefits of user modeling with a very simple modeling system, cutting down on development costs and performance overheads.

Traditional user modeling systems often make use of Knowledge Representation (KR) techniques. KR formalisms offer facilities for maintaining knowledge bases (using representation formalisms) and for reasoning (using the inference procedures of representation formalisms). For user modeling, these facilities are typically employed as follows: assumptions about individual characteristics of the user are maintained in a knowledge base, using a representation formalism. Since this knowledge base may additionally contain system knowledge about the application domain or meta-knowledge for inferring additional assumptions about the user from his/her current model (including predefined group models, the so-called stereotypes), it has been called User Modeling Knowledge Base (UMKB, (Pohl *et al.* 2001)). If available, inference procedures of the representation formalism or meta-level inferences can be used to expand the user model.

Two main problems arise from the use of KR user models with predefined knowledge acquisition rules. First, it is quite difficult to create these rules and second, it is difficult to maintain these user models. In order to overcome these difficulties machine learning techniques are currently widely used in user adaptive systems.

4.2   Machine Learning and User Modeling

More recently, quite a large number of systems using machine learning for personalized information have been described in the literature, like Syskill&Webert (Pazzani and Billsus 1997) or Letizia (Liebermann 1995). In general, Machine Learning (ML) methods process training input and offer support for decision (mainly classification) problems based on this input. Hence, ML-based user-adaptive systems work quite differently from KR-based ones. Instead of a knowledge base, learning results are the central source of information about the user. Observations of user behavior (e.g., reactions to meeting proposals or document ratings) are used to form training examples. Learning components do model acquisition by running their algorithms on these examples. Representation is implicit: formats of learning results are specific to the learning algorithm used (decision trees, probabilities, etc.) which makes them difficult to be reused for other purposes. Owing to the lack of an independent representation formalism, there is no further reasoning based on already acquired data. However, decisions are directly supported, e.g., the meeting scheduling assistants let their learning components predict the user's reaction to new meeting proposals and use this prediction for their individualized suggestions.

The main advantage of using machine learning techniques in user adaptive systems, is their ability to support (history-aware) acquisition and decisions dynamically. Yet there are also problems. It is not easy and is sometimes nearly impossible for several different decision processes to take advantage of learning results when these results reflect usage regularities but do not explicitly represent individual user characteristics. Thus it is difficult to communicate learning results to the user for inspection and explanation purposes. In KR-based user modeling systems with their explicitly represented user models, these problems can be handled more easily. We propose to integrate features of KR-based and ML-based user modeling, as we see in the next sections (Pohl *et al.* 2001).

In order to take advantage of the two approaches described earlier, there are several hybrid approaches that combine both technologies.

The LaboUr system (Pohl *et al.* 2001) stores certain observations about the user. It is composed of both Learning Components (LCs) and Acquisition Components (ACs) based on some predefined rules.

4.3   aLF User Modeling

As we have mentioned before, we propose a hybrid approach for user modeling. We combine the techniques of Knowledge Representation (KR) and the Machine Learning (ML) models. Moreover, in order to improve the response given by the ML-based components we propose a combination of several machine learning techniques.

In addition, this user model is based on the services and interactions observed in aLF, so it is easily usable in any course being taught through this environment.

As we have already mentioned, a key feature of aLF is that it is able to track user navigation and actions through the site and dynamically generate different views. The TCL scripting language allows all kinds of information about users to be gathered. It interfaces with the database so that this information can be easily stored and retrieved on demand.

With these mechanisms, aLF monitors student actions on the platform and stores this data in the database. From this data the system may infer student requirements or interests. To make all these inferences, aLF maintains a knowledge base quite separate from the database to represent the models considered in the system, such as user model or content model. These models are composed of several entities and are represented in THEO (Mitchell *et al.* 1990), a framework for learning and problem solving. Each entity in the knowledge base has several attributes that describe the characteristics of the entity, for example, we can define an entity named user which will have several attributes such as name or address. The value of these attributes can be defined in three different ways:
- The attribute value is directly assigned by the user or the tutor (for example, the name) or it is the result of a particular function

(for example, the age of the student is determined from the date of birth and the date of the interaction).

- The attribute value can be determined by applying a specific rule predefined by the tutor. The syntax of these rules is similar to PROLOG logical programming language rules. An example of one of these rules can be found in Figure 7. One key feature of THEO is consistency, i.e., if a rule is dependent on one particular attribute and the value of this attribute changes in a later interaction, then the value of the attribute associated with that rule also changes.

IF (preferred-text-only preferences-id-user)

THEN (take-only-alt <image> <page-html>)

Figure 7. Example of a rule in THEO, it expresses user preference in the presentation of pages. This rule depends on the attribute preferred-text-only.

- The attribute value can be the result of a machine learning task. When an attribute is dependent on a machine learning task, THEO sends a request to a special module in charge of executing this task. We have implemented the learning module as a combination of several machine learning methods, a decision tree learner (C4.5), a rule set learner (C4.5Rules) and a Bayesian learner (Naive Bayes). This design lies in the assumption that it has to be capable of performing well in a wide range of relatively complex learning problems. Since it is well known that no single machine learning algorithm is better for every domain, at first sight it appears that using a single method will not provide a reasonable performance for all the problems. Furthermore, given that these problems are not likely to be easy because of the heterogeneous nature of web users, we can expect every algorithm to perform well only in some regions of the instance space. In other words, for each algorithm there will be a possible subset of instances outside of its competence region, for which the algorithm will not be able to be accurate in its predictions. If we assume that different algorithms have different competence regions, optimal performance will be obtained by selecting the best algorithm for each particular instance presented to the system. This feature would be improved if each learning method were executed by a different agent forming a multi-agent architecture. The multi-agent architecture is thus suitable for introducing negotiation, for example between several user modeling agents to get the best response.

We will now describe the adaptive tasks for the course described above.

5   aLF Course Adaptive Tasks

5.1   Models

To carry out the adaptive tasks described in Section 4, we define three models, a user model, a pedagogical model and a contents model. In addition, as a result of the user action tracking performed by aLF we have the following data: pages visited, messages visited in the bulletin boards, chat conversations visited or participated in, FAQs (Frequently Asked Questions) read, and presentations bookmarks of other users, news, personal pages visited by the user and files visited.

The contents model is composed of XML and the conceptual network described in Section 3.3.

To form the pedagogical model, each page in the course is represented in the knowledge base as an entity in THEO. In this representation, the course designer specifies (by means of a PROLOG rule) the ideal path that the student may follow through the course contents. We will see this representation in more detail in Section 5.2.

The pedagogical model also includes a representation of several predefined stereotypes (Rich 1979) (see Section 4.3). At the moment we have defined the following stereotypes:

- Students with no-knowledge in the course and very active once they become familiar with the platform.
- Students (not active) with some background in the use of the Internet but they have never used it in education.
- Students very active with some background in the use of Internet but they have never used it in education.
- More advanced students but not active.
- More advanced active students.

When the students start the course we ask them to complete a questionnaire to find out what they know about the Internet. We then initialize their user model according to the results of this survey.

As we will describe later, we can predict the level of activity of a user with only two interactions. We assign a different stereotype to a particular student if he/she has progressed in the course contents or if he/she has increased or decreased his/her collaboration. The main disadvantage of the stereotypes is that they are very rigid and static. Machine learning techniques could be a good alternative to avoid these inconveniences.

Regarding the user model, there are basically two groups of data:

- Personal data: Student personal data, Background knowledge obtained from the survey.
- Interaction data and student knowledge state. We distinguish between:

- Overlay model. We formed an overlay model for each student. The overlay model models the student's knowledge as a subset of that of an expert. The overlay model is more applicable when the subject matter to be learnt can be represented as a prerequisite hierarchy. In the prerequisite hierarchy, the subject has a number of concepts and for each concept there are a set of prerequisites. The overlay model indicates how far the student has progressed in acquiring the subject knowledge in comparison with that of the expert.
- Social characteristics: It groups those attributes that characterize student collaboration. At the moment we have only defined one attribute, the *level of activity* and its value is the result of a learning task.

5.2   Course Adaptive Navigation and Adaptive Collaboration Support

With respect to the adaptive navigation support task, the system guides students through the course contents via adaptive link annotation. In this instance, the pedagogical model monitors the adaptive navigation support task, which consists of guiding students through Web contents via link annotations. The pedagogical model thus represents the content pages as shown in Figure 8. The attributes title and source-int define the title and the path to the file containing the page constructed beforehand by a lecturer.

The attribute next-link-advised is the one that determines which link the system will suggest. This attribute is calculated using a rule defined in the knowledge base as shown in Figure 8. As we have mentioned before, the syntax is similar to PROLOG logical programming language rules. The lecturer defines the possible links to be recommended in the attribute links-opc. These links are defined using a list of values where the link identifier is defined, which will be used after in the rule (in the example: "Fun"), the text appearing in the link (in the example: "Fundamentos de Internet"), the link destination (in the example: "fundamentos.html") and the text, icon,... appearing as a link annotation to indicate it as a recommended link (in the example: "Quiero saber más de Internet"). The lecturer can thus justify why this is the advised link.

```
(introducion.html *novalue*
        (id-user anonymous)
        (title "Introduccion ")
        (links-opc (("Fun" "Fundamentos de Internet"
                "Fundamentos.html" "Quiero saber mas de Internet")
                ))
        (source-int "fundamentos.html")
        (annotations-allowed yes)
        (next-link-advised *novalue*
        (all.prolog.clauses (
                ((next-link-advised ?r ?value):-
                        (id-user ?r ?user)
                        (eval (visited-page '?user "survey.html") nil)
                                (eval "Fun" ?value))
                ) ) ) )
```

Figure 8. Representation in THEO of a course page (in Spanish).

As can be seen in the PROLOG rule in Figure 8, the recommendation is based on the user navigation trace, i.e., if the user has visited some specific page then the recommendation is another specific page. The recommendation is obviously limited since it is based on a predefined topic network.

We do not consider any other goal than the one predefined by the tutor. We only provide adaptive annotation of the links recommended by the system but we do not yet identify an erroneous situation if the student does not follow our recommendations. However, with the data gathered by aLF, such as the pages accessed by the user, we have the user navigation trace through the course contents. By simply matching the user trace with the one predefined by the tutor, we can determine if the student follows a correct navigation.

As we have already mentioned, the only goal considered is "to learn some concept" predefined by the tutor. This goal can be improved in an environment like aLF, distinguishing whether the student has some other subgoal, such as do some exercise, obtain some reference or contact with someone able to help. This must be determined in a more sophisticated way by comparing the user trace with other user traces and trying to categorize these traces.

With respect to the adaptive collaboration support task, the system is responsible for guiding cooperation and communication among students and with lecturers. From the data stored on the user, the system can determine all the information regarding his/her collaboration in the workgroups in which he/she participates. This is because aLF stores in the database all the annotations made by the user, every message sent to the forums and to the group components, and all the group interactions. Therefore, the system can include in the user model certain attributes that reflect his/her interaction and collaboration profile, such as the level of group activity (low, medium or high) mentioned in Section 5.1. At the moment this profile is constructed from the data that we have on the interactions that the user has made in the forums, but it will be extended to the rest of interactions that the user can make, such as annotations on the pages or the actions done to public files in the file storage area (also mentioned in Section 5.1).

The point here is to determine the user interaction profile. It is not like the model used in an adaptive navigation support task because this one must be constructed without a predefined interaction model or a quite rigid one.

Taking into account this profile, at the moment the system may provide adaptive collaboration support by recommending a user to perform some action in the forums from his/her earlier interactions (see (Vassileva *et al.* 1999) for related work). With the first two forum interactions, the module in charge of user modeling (see Section 4.1) can determine if the level of activity of that user is low, medium or high. Once this value is obtained, if the activity of the user is low, the system may recommend visiting the help pages to learn how to use the forums or visiting a specific forum instead. Once this attribute is determined, the system may use it to construct the appropiate recommendation.

6 Summary and Related Work

aLF, the platform described in this chapter, is especially for developing Web workgroups. Nowadays, there are more and more Web initiatives to facilitate the development of communities of Web users, such as ThirdVoice[4] or Gooey[5]. What differentiates aLF from all other initiatives is that it provides an integrated framework for all Internet services through HTML pages, storing all the information about user interactions in a database which allows that data to be processed.

Although aLF is not solely for educational purposes, it is specially useful in the establishment of on-line courses, since it provides many integrated services such as forums or file storage areas. However, supporting distance education with educational web sites does not guarantee that the students will find the required information or will engage in effective collaborative learning behavior.

The users registered in aLF may feel somewhat overwhelmed by the amount of services provided and the complexity and variety of tasks they are expected to solve, such as self-assessment exercises, collaborative tasks, or practical exercises. In this chapter we de-

---

[4] www.thirdvoice.com
[5] sourceforge.net/projects/gooey/

scribe our proposal for a user modeling system framed within aLF, in order to carry out the adaptive tasks needed to support the users in their interaction with aLF.

The Web-based adaptive educational systems seem to be the best solutions to support students in their interactions with the educational web sites, since they can adapt the information and the services to user requirements and interests. Such adaptation is done through user modeling representing the user's knowledge state, preferences and goals. We have seen that the development of the web-based adaptive educational systems borrows heavily from the Intelligent Tutoring Systems (ITS) and Adaptive Hypermedia (AH) systems. Some of the best known web-based ITS are CALAT (Nakabayashi 1996), ELM-ART (Brusilovsky *et al.* 1996a), PAT Online (Ritter 1997), Albatros (Lai *et al.* 1995) and some of the most well-known adaptive hypermedia systems are Interbook (Brusilovsky *et al.* 1996b) and AHA (De Bra and Calvi 1998).

Among the systems combining both techniques, ITS and AH, we find ELM-ART (Brusilovsky *et al.* 1996a) and PAT-InterBook (Brusilovsky *et al.* 1997). These systems facilitate course delivery over the Internet guiding the students through the course contents (by adapting the contents and the hypermedia page links to the student), analyzing student errors, checking which concepts have been learnt and which have not, etc. The precise objective of the development of the PAT-Interbook system was to construct an integrated system incorporating two different systems with their respective functions (conceptual instruction through InterBook, and problem-solving interaction through PAT Online) where the emphasis was on providing the systems with sufficient flexibility to facilitate their integration (shared data concerning user progress, user model, etc.).

In this proposal, the only adaptive tasks considered are adaptive navigation and collaboration support. More specific ITS techniques are not yet required, since given the amount of services provided in aLF, it is more important to provide support to the user in the interaction with the web site.

Systems developed within these areas are usually based on a static representation of the domain knowledge and student model. Yet if we want a user model to adapt from experience, it should incorporate *learning* capabilities.

The application of machine learning techniques to student modeling has focused on learning some already defined student model attributes or on including some data which are not used traditionally (the difficulty of particular problems, student beliefs about their own abilities).

Machine learning techniques have been applied to the construction of student models in order to determine, for example, whether a student had a particular misconception (Chiu and Webb 1997), to determine the steps where the student would need help (Gertner *et al.* 1998) and to select which advanced level teaching action to perform next (Quafafou *et al.* 1995).

In this chapter we have seen that some user model attributes are learned from observations of student interaction. The learning approach has been chosen because the wide range of services are used for very different kind of users and for a variety of purposes which cannot be anticipated by several user *profiles* or *stereotypes* predefined by the course tutor. Given the difficulty of the tasks involved in learning a web-based user model, we assume that optimal performance would be obtained by selecting the best algorithm for each particular learning task.

The selection of the best algorithm would be improved if each learning method were executed by a different agent forming a multi-agent architecture. The multi-agent architecture is thus suitable for introducing negotiation, for example between several user modeling agents to get the best response.

Machine learning multi-agent architectures have also been used in the development of intelligent tutoring systems. For example, the ADVISOR system (Beck *et al.* 2000) is composed of a two-agent machine learning architecture for intelligent tutoring systems. The first agent is responsible for learning a model (by linear regression) of how students perform while using the tutor in a variety of contexts. The second agent is provided with this model of student behavior and a goal specifying the desired educational objective to obtain a teaching policy which meets the specified educational goal (by reinforcement learning).

Generally speaking, when using learning agents for the construction of user models, a specific machine learning technique is selected (Beck and Woolf 2000) depending on the problem to be solved.

Another multi-agent approach to the design of collaborative environments is I-Help (Vassileva *et al.* 1999). I-Help is a user-adaptive distributed system deployed to support a collaborative community of learners to locate help resources (electronic resources and human peer helpers) on a long university introductory computer science course. The adaptation within the multi-agent I-Help system is based on models of human users and models of involved software applications. These are maintained by two classes of agents: personal agents (human users) and application agents (software applications). Thus the adaptive behavior (location of resources) of the heterogeneous distributed system I-Help is the result of goal-oriented autonomous cognitive agents.

References

Beck, J.E. and Woolf, B.P. (2000), "High-level student modeling with machine learning," *Proceedings of the Fifth International Conference on Intelligent Tutoring Systems*, Springer.

Beck, J.E., Woolf, B.P., and Beal, C.R. (2000), "Advisor: a machine learning architecture for intelligent tutor construction," *Proceedings of the Seventeenth National Conference on Artificial Intelligence*.

Boticario, J.G. and Gaudioso, E. (2000), "Adaptive web-site for distance learning," *Campus-Wide Information Systems*, vol. 17, issue 4, MCB University Press.

Boticario, J.G., Gaudioso, E., and Hernandez, F. (2000), "Adaptive navigation support and adaptive collaboration support in webdl," *Proceedings of the International Conference on Adaptive Hypermedia and Adaptive Web-based Systems*, Trento, Italy, August, Springer Verlag, Lecture Notes in Computer Science (LNCS) no. 1892, pp. 51-61.

Boticario, J.G., Gaudioso, E., and Hernandez, F. (2001), "A machine learning architecture for user model acquisition," *Proceedings of the AIED 01. Frontiers in Artificial Intelligence and Applications*, San Antonio, USA, IOS Press.

Brusilovsky, P. (1995), "Intelligent tutoring systems for World-Wide Web," in Holzapfel, R. (ed.), *Proceedings of Third International WWW Conference (Posters)*, Darmstadt, Fraunhofer Institute for Computer Graphics, pp. 42-45.

Brusilovsky, P. (1996), "Methods and techniques of adaptive hypermedia," in *User Modeling and User-Adapted Interaction*, Kluwer Academic publishers, pp. 87-129.

Brusilovsky, P. (1998), "Adaptive educational systems on the World-Wide-Web: a review of available technologies," *Proceedings of Workshop WWW-Based Tutoring at Fourth International Conference on ITS (ITS'98)*, San Antonio, TX, August, MIT Press.

Brusilovsky, P., Ritter, S., and Schwarz, E. (1997), "Distributed intelligent tutoring on the web," in du Boulay and Mizoguchi (eds.), *Artificial Intelligence in Education: Knowledge and Media in Learning Systems*, Amsterdam, IOS, pp. 482-489.

Brusilovsky, P., Schwarz, E., and Weber, G. (1996a), "Elm-art: an intelligent tutoring system on world wide web," *Proceedings of the Third International Conference on Intelligent Tutoring Systems*, Montreal, Springer Verlag, pp. 261-269.

Brusilovsky, P., Schwarz, E., and Weber, G. (1996b), "A tool for developing adaptive electronic textbooks on WWW," *Proceedings of WebNet96*, San Francisco, CA, October, World Conference of the Web Society, pp. 64-69.

Chiu, B. and Webb, G. (1997), "Using c4.5 as an induction engine for agent modelling: an experiment of optimisation," *Machine Learning for User Modeling Workshop at the Seventh International Conference on User Modeling*.

De Bra, P. and Calvi, L. (1998), "Aha! an open adaptive hypermedia architecture," *The New Review of Hypermedia and Multimedia*, vol. 1, no. 4, pp. 115-139.

Gertner, A.S., Conati, C., and Vanlehn, K. (1998), "Procedural help in Andes: generating hints using a Bayesian network student model," *Proceedings of the Fifteenth National Conference on Artificial Intelligence*, pp. 106-111.

Jermann, P., Soller, A., and Muehlenbrock, M. (2001), "From mirroring to guiding: a review of state of the art technology for supporting collaborative learning," in Hakkarainen, K. Dillenbourg, P., and Eurolings, A. (eds.), *European Perspectives on Computer-Supported Collaborative Learning. Proceedings of the First European Conference on Computer-Supported Collaborative Learning*, Maastricht, McLuhan Institute, pp. 324-331.

Lai, M.C., Chen, B.H., and Yuan, S.M. (1995), "Toward a new educational environment," *Proceedings of 4th International WWW Conference*, Boston, USA, December.

Liebermann, H. (1995), "Letizia: an agent that assists Web browsing.

Mitchell, T.M., Allen, J., Chalasani, P., Cheng, J., Etzioni, O., Ringuette, M., and Schlimmer, J.C. (1990), "Theo: a framework for self-improving systems," in VanLehn, K. (ed.), *Architectures for Intelligence*, Erlbaum, Hillsdale, NJ.

Nakabayashi, K. (1996), "An intelligent tutoring system on the WWW supporting ubteractive simulation environments with a multimedia viewer control mechanism," *Proceedings of WebNet96*, San Francisco, CA, October, World Conference of the Web Society, p. 366.

Pazzani, M. and Billsus, D. (1997), "Learning and revising user proles: the identification of interesting Web sites."

Pohl, W., Schwab, I., and Koychev, I. (2001), "Learning about the user: a general approach and its application."

Quafafou, M., Mekaouche, A., and Nwana, H.S. (1995), "Multiviews learning and intelligent tutoring systems," *Proceedings of Seventh World Conf. on Artificial Intelligence in Education.*

Rich, E. (1979), *User Modelling via Stereotypes*.

Ritter, S. (1997), "Pat online: a model-tracing tutor on the World-Wide Web," in Brusilovsky, P., Nakabayashi, K., and Ritter, S. (eds.), *Proceedings of Workshop Intelligent Educational Systems on the World-Wide Web at AI-ED97, 8th World Conference on Artificial Intelligence in Education*, Kobe, Japan, pp. 11-17.

Ross, E. (2000), "Intelligent User Interfaces: Survey and Research Directions," Technical Report CSTR-00-004, kk, 1.

Schank, R.C. and Cleary, C. (1995), *Engines for Education*, Lawrence Erlbaum Associates, Hillsdale, New Jersey.

Vassileva, J., Greer, J., McCalla, G., Deters, R., Zapata, D., Mudgal, C., and Grant, S. (1999), "A multi-agent approach to the design of peer-help environments," in Lajoie, S.P. and Vivet, M. (eds.), *Proceedings of the International Conference on Artificial Intelligence in Education*, Le Mans, France, July, vol. 50 of *Frontiers in Artificial Intelligence and Applications*, IOS Press, pp. 38-45. Available on-line at http://julita.usask.ca/Texte/AIED '99.zip .

Chapter 10

An Intelligent System for Capturing Presentation on Desktop Manipulations — Supporting for Video Contents Production

Y. Nakamura, M. Ozeki and Y. Ohta

Although the use of video is essential for Internet education, it is difficult for non-professionals to take good videos. We need assistance for capturing and editing videos. We are tackling this problem by developing an automated system for taking videos on desktop manipulation. In this system, multiple cameras automatically track and shoot at important targets. The system selects the relevant views by recognizing human behaviors. Thus the effective presentation videos are automatically obtained.

In this chapter, we introduce the framework of our system. We first categorize the targets and purposes of shooting, and discuss the appropriate cameraworks. We propose camera control algorithms to realize such cameraworks. Next, we discuss the algorithms for detecting typical human behaviors, for example, deictic movements. Then, we introduce some experiments of recording presentations, and the user's evaluations and impressions.

1   Introduction

The use of video is essential for Internet education. Movie clips can be used effectively to teach in a wide variety of fields, and distant learning utilizes live videos. Many university courses are now recorded on video.

Taking good video is a difficult task that requires considerable skill and that can be costly. For example, several people may be involved in the videotaping and editing a video for audiovisual education. Thus, it is widely recognized that automated video production is one of the key technologies in multimedia.

For this purpose, we are investigating a framework for effectively capturing presentations, and producing comprehensible video contents. This requires an integration of intelligent works. Let us consider the process of making movies or TV programs. Camera operators move their cameras and change the camera angles and zoom factors. By this framing work, important portions are tracked and captured in an image frame. Editors select the best view. They determine which image to use out of the images from multiple cameras.

To realize such functions, we first developed a multi-camera system and its algorithm that automatically and intelligently tracks the candidates for the focus of attention. Then, we investigated event recognition for detecting the focus of attention, and editing for presenting the focused portions. Thus, we built a prototype system for communicating desktop manipulations. We applied the system to typical presentations of desktop manipulations and then verified the performance of the system.

2   Communicating the Focus of Attention

2.1   Communication and Attention

Let us consider a situation wherein a person is demonstrating the usage of a complicated machine, as shown in Figure 1. When the speaker explains an important device by holding it out toward us, we need to carefully look at it. In this case, we usually prefer a close-up shot (Figure 2(a)) or an extreme close-up shot (Figure 2(b)). Similarly, when the speaker demonstrates an important skill, we should carefully watch the speaker's hand or body motions. A closer shot of the workspace is necessary for good understanding of the manipulation.

Figure 1. Example behaviors in a presentation.

(a) close-up   (b) extremely close-up

Figure 2. Example of appropriate views.

To automatically obtain these shots and present them, we need to computerize the following functions:

Camera Control: Shooting and tracking of important portions with appropriate camerawork.

Focus Recognition: Recognition of the events occurring in a presentation, and detecting the focus of attention.

Selection and Emphasis: Selection of the best views and emphasizing important portions.

Before discussing the actual method, we will first clarify the problems we are tackling.

2.2 Important Behaviors

This research deals with *desktop presentations* in which a person demonstrates manipulations on a desk or a table. We assume the following situation:

- One person is speaking and presenting the manipulation.
- There is an audience, but the person giving the presentation does not get questions from audience members in realtime.
- The person may monitor the state of the system, such as camera motions or editing results.

This situation is common in a variety of video productions, *e.g.*, video instruction manuals or cooking shows.

The following behaviors frequently appear in this situation, and they are designed to capture the viewers' attention:

Pointing: Pointing with one's hand. It forces the audience to look in the directed indicated, as shown in Figure 3(a). This corresponds to *deictic movement* in Ekman's classification (Ekman and Friesen 1969). The focus is on the pointed object, location, or direction.

Holding-out: Holding out an object toward the audience, usually at a position higher than the waist and lower than the eyes (Figure 3(b)), invites the viewer to focus on the held object.

Manipulation: Demonstrating important operations is a typical behavior, as shown in Figure 3(c). What may occur is virtual manipulations such as *illustrators* in Ekman's classification. The focus is on the manipulation.

Illustration: Illustrating a shape, size, or motion by moving hands draws attention to it. This also corresponds to *illustrators* in Ek-

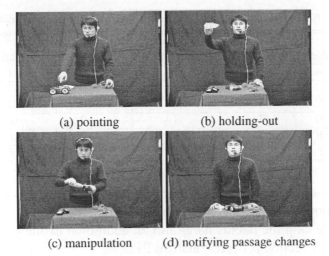

(a) pointing	(b) holding-out

(c) manipulation   (d) notifying passage changes

Figure 3. Important behaviors in presentations.

man's classification. The focus is the locus or the motion of the hands.

Notifying passage change: This refers to informing the audience that a speaker is beginning the next passage of an explanation (Figure 3(d)). While the purpose is rather vague, we can usually think that the focus is on the speaker.

Since discrimination between manipulation and illustration is sometimes difficult in actual presentations and their functions are similar, hereafter we group them together in this paper. Regarding pointing, we currently deal with only pointing at an object within the reach[1]. Since this makes the difference between pointing and holding-out obscure, we also put these two behaviors together in this discussion.

To get a rough idea of the frequency of these behaviors, we present an actual experiment. We asked several people to give a natural explana-

---

[1]Pointing beyond the speaker's reach are left for future research, since additional research is required for delineating the location of the pointed object.

Table 1. Behaviors that appeared in presentations on desktop manipulations.

subject	pointing, holding-out	manipulation, illustration	notifying passage changes	total
A	14	2	5	21
B	24	0	3	27
C	13	4	7	24
D	11	3	2	16
E	13	5	0	18
F	13	1	4	18

tion for assembling a toy car. The presentation was about 4 minutes long, although the length varied slightly among the people. For simplicity, we skip the details here, and an additional explanation will be given in Section 6.2 (presentation P1).

The rough statistics of the behaviors listed above are shown in Table 1. Each row shows the subject (A–F), and each figure shows the number of occurrences. As we can see here, the above behaviors appear around 20 times in 4 minutes. This implies that on average one of the behaviors appears every 12 seconds. Among them, holding-out behavior most frequently appears, and we need to intensively deal with it.

We also consulted our database (Nakamura *et al.* 1998) that stores presentations and TV programs about desktop presentations. Although quantitative analysis was difficult for TV programs[2], the types of behaviors we observed are similar to the above example.

2.3   System Design

Figure 4 shows an overview of our system. Multiple pan-tilt cameras shoot at important portions. Each camera is assigned a unique target and an objective for shooting. Videos taken by those cameras are

---

[2]TV programs often use shots without a speaker, close-up shots, and so on. We cannot tell certainly what a speaker is doing offscreen.

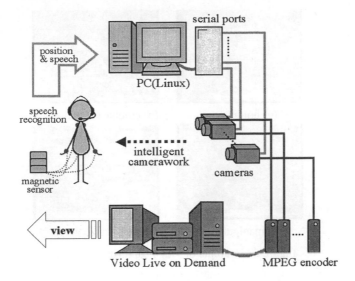

Figure 4. Overview of the system.

transmitted, switched, or recorded in MPEG format. This framework is essential for effective communication, since important portions are often scattered in a scene, and some of the important portions such as hands or important objects often moves arbitrarily. For camera control and behavior recognition, we have magnetic sensors for detecting the speaker's position.

This framework also includes event recognition whose outputs are used for video editing. For this purpose, the system has a speech recognition module and the above-mentioned magnetic positional sensors. Integration of speech and movement recognition is the key technique to realize automated editing for producing comprehensible videos. According to the recognition results, the system emphasizes the focus of attention by switching the views or choosing the relevant portions. Thus, the system gives views that a speaker wants to show or that viewers want to see.

(a) holding out   (b) emphasize the object

(c) manipulation   (d) emphasize the work

Figure 5. Example of video capturing and editing.

Figure 5 shows an example, in which an object is held out by a speaker. One camera always tracked the right hand of the speaker, and when he held out an object, as shown in Figure 5(a), the system switched the video to the close-up view, as shown in Figure 5(b). Thus, the focused object drew the attention of the audience.

3   Related Work

There are several kinds of research that are closely related to our framework.

A historical starting point may be teleconference systems. Teleconferencing with fixed cameras is tiring and frustrating, since an important portion is often out of the field of view or too small to hold the viewer's attention, and manual camera control by the attendee is difficult. Consequently, it is widely recognized that automated camera control and view switching are essential for comfortable and effective communication.

As for capturing presentations, Bobick's group first proposed an advanced framework. They proposed the idea of *smartcam* that automatically tracks human faces, hands, and so on (Bobick 1997, Bobick and Pinhanez 1997). Recently, a number of researchers have reported their works regarding distant learning (He *et al.* 1999, Miyazaki and Kameda 1998, Mukhopadhyay and Smith 1999, Ohno and Ikeda 1999, Kameda *et al.* 2000).

Although cameras are automatically controlled in some of those systems, we usually need much more sophisticated camerawork to effectively capture desktop presentations on desktop manipulations.

- Close-up shots are necessary to show the details of important objects or important manipulations. We need smart camera control to take relevant views, because targets, *e.g.*, a hand or an important object, move fast and sometimes go out of the viewing field quickly.
- We have various targets we want to pay attention to, for example, the speaker's face, behaviors, hands, objects, and so on. The camerawork required for each target is different.

We also investigated focus detection, which we implemented by multimodal recognition of the above-mentioned behaviors. Those processes have not been well explored in the context of automated communication supports. In this sense, our framework contributes to clarifying what kind of behaviors are important clues for effectively communicating and emphasizing desktop presentations.

4   Camera Control

The main purpose of camera control is basically to capture a target with appropriate size and at a good position in an image frame. The problem of tracking a target, however, is not so simple. For example, when we are shooting at a hand manipulation, the camerawork will involve: (a) emphasizing the appearance of the object, and (b) emphasizing the manipulation. For purpose (a), we prefer an extremely close-up shot in which the object is always kept at the center of the screen. In the case of (b), however, we prefer a fixed view for looking at the movements of the hand or the object.

Therefore, there is a certain trade-off between "quickness" and "smoothness" in tracking. Watching a video with shaky tracking can make viewers feel sick, and the frequent change in field of view disturbs our spatial cognition. We have to adjust the camerawork in response to the target and the purpose of a shot. Before discussing camerawork, we first categorize the target of video capturing.

4.1   Target and Aspect-of-Target

We consider camerawork from two points of view: what *target (subject)* we want to shoot, and what *aspect-of-target* we want to capture. The target is the object to be tracked by a camera, and the aspect-of-target determines how to track it.

Target:

As discussed in Section 2.2, there are several important behaviors in presentations in which the focus of attention can be an object, a hand, a speaker, and so on.

For our purposes, we currently consider the following four kinds of targets.

<speaker>   a speaker, a lecturer, or an instructor.

<workspace>   a *dynamic* space where a manipulation such as assembling or cooking is going on.

<object>   an important object to which attention is to be paid.

<place>   an important *static* place to which attention is to be paid.

For each target, we prepare three types of shots: long or wide-angled shot, medium shot, and close-up shot.

Aspect-of-Target:

Next, we categorized aspect-of-target considering the focus of attention as follows:

<circumstance> The target's circumstance includes its position, trajectory, or spatial relationship to other objects. This is suitable for giving the overview of a presentation or manipulation with a wide-angled view.

<movement> The target movements may include frequent small motions such as hand motions in manipulations.

<appearance> The target's appearance will include its shape or color.

For the <circumstance> camerawork, the camera must remain fixed as long as possible so that a viewer could easily observe target's position in a scene. The <movement> camerawork requires quick tracking while suppressing small camera movements in order to get a stable view. The <appearance> camerawork requires a camera to track a target as quickly as possible while keeping the target at the center of the field of view.

4.2   Filtering and Virtual Frame

Considering the requirements just described, we propose (a) camera motion smoothing by the Kalman filter and (b) camera motion suppression by the *virtual-frame control*. We can adapt camerawork for various purposes by tuning the parameters described above.

Smoothing by Kalman Filtering:

With smoothing, we expect that sensor noise and small irritating motions such as trembles are eliminated. For that purpose, we use the

Kalman filter with the rigid body motion model as system dynamics. A state variable $\mathbf{x}_t$ and a state transition matrix F are determined as follows:

$$\mathbf{x}_k = \begin{pmatrix} x \\ \dot{x} \\ \ddot{x} \end{pmatrix} \qquad F = \begin{pmatrix} 1 & \Delta & \frac{1}{2}\Delta^2 \\ 0 & 1 & \Delta \\ 0 & 0 & 1 \end{pmatrix} \tag{1}$$

where Δ is the sampling interval of a measurement, $\mathbf{x}_t$ is a state vector containing the current values of position, velocity, and acceleration.

The Kalman filter is represented by the following formulae:

$$\begin{aligned} \hat{\mathbf{x}}_{t|t} &= \hat{\mathbf{x}}_{t|t-1} + K_t(y_t - H\hat{\mathbf{x}}_{t|t-1}) \\ \hat{\mathbf{x}}_{t+1|t} &= F\hat{\mathbf{x}}_{t|t} \\ K_t &= P_{t|t-1}H^T(I + HP_{t|t-1}H^T)^{-1} \\ P_{t|t} &= P_{t|t-1} - K_t HP_{t|t-1} \\ P_{t+1|t} &= FP_{t|t}F^T + \frac{\sigma_u^2}{\sigma_w^2}\Lambda \end{aligned} \tag{2}$$

$$H = (\,1,0,0\,), \qquad \Lambda = \mathrm{diag}\{0,0,1\}$$

where $\hat{\mathbf{x}}_t$ is an estimator of the target's state, σ_u^2 is a process noise variance, σ_w^2 is a measurement noise variance, and H is a measurement matrix.

The behavior of the above Kalman filter depends on the ratio of the process noise variance (σ_u^2) to the measurement noise variance (σ_w^2). We consider this ratio (hereafter abbreviated as *noise_variance_ratio*) as one of the camera control parameters that govern the smoothness of tracking. If the ratio is small, the camera tracks more smoothly.

Virtual-Frame Control:

The virtual-frame control algorithm switches the tracking mode to *immediate tracking mode* when the target goes outside the virtual frame, and it switches back to *motion suppressing mode* when the target stays still or repetitive motions are observed. In immediate tracking mode, a camera quickly and exactly tracks the target. In motion suppressing mode, camera motion is suppressed while a target stays in a virtual frame. This virtual frame is a rectangle placed at the center of an image, and its size (*virtual frame size*) is specified by the ratio to the image size. A camera is moved so that the center of a virtual frame is located at the target's average position for a certain period (*frame refresh interval*), e.g., a few seconds.

The following are the conditions for switching from immediate tracking mode to motion suppressing mode.

Stationary target position: A target stays within a small region (*stationary range th*) for a certain period of time (*stationary time th*).

Repetitive target motion: A target is moved repeatedly over a certain count (*repetition count th*). For example, an object is shaken by a hand. This repetition is detected by checking the sign changes of the target's motion vector.

Figure 6 shows the flow of the algorithm. If *virtual frame size* or *frame refresh interval* is large, a camera angle tends to be fixed. This causes inexact tracking and fixed views. Similarly, if we make *stationary time th*, *stationary range th*, or *repetition count th* small, we also get more stable views.

Figure 7 shows the result of shooting at a desktop manipulation in which a person opens a box. The left column shows the sequence of images captured with the virtual-frame control, and the right column shows the sequence without the virtual-frame control. As we can see here, most of the uncomfortable field of view movements are eliminated in (a).

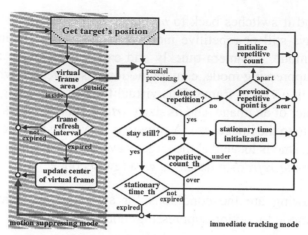

Figure 6. Flow of the virtual-frame control algorithm.

4.3   Parameter Setting

The relations between aspect-of-target and the camera control parameters are shown in Figure 8. In the case of <circumstance>, we set large *virtual_frame_size*, long *stationary_time_th*, and small *noise_variance_ratio* so that the viewers can easily grasp the circumstances because they are provided with a stable view. Since the tracking becomes inexact with large *virtual_frame_size*, we need to make *stationary_time_th*, *stationary_range_th*, and *repetition_count_th* large so that the tracking mode cannot easily be switched to motion suppressing mode. In the case of <movement>, *repetition_count_th* is set small in order to quickly detect repetitions. *Virtual_frame_size* and *frame_refresh_interval* are also set small expecting that the target is captured at the center of the image. For <appearance>, *virtual_frame_size* and *frame_refresh_interval* are set small, as we expect the target to be captured in the center of the image as long as possible. Additionally, to quickly stop the camera motion when a target stops, *stationary_time_th* and *stationary_range_th* are set small, and *noise_variance_ratio* of the Kalman filter is set large.

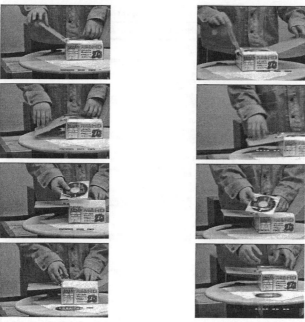

(a) With the virtual-frame control   (b) Without the virtual-frame control

Figure 7. Manipulation on opening a box (the right hand is tracked).

Since it is not easy for non-expert users to determine the above parameters, we prepared a set of parameters for every purpose. The users can choose one on a GUI panel. Figure 9 shows the upper half of the panel.

5 Behavior Recognition for Focus Detection

5.1 Behavior Recognition

The purpose of behavior recognition is to detect the focus of attention. By using the result, the system can switch the view or empha-

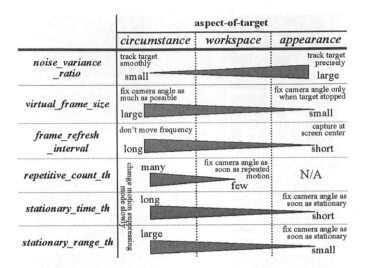

Figure 8. Correspondence between the aspect-of-target and the camera control parameters.

size the focus at an appropriate time. We are currently dealing with five kinds of behaviors, as shown in Section 2.2. To detect those behaviors, we need multimodal processing. Human motions or poses are rather ambiguous, and they may represent different things in different contexts. With the integration of motion and speech analysis, we can greatly reduce the ambiguity. We will briefly describe our basic idea in the following paragraphs.

Clues from Speech

There are simple and useful clues in speech. For example, phrases that include a demonstrative pronoun/adjective/adverb, such as "this (is a ...)," "this (switch)," or "this long," frequently appear in speech, and they strongly suggest the focus of attention. Words for representing space/location, *e.g.*, "here," suggest that the focus is around the space/location.

Table 2 shows the speech clues that we are currently using, and it

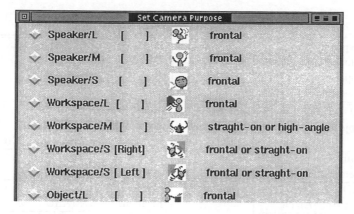

Figure 9. GUI menu for camera setting(cropped) (target category, icon, view point).

indicates the focus suggested by the clues. The first column gives the words, the second gives the behaviors, and the third gives the focus of attention. In each pair of rows, the upper row shows Japanese expressions, and the lower row shows English expressions. Since this system is designed for Japanese, the words in the upper row are actually the targets of speech recognition.

Clues from Motion:

A speaker's motions or postures, *e.g.*, hand position or velocity, are the most useful clues. The following features are simple and do not need any sophisticated analysis, and efficient real-time processing is possible.

For pointing, the following two features are checked.:
- local maxima of arm stretch
- local minima of pseudo velocity change of a hand

Arm stretch change ($EXTC$) and pseudo velocity change ($VELC$) are calculated as shown in Figure 10.

$$EXT_t = |\mathbf{P}_t - \mathbf{P}_o|$$

Table 2. Typical examples of speech, behaviors, and focus.

	Typical Words (upper row: Japanese, lower row: English)	Behavior	Focus	Example
(a)	KORE, KONO (+ object name), etc.	pointing, holding-out	object	KONO NEJI-MAWASHI WO TSUKAIMASU
	(this + object name), this, etc.			use this screw driver
(b)	KOKO, KONO (+ place name), etc.	pointing	place, location	KOKO NI OKI-MASU
	(this + location name), here, etc.			put it here
(c)	KONOYOUNI, KOUSHITE, etc.	manipulation, illustration	manipulation, hand motion / locus	KONOYOUNI NEJI WO MAWASHIMASU
	in this way, like this, etc.			drive the screw in this way
(d)	KOKODE, SORE-DEHA, TSUGINI, etc.	notifying passage changes	speaker	SOREDEHA TSUGI NO STEP WO HA-JIMEMASU
	So, OK, Next, etc.			OK, go on to the next step

$$EXTC_t = EXT_t - EXT_{t-1}$$
$$VEL_t = |\mathbf{P}_t - \mathbf{P}_{t-1}|$$
$$VELC_t = VEL_t - VEL_{t-1} \qquad (3)$$

If the arm stretch change at a local maxima is larger than a threshold value, which means $EXTC_t > Th_{ext}$, the first condition is satisfied.

For detecting that both hands are on/above the desk, the distance between the body and a hand is calculated. The value is checked if it is larger than a certain threshold (Th_{wh}).

$$|\mathbf{P}_w - \mathbf{P}_h| > Th_{wh} \qquad (4)$$

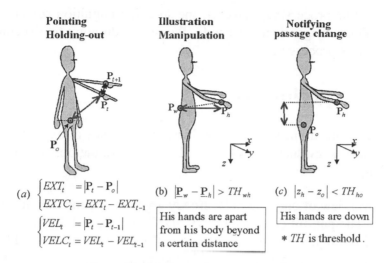

Figure 10. Motion and posture detection.

Similarly, $|\mathbf{Z}_w - \mathbf{Z}_h| < Th_{ho}$ is enough for checking that both hands are down.

5.2   Detection Process

The condition for detecting each behavior is as follows:

pointing/holding-out: Table 2(a), (b) and Fig. 10(a)

manipulation/illustration: Table 2(c) and Fig. 10(b)

notifying passage changes: Table 2(d) and Fig. 10(c)

If the system detects both speech clues and motion clues within a certain period, the system accepts the corresponding behavior. We previously investigated the occurrence time difference between speech and motion (Nakamura *et al.* 1998). The statistics showed that, in around 90% of cases, speech clues and motion clues occur within 2 seconds of each other This duration is enough for off-line processing.

For on-line processing, however, the speech recognition sometimes has a delay longer than 2 seconds. We set the duration to 3 seconds for on-line processing.

6   Experiments

To verify our framework, we conducted three kinds of experiments: camerawork evaluation, behavior detection evaluation, and video editing.

The overview of our system is already given in Section 2.3 and Figure 4. The pan-tilt cameras are EVI-D30 (Sony), and they are controlled through serial communication. The position sensor is Flock of Birds (Ascension Technology Corporation), and it was used with the frequency of 30 Hz in the following experiments. The speech recognition module is built on ViaVoice (IBM). The system also has a video selector to switch the views for producing a video in real-time.

6.1   Camerawork Evaluation

First, we evaluated the camera motions. Since some papers (Kato and Yamada 1996, Kato *et al.* 1997) reported the camera operator's characteristics in tracking objects, we compared the characteristics of our system with those. The scene is shown in Figure 7.

The results are shown in Figure 11. In this figure, we plotted the apparent (image) position[3] where a stationary point in the scene is located. With the virtual-frame control, the apparent velocity[3] almost always is less than the maximum value by professional camera operators. Without the virtual-frame control, on the other hand, the appar-

---

[3]The apparent position is plotted using normalized screen size. The apparent velocity is the ratio of the difference in normalized position between two consecutive video frames.

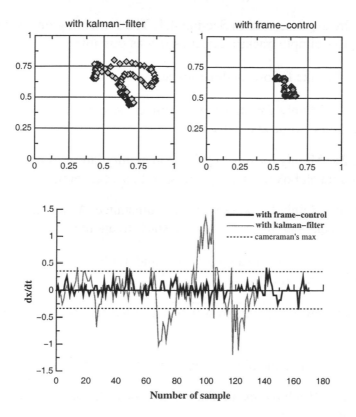

Figure 11. Target's normalized position and velocity with/without frame-control (upper: normalized position, lower: normalized horizontal velocity).

ent velocity can easily exceed the maximum. This causes shaky and irritating views. Thus, our camera control algorithms are effective for recording manipulations.

Subjective Evaluation:

Next, we present an experimental result of subjective evaluation. We took the following presentations by four types of camerawork, three of which, <appearance>, <movement>, and <circumstance>, were already described in Section 4.1. The remaining one is camerawork that simply tracks a target as fast as possible.

We devised the following three scenes:

Scene 1: Mainly for showing an object. A person shows a small seasoning bottle and moves it.

Scene 2: Mainly for showing desktop manipulation. A person takes out a lunch box from a bag and sprinkles seasoning on the lunch.

Scene 3: Mainly for presenting a circumstance. A person is moving toy blocks step by step from one stack to another.

Figure 12 shows the example views, and Table 3 shows the camera control parameters.

We asked seven students to watch the video for the following purposes:

Scene 1: Notice the object's appearance, *e.g.*, color or shape.

Scene 2: Watch the manipulation, *e.g.*, how the person does something.

Scene 3: Watch the situation, *e.g.*, the spatial relationships among the person and two stacks.

Our evaluation was based on Thurstone's method of paired comparison (Ohkushi *et al.* 1991). We showed seven subjects a pair of videos and asked them to choose which is more "preferable or comfortable." We repeated this process, presenting the subjects different pairs. Then we calculated a subjective scale of values.

The result is shown in Figure 13, in which larger values mean "preferable." The result is quite satisfactory. For all scenes, the cameraworks that we prepared for each purpose got good evaluation val-

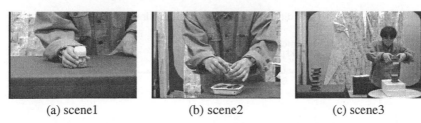

| (a) scene1 | (b) scene2 | (c) scene3 |

Figure 12. Videos used for evaluation (left: showing object, middle: desktop manipulation, right: manipulation with significant human position change).

ues. Moreover, the bad evaluation values on simple tracking clearly show the necessity of sophisticated camerawork as we have noted in this paper.

Table 3. Parameter sets for the camera control methods.

	\<appearance\>	\<movement\>	\<circumstance\>
noise_variance_ratio	10	4	3
virtual_frame_size	0.45	0.7	0.9
frame_refresh_interval	2.5 sec	3.5 sec	5.0 sec
stationary_time_th	0.04 sec	3.0 sec	4.0 sec
stationary_range_th	60 mm	150 mm	300 mm
repetition_count_th	-	2	6

6.2 Behavior Detection Evaluation

We examined the behavior detection by applying our system to real presentations. We gathered six students without any professional experiences in teaching or giving instructions. Each subject was asked to give the following two presentations on the same topic, which is assembling a toy car.

Natural presentation (P1): Each subject was asked to give a presentation on a specified topic. He/she had no detailed knowledge about our system, and each subject was asked to behave as they usually do. To make the presentation as natural as possible, we

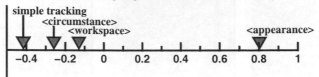

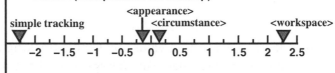

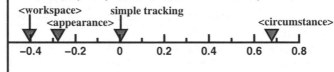

Figure 13. Result of the paired comparison method (positioned by evaluation scores).

did not attach magnetic sensors to the subject.

Adapting the system (P2): Before the presentation, a subject is told how the system works and is asked to express their intention clearly by motions and speech. A subject can see the system response, which is currently the switched view indicating the focus of attention.

In both presentations, we assumed that several people are watching the video. Table 4 shows the summary of P1[4] and details of P2. For P1, only the numbers of appeared movements are counted, since be-

---

[4]Table 1 already gave the result of P1.

havior recognition was not possible due to the lack of motion data. As for P2, once we explained the system mechanism, all subjects quickly adjusted themselves to give presentations on the system. They were able to keep giving the presentation with checking the responses from the system. As a result, even though subjects had not had a prior training phase, around 70% of their behaviors were correctly recognized. If we omit small and short movements that are hard to become the foci of attention, the detection rate (recall) is around 80%. This modification is reasonable because a considerable number of pointing/holding-out behaviors appear even though a speaker does not intend to call attention to anything with that movement. In this case, the movements are usually small and short. We need further investigation to determine how to detect them and discriminate among them.

Roughly speaking, the subjects had good impressions of the system; most of the subjects stated that they were not severely constrained by it. In most cases, they just tried to speak a little more clearly and made their motion a little bigger. Those efforts were successful, as we can see in Table 4. One significant difference between P1 and P2 is the increase of manipulation/illustration behaviors. Once the subjects noticed that the system recognizes their movements well, they tend to in a way that works with the system. On the other hand, some of them stated that they felt a little uneasy during their movements, wondering if those movements were recognized. This was mainly caused by the error and the delay of recognition. In this sense, we need to improve detection rate and detection delay.

6.3   Video Editing Experiments

By selecting the most relevant view by using the behavior recognition results, we obtain a comprehensible video. This selection is fully automated by an electronic video selector controlled by a host computer.

Table 4. Behavior recognition results on on-line presentations.

	P1	P2			
	N	N	R(%)	P(%)	R'(%)
pointing, holding-out	88	94	41	100	67
manipulation, illustration	15	44	82	95	82
notifying passage changes	21	21	62	92	62
total (average)	125	137	70	97	83

N: number of occurrences, R: recall (detection rate),
P: precision (accuracy), R': modified recall

Table 5. The camera setting using examples of shoot.

Camera	Target	Camerawork	Target Position
Camera1	<speaker>/M	<circumstance>	a point on waist
Camera2	<object>/C	<appearance>	a point on the right hand
Camera3	<workspace>/M	<movement>	a middle point of both hands

M: Medium,   C: Close-up

Here we show editing examples. Three cameras are used for capturing presentations, and their setting is shown in Table 5. Camera 1 captures the speaker's behavior with <circumstance> camerawork. Camera 2 shoots at the reference object that the speaker holds, which draws the viewers' attention. Camera 3 shoots at the workspace from a high position (around 2 m high) so that it can capture a better view of the desktop that is sometimes difficult to see from the position of Camera 1 or Camera 2. It is important to note that we considered the middle point of both hands as the center of <workspace> in two-handed manipulations. Similarly, we consider the position of a hand[5] holding a target as the center of the <object> to which a speaker wants to lead our attention.

---

[5]Strictly speaking, a point that has a certain offset toward the fingers from the wrist.

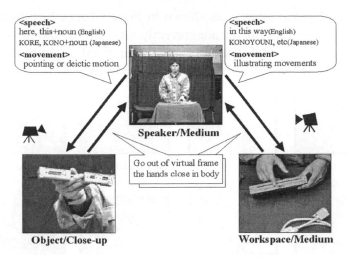

Figure 14. Video switching condition

The switching condition is shown in Figure 14. When pointing or holding-out behaviors appear, the system selects the <object> view through Camera 2. Similarly, in the case of manipulation or illustration behaviors, the <workspace> view through Camera 3 is selected.

Figure 15 shows some examples of the portions of video. The left column shows the cases in which the <object> view is chosen, and the right column shows the cases of <workspace> view. In each sub-figure, the left image shows the image just before switching and the right image shows the selected view after the switching. The phrases below the images are the transcribed speech. The upper phrase is actually spoken in Japanese, and the lower is translated into English. Although nuances differ between Japanese and English, we believe that these examples show the effectiveness of our system.

Figure 16 shows a simple example. A person explained how to attach a monitor cable to a small notebook PC. By capturing the presentation through the three cameras we have described, we obtained three streams of video images, as shown in Figure 16(a). In this experiment, all clear movements are correctly recognized, and the switching is very successful. We can easily understand the improvements by comparing the videos in Figure 16(a) and (b).[6]

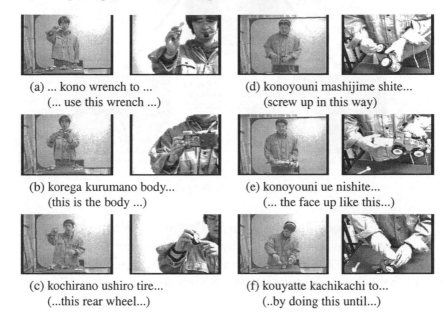

(a) ... kono wrench to ...
(... use this wrench ...)

(d) konoyouni mashijime shite...
(screw up in this way)

(b) korega kurumano body...
(this is the body ...)

(e) konoyouni ue nishite...
(... the face up like this...)

(c) kochirano ushiro tire...
(...this rear wheel...)

(f) kouyatte kachikachi to...
(..by doing this until...)

Figure 15. Example of view switching. For each sub-figure, the left image shows the image just before switching, and the right image shows the selected view. The phrases below the images are the speech. The upper phrase is actually spoken in Japanese, and the lower is translated into English.

7   Conclusion

This paper introduced our framework for intelligent video capturing and presentation. We concentrated on two points: camerawork for shooting at the focus of attention and behavior recognition by using speech and motion. Through the experiments, we proved that the

---

[6]MPEG files are available on our Web page
(http://image.esys.tsukuba.ac.jp/~yuichi/VETL/)

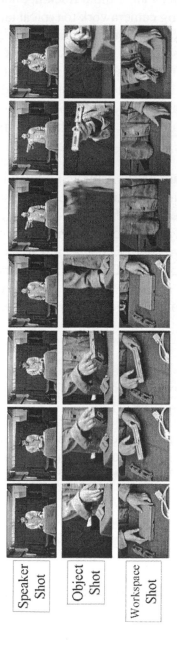

(a) Videos captured by three cameras

(b) Result of camera switching

Figure 16. Result of presentation capture.

proposed camerawork is much better than simple tracking, and our parameter sets are useful for adjusting camerawork to typical targets. The behavior recognition also works well for presentations on desktop manipulations. Although the users who give presentations need to know a little about our system's mechanism, it is easy to get used to the system. Once the user is accustomed to the system, the detection rate is around 80%, which is satisfactory as a prototype system. Thus, the switched video looks natural, and it is useful for communicating presentations.

We have many options area for future work. Although we can imagine a wide variety of applications such as video production systems, teleconferencing, or CSCW, we need to further investigate on many points, including how to handle a wider variety of behaviors, how to achieve better accuracy, how to have shorter delays, how to develop effective video presentations, and so on. Additionally, behaviors will be different if we have two or more speakers. Dealing with the questions from the audience is also an interesting problem to tackle.

References

Bobick, A. (1997), "Movement, activity, and action," *MIT Media Lab Preceptual Computing Section*, vol. TR-413.

Bobick, A. and Pinhanez, C. (1997), "Controlling view-based algorithms using approximate world models and action information," *Proc. Conference on Computer Vision and Pattern Recognition*, pp. 955-961.

Ekman, P. and Friesen, W. (1969), "The repertoire of nonverbal behavior: categories, origins, usage, and coding," *Semiotica*, vol. 1, pp. 49-98.

He, L. *et al.* (1999), "Auto-summarization of audio-video presentations," *Proc.ACM Multimedia*, pp. 489-498.

Kameda, Y., Ishizuka, K., and Minoh, M. (2000), "A live video imaging method for capturing presentation information in distance learning," *Proc. Int. Conf. on Multimedia and Expo*, pp. WA0-5.

Kato, D. and Yamada, M. (1996), "Analysis of the camera work of television cameramen while tracking subjects," *The Journal of the Institute of Image Information and Television Engineers*, vol. 50, no. 12, pp. 1941-1948.

Kato, D., Yamada, M., *et al.* (1997), "Analysis of the camerawork of broadcasting cameramen," *SMPTE Journal*, pp. 108-116, Feb.

Miyazaki, H. and Kameda, Y. (1998), "A real-time method of making lecture video using multiple cameras," *MIRU'98*, pp. 123-128. (In Japanese.)

Mukhopadhyay, S. and Smith, B. (1999), "Passive capture and structuring of lectures," *Proc.ACM Multimedia*, pp. 477-487.

Nakamura, Y. *et al.* (1998), "MMID: multimodal multi-view integrated database for human behavior understanding," *Proc. IEEE International Conference on Automatic Face and Gesture Recognition*, pp. 540-545.

Ohkushi, K., Nakayama, T., and Fukuda, T. (1991), *Evaluation Techniques for Image and Tone Quality*, SHOKODO. (In Japanese.)

Ohno, N. and Ikeda, K. (1999), "Video stream selection according to lecture context on remote lecture," *5th Symposium on Intelligent Information Media*, pp. 31-38. (In Japanese.)

Index

List of Contributors

Ferda N. Alpaslan
Computer Engineering Department
Middle East Technical University
06531, Ankara
Turkey

M.V. Belmonte
Departamento de Lenguajes y Ciencias de la Computación
E.T.S.I. Informática
Universidad de Málaga
Apdo. 4114, Málaga 29080
Spain
belmonte@lcc.uma.es

Jesús G. Boticario
Artificial Intelligence Department
Facultad de Ciencias
Universidad Nacional de Educación a Distancia
C/Senda del Rey, 9, 28040 Madrid
Spain
jgb@dia.uned.es

R.M. Carro
Escuela Técnica Superior de Informática
Universidad Autónoma de Madrid
Campus de Cantoblanco, 28049 Madrid
Spain

Stephen Chan
Hong Kong Polytechnic University
Hong Kong

Jeffrey T. Clark
Department of Sociology/Anthropology
North Dakota State University
Fargo, ND 58105
U.S.A.

Lisa M. Daniels
Department of Teacher Education
North Dakota State University
Fargo, ND 58105
U.S.A.

Zippy Erlich
The Open University of Israel
Israel

Judith Gal-Ezer
The Open University of Israel
Israel

Elena Gaudioso
Artificial Intelligence Department
Facultad de Ciencias
Universidad Nacional de Educación a Distancia
C/Senda del Rey, 9, 28040 Madrid
Spain
elena@dia.uned.es

E. Guzmán
Departamento de Lenguajes y Ciencias de la Computación
E.T.S.I. Informática
Universidad de Málaga
Apdo. 4114, Málaga 29080
Spain
guzman@lcc.uma.es

Curt Hill
Department of Computer Science
North Dakota State University
Fargo, ND 58105
U.S.A.

Anita Hung
St. Teresa Secondary School
Kowloon
Hong Kong

T. Ichimura
Faculty of Information Sciences
Hiroshima City University
3-4-1, Ozuka-higashi, Asaminami-ku, Hiroshima 731-3194
Japan

Mizue Kayama
University of Electro-Communications
Graduate School of Information Systems
Chofugaoka 1-5-1, Chofu, Tokyo 182-8585
Japan

Raymond Lee
Hong Kong Polytechnic University
Hong Kong

James Liu
Hong Kong Polytechnic University
Hong Kong

David Lupo
The Open University of Israel
Israel

K.J. Mackin
Fujitsu Limited
3-9-18 Shin-Yokohama, Yokohama 222-0033
Japan

L. Mandow
Departamento de Lenguajes y Ciencias de la Computación
E.T.S.I. Informática
Universidad de Málaga
Apdo. 4114, Málaga 29080
Spain
lawrence@lcc.uma.es

Phil McClean
Department of Plant Sciences
North Dakota State University
Fargo, ND 58105
U.S.A.

E. Millán
Departamento de Lenguajes y Ciencias de la Computación
E.T.S.I. Informática
Universidad de Málaga
Apdo. 4114, Málaga 29080
Spain
eva@lcc.uma.es

Yuichi Nakamura
University of Tsukuba
Tsukuba 305-8573
Japan
and
PRESTO, JST
Japan
yuichi@esys.tsukuba.ac.jp

M. Nakamura
Faculty of Information Sciences
Hiroshima City University
3-4-1, Ozuka-higashi, Asaminami-ku, Hiroshima 731-3194
Japan

Yuichi Ohta
University of Tsukuba
Tsukuba 305-8573
Japan

Toshio Okamoto
University of Electro-Communications
Graduate School of Information Systems
Chofugaoka 1-5-1, Chofu, Tokyo 182-8585
Japan

S. Otsuki
Faculty of Information Sciences
Hiroshima City University
3-4-1, Ozuka-higashi, Asaminami-ku, Hiroshima 731-3194
Japan

Bülent Özdemir
Computer Engineering Department
Middle East Technical University
06531, Ankara
Turkey

Motoyuki Ozeki
University of Tsukuba
Tsukuba 305-8573
Japan

J.L. Pérez de la Cruz
Departamento de Lenguajes y Ciencias de la Computación
E.T.S.I. Informática
Universidad de Málaga
Apdo. 4114, Málaga 29080
Spain
perez@lcc.uma.es

E. Pulido
Escuela Técnica Superior de Informática
Universidad Autónoma de Madrid
Campus de Cantoblanco, 28049 Madrid
Spain

P. Rodríguez
Escuela Técnica Superior de Informática
Universidad Autónoma de Madrid
Campus de Cantoblanco, 28049 Madrid
Spain

Bernhardt Saini-Eidukat
Department of Geosciences
North Dakota State University
Fargo, ND 58105
U.S.A.

Donald P. Schwert
Department of Geosciences
North Dakota State University
Fargo, ND 58105
U.S.A.

Brian M. Slator
Department of Computer Science
North Dakota State University
Fargo, ND 58105
U.S.A.

Alan R. White
Department of Biological Sciences
North Dakota State University
Fargo, ND 58105
U.S.A.

T. Yamashita
Graduate School of Engineering
Tokyo Metropolitan Institute of Technology
Tokyo
Japan

K. Yoshida
Department of Preventive Medicine
St. Marianna University
Japan